STUDY GUIDE
for use with

INTRODUCTION
to
FINANCIAL MANAGEMENT

CHARLES P. JONES

Prepared by
Thomas A. Bankston
Angelo State University

IRWIN

Homewood, IL 60430
Boston, MA 02116

Printed in the United States of America

ISBN 0-256-07872-6

1 2 3 4 5 6 7 8 9 0 EB 8 7 6 5 4 3 2 1

PREFACE

This *Study Guide* is to accompany *Introduction to Financial Management* by C. P. Jones. The purpose of this *Study Guide* is to help students derive the most benefit from the textbook.

Use of the Study Guide

You should study the textbook first, using your best study techniques. You may use any or all of the following for each chapter: preview, outline, study, answer end-of-chapter questions and problems, and review. The *Study Guide* should be of particular help in reviewing concepts, vocabulary, and notation and in working problems.

Study Features

There are five to seven sections in most chapters of the *Study Guide* oriented to specific aspects of your study.

Concepts You Should Understand highlights the major themes running throughout the chapter. This should provide an organizational framework for the material in the chapter.

A Second Look restates many of the ideas contained in the chapter, providing a review of the main ideas. The perspective or viewpoint is intentionally somewhat different from the textbook in the hopes that a different view may bring increased understanding.

Chapter Summary concentrates on terminology and vocabulary and allows you to test yourself in a fill-in-the-blank format. You may want to pencil in answers in the spaces provided.

Answers to Chapter Summary provides answers for the fill-in-the-blank questions.

Acronyms and Notation You Should Know lists symbols and acronyms found throughout the chapter. Often these are critical not only to the immediate chapter but also throughout the book.

Equations You Should Know lists the equations in the chapter that are necessary to work the problems. Equations used in deriving other equations are omitted, leaving only the equations that are most useful for the problems. This is for the convenience of having them all together for easy reference and may be helpful for the problems in the textbook as well as for those in the *Study Guide*.

Problems is a group of problems carefully selected to complement the examples and end-of-chapter problems in the textbook.

Problem Solutions presents solutions step-by-step with a narrative explaining where each figure came from and the reasoning behind it.

Lotus Notes is a section included only in chapters where an electronic spreadsheet can be especially useful.

To repeat, you will gain the most by first studying the textbook, and then the *Study Guide*. It should help you review and consolidate the text materials and give you practice on problems. I shall be glad to hear your comments for future improvements.

Acknowledgments

This *Study Guide* was formulated with the input and insight of many colleagues and students over many years. Editors Mike Junior and Tom Sharpe of Richard D. Irwin, Inc., were most helpful and considerate throughout the writing process. Thanks to the reviewers who added thoughts and corrected mistakes in my original manuscript. I wish to thank Susan Dunnam and Brenda Huisenga for their assistance in preparing the manuscript for publication. And thanks to my daughters, Celia and Brittany, and my family and friends who allowed me the time to work on this project.

Thomas A. Bankston
July 22, 1991

CONTENTS

Contents

CHAPTER 1
FINANCIAL MANAGEMENT DECISION MAKING

Concepts You Should Understand

* The study and practice of finance may be divided into three major categories: financial management, investments, and financial markets (money and capital markets).

* Financial management is a dynamic field as evidenced by its evolution from the study of legal aspects of raising funds during the early part of this century to the application of financial theory utilizing computer models toward the end of this century.

* A decision framework consists of (1) a goal, (2) the identification of significant variables and constraints, and (3) some decision rules.

* The appropriate goal for financial management of the firm is the maximization of shareholders' wealth through stock price maximization over the long run in a socially responsible manner.

* Shareholder wealth maximization is subject to certain constraints, including the agency problem, the possibility of hostile takeovers, and social responsibility.

* Expected return and risk are important variables in the framework for financial decisions. Risk averse investors invest in more risky assets only in expectation of higher returns.

* Profit maximization alone *is not* an appropriate goal for financial management of the firm because the term profit can be interpreted several ways and because it does not specifically consider either the timing or the risk involved.

A Second Look

The field of finance can be separated into three major categories: financial management, investments, and financial markets. Financial management deals with the financial decisions faced by business managers on both a day-to-day and occasional basis. Investments deals with the analysis of financial securities from an investors viewpoint. Financial markets consists of money markets, which are markets for short-term securities, and capital markets, which are markets for long-term securities. The focus of the textbook is financial management, which is essentially applied microeconomics, utilizing accounting data.

1

Chapter 1: Financial Management Decision Making

The study of finance during the first half of this century was largely descriptive in nature, emphasizing important topics of the day. A great deal of financial theory was developed and tested during the three decades beginning with 1950. The widespread availability of personal computers during the 1980s expanded research and allowed application of many theoretical concepts which had previously required too many calculations to be practical or economically feasible.

Financial management decisions fall into two broad categories: investing in assets and raising funds. Managers may invest in financial assets and real assets needed to pursue the business interests of the firm. But there must be funds if there are to be investments. The other side of the manager's job, then, is to get the funds required for the necessary investments. Some needs are ongoing in that the needs recur on a regular basis. Other needs arise only occasionally and are referred to as episodic needs. Dividend policy is one aspect of the financing decision.

A framework for making financial decisions requires (1) a goal, (2) identification of relevant variables, and (3) decision rules. The appropriate goal of financial management is the maximization of stockholders' wealth. Stockholders' wealth is best measured by the market price of shares of the firm's stock. Profit maximization, per se, is not an appropriate goal because it is vague and does not include all relevant variables. Management of the large corporation must be pursued within constraints for the benefit of the shareholders and of society in general. Ethical and socially responsible behavior by management will be in the long-run best interests of the business as well as of the community.

The second part of the decision framework identifies expected return and risk as the major variables to be considered in financial decisions. Risk averse managers invest in more risky projects only in expectation of higher returns.

The third part of the decision framework involves decision rules. Much of this book is devoted to understanding and applying decision rules that will help management achieve the specified goal of maximizing stockholders' wealth.

A modern business is affected by international economic events, financial markets, suppliers, and competition. The financial implications of the international arena are to be considered in decision making.

The textbook, like the financial manager's job, is organized around the balance sheet. Short-term investing and raising short-term funds are viewed together. The analysis of long-term investments is followed by considerations in raising long-term funds. Mergers and acquisitions and international financial management conclude the text.

Chapter Summary

The field of finance can be separated into three main areas: (1) _____, (2) _____, and (3) _____. The study of how a company's financial resources are allocated is called (4) _____.

The evolution of the study of finance during the Twentieth Century began with descriptive material concerning the (5) _____ of financial problems and the types of (6) _____ issued by a firm. During the 1930s the study of (7) _____ came to the forefront. The analysis of the firm from an (8) _____ viewpoint was important during the 1940s. Several theoretical cornerstones were laid during the 1950s and emphasis switched to the (9) _____ viewpoint and the (10) _____ side of the balance sheet. During the 1960s theoretical developments continued and the goal of (11) _____ became more widely accepted. Research broadened in scope during the 1970s, leading to integration of (12)_____ and financial management. The application of (13) _____ to financial problems became widespread during the 1980s, as did the study of (14) _____ and (15) _____.

Financial management decisions can be categorized as either (16) _____ decisions or (17) _____ decisions. Investment decisions are reflected on the asset side of the balance sheet, including both (18) _____ and (19) _____. Financing decisions must be made in order to secure funds for the firm's investments. Financing decisions are reflected on the (20) _____ side of the balance sheet. The best mix of (21) _____ is considered along with the (22) _____ decision.

A framework for financial decisions consists of three parts: (23) _____, (24)_____, and (25)_____. The appropriate financial goal of maximizing stockholders' wealth can also be stated as maximizing (26)_____. Profit maximization alone is not an appropriate goal because it is (27)_____, it ignores the (28)_____ of cash flows, and it does not specifically account for (29)_____. The goal of stockholder wealth maximization is both (30)_____ and (31)_____, making it good in practice as well as in theory.

Numerous factors constrain management in their pursuit of stock price maximization. The (32)_____ deals with the fact that stockholders, management, and creditors all have their own interests at stake and that these interests may conflict with one another. The threat of a (33)_____ may cause management to make different decisions than it would without this constraint. A third type of constraint involves (34)_____. In the long run these constraints should benefit both the stockholders and society.

The two most important variables identified in the second part of the decision

Chapter 1: Financial Management Decision Making

framework are (35)_____ and (36)_____. Managers invest in more risky assets because they expect more return. This upward sloping relationship is know as the (37)_____. This relationship is recognized throughout the decision rules developed in the third section of the decision framework.

Business firms no longer operate on a strictly domestic level. They are influenced by (38)_____ through their suppliers, customers, investments, and sources and costs of financing. Financial management is, thus, forced to consider the international scene in business decisions.

Answers to Chapter Summary

1. financial management
2. investments
3. money and capital markets
4. financial management
5. legal aspects
6. bonds and stocks
7. bankruptcy and reorganization
8. outsider's
9. manager's
10. asset
11. maximization of stockholders' wealth
12. investments
13. computers
14. financial deregulation
15. new financing methods
16. investment
17. financing
18. financial assets
19. real assets

20. liability
21. debt and equity
22. dividend
23. a goal
24. the identification of important variables
25. decision rules
26. stock price
27. vague
28. timing
29. wealth
30. quantifiable
31. operational
32. agency problem
33. hostile takeover
34. social responsibility
35. risk
36. expected return
37. risk-expected return tradeoff
38. international events

CHAPTER 2
THE ROLE OF FINANCIAL MARKETS

Concepts You Should Understand

* Maximizing stockholder wealth involves management decisions, the economic environment, and how the financial markets react to determine stock prices.

* Investors in the financial marketplace determine stock and bond prices by the amount for which they are willing to buy and sell the stocks and bonds. That is, prices are determined by supply and demand.

* Financial intermediaries provide a means by which savers can lend to borrowers by going through the intermediaries.

* Financial markets provide a means by which savings are allocated to borrowers through the trading of financial assets.

* The nominal interest rate includes three components: a real interest rate, a premium for expected inflation, and a risk premium.

* Investors buy stocks and bonds based on expectations about the future. They consider the amount of expected future cash flows, the timing of those expected future cash flows, and the risks involved.

A Second Look

Maximizing owners' wealth is the appropriate goal for financial management regardless of the form of business organization. The same financial principles apply to all profit-oriented organizations, but the mechanics may vary depending on the size and type of organization.

Businesses are classified according to who owns them and what the legal arrangements are. One of the most important differences between the types of organizations is the personal liability of the owners. If a proprietorship or partnership owes someone money and cannot pay it out of business funds, the owners may have to pay out of their personal assets, such as their savings. If a corporation is bankrupt, on the other hand, the creditors cannot ask the owners to use personal assets to pay off the corporation's debts.

Very often it is impossible for savers and borrowers to get together individually to make a financial deal. In the first place, they do not know where to find each other. In the second place, the lender does not have the exact amount of funds that the borrower wants. And the lender does not want to make a loan for the same length of time that the borrower wants the funds. So financial intermediaries came into existence to fulfill the need of satisfying both borrowers and lenders. The saver can make a deal with the intermediary, and the intermediary can make an entirely different deal with the borrower. Intermediaries are one means of facilitating the allocation of financial resources within our economy.

Financial markets are another means of allocating financial resources. One type of market is a registered exchange, which is somewhat like a private club; a person has to be a member before going there and buy or sell securities. Certain exchange members can do business with the public. The over-the-counter market, by contrast, is a group of independent securities dealers that do business with each other and the public.

Financial markets facilitate the acquisition and investment of money and encourage capital formation simply by giving savers a means by which to invest their money. If you have a few thousand dollars to invest, and decide you would like to invest in a business, what are your options? It is easier to call your stockbroker than to ask around town until you find an individual who needs a partner. And if you did find an individual who would sell you a part of his/her business, how would you know if he/she was asking a fair price? The market establishes a price, and at least you know you are paying what others are willing to pay when you buy a stocks or bonds.

Debt

When people are borrowing and lending, they are buying and selling money. The price of money is the interest rate that the borrower pays and the lender receives. Interest rates are determined by the supply and demand for money, where the quantity is measured in dollars and the price in percentages.

The interest rate that you hear on the news or that your banker tells you your student loan will have is called the nominal interest rate (NIR). Thinking about it from the lenders viewpoint, how much would you expect to receive in order to entice you to lend your money? You would want a basic rate of return, called the real rate (RR), plus an additional return to offset expected inflation (EI), plus an additional risk premium (RP) to reward you for risk, such as business risk and financial risk. This relationship is summarized by the equation: $NIR = RR + EI + RP$. The risk-free rate is defined as the real rate plus the expected inflation premium: $RF = RR + EI$. These rates will be used throughout your study of financial management.

Equity

How are stock prices determined by supply and demand? Consider a company which has ten million shares of stock outstanding. Only a few of these shares are bought and sold on any one day. Investors who want to buy shares of the stock must decide how much they are willing to pay for the stock. Likewise, investors who own the stock and want to sell it must decide how much to ask for it. When the buyer and seller agree on a price, the sale is made. The mechanism through which this agreement and sale takes place may be a simple one-on-one transaction or may go through a complex stock exchange. Either way, the price is taken as the market value of the stock and represents the owners' wealth.

An important concept to understand in the valuation process is that investors buy stocks or other securities for the cash they expect to receive from that investment in the future. Investors may use the past as a starting point for projecting the future, but they do not buy a security for what it paid in the past. They buy a security for what they expect to receive from it in the future. In the case of common stock, investors normally expect cash dividends and a price increase. Sometimes they get what they expect; sometimes they do not. The fact that investors do not always get what they expect is the risk aspect of the investment. Financial managers need to understand the roles of investors and financial markets in determining the stockholders' wealth.

Chapter Summary

Shareholders' wealth is measured by a company's (1) _____, which is determined by management's actions and investor reactions in the financial markets. The economic principle of (2) _____ sets stock prices.

There are three major forms of business organizations: (3) _____, (4) _____, and (5) _____. About (6) _____ percent of the businesses in the United States are sole proprietorships, but (7) _____ account for about 80 percent of the sales. Proprietorships and partnerships share three common advantages: (8) _____, (9) _____, and (10) _____; and two common disadvantages: (11) _____ and (12) _____. Partnerships offer the added advantage of (13) _____. Corporations offer three advantages: (14) _____, (15) _____, and (16) _____; and three disadvantages: (17) _____, (18) _____, and (19) _____.

In analyzing financial markets, savers are also referred to as lenders and (20) _____; whereas, users are referred to as borrowers and (21) _____. (22) _____ are the major savers, and (23) _____ are the main users.

Funds are often channeled through financial intermediaries, of which there are three main types: (24) _____, (25) _____, and (26) _____. When a saver pays money to a financial intermediary, an (27) _____ security is formed. A (28) _____ security is formed when the intermediary loans funds to a borrower.

Three broad purposes are served by financial markets: (29) _____, (30) _____, and (31) _____. The mechanics by which small, unincorporated firms and large corporations participate in financial markets often differ according to legal and institutional parameters. A large firm, for example, may borrow money by selling (32) _____ to the general public; whereas, a small firm may borrow money from a (33) _____ or insurance company. Another example of a difference between a proprietorship and a publicly held corporation is the price setting function of the market. The corporation's (34) _____ may be bought and sold every few minutes, so one can find out the market value by checking the most recent price. The market value of a (35) _____, by contrast, is never really known until the proprietor reaches an agreement to sell the business, which is not feasible for businesspeople who want to know their net worth.

Interest rates are also determined in the financial marketplace. The nominal rate is the sum of the (36) _____ plus the (37) _____ plus a (38) _____.

The markets for short-term securities, such as Treasury bills and commercial paper, is called the (39) _____, while the market for long-term securities, such as 30-year bonds and common stock, is known as the (40) _____. The (41) _____ involves the issue of new securities, and the (42) _____ facilitates the trading of previously issued securities.

Only listed securities are traded on (43) _____. Buying and selling is done by (44) _____ on the exchanges. NASDAQ is the acronym for the (45) _____ but is widely used in referring to the international market for over-the-counter stocks.

Government regulation of securities and markets is carried out on both the (46) _____ and (47) _____ level. The two major regulatory acts are the (48) _____, which addresses new issues, and the (49) _____, which addresses the secondary markets. The federal regulatory body is the (50) _____.

Investors place a value on a stock or other financial asset based on the (51) _____ and (52) _____ of cash flows expected in the (53) _____ in conjunction with an assessment of the (54) _____ involved. Valuation and rates of return are interrelated. Studies have shown that over the long run, returns on common stocks have averaged (55) _____ percent, while returns on long-term corporate bonds have averaged (56) _____ percent.

Acronyms and Notation You Should Know

EI	Expected inflation
NIR	Nominal interest rate
RP	Risk premium
RR	Real rate of interest
NASD	National Association of Securities Dealers
NASDAQ	National Association of Securities Dealers Automated Quotations
NYSE	New York Stock Exchange
Amex	American Stock Exchange
OTC	Over the Counter
TR	Total return
SEC	Securities and Exchange Commission

Equations You Should Know

$$NIR = RR + EI + RP \tag{2-1}$$

$$RF = RR + EI \tag{2-2}$$

$$\text{Total return} = \frac{\text{cash dividends}}{\text{purchase price}} + \frac{\text{sale price - purchase price}}{\text{purchase price}} \tag{2-3}$$

Problems

2-1.   *Interest rates.* The real rate of interest is 0.5 percent, the expected inflation is 3.1 percent, and the risk premium on long-term corporate bonds is 1.6 percent. The nominal rate of return observed on common stock is 10.3 percent.
A. Calculate the risk-free rate of return.
B. Calculate the nominal rate on corporate bonds.
C. Calculate the risk premium on common stocks.

2-2.   *Interest rates.* The nominal return observed on Acme Automotive Corporation's stock is 15 percent. The real rate is one percent, and the risk premium is 10 percent.
A. Calculate the expected rate of inflation.
B. Calculate the risk-free rate.

2-3.   *Total return.* You purchased 100 shares of common stock of Ace Biscuit Company at $30 per share. During the year you received $1.50 per share in dividends. You sold the stock at the end of the year for $28.50 per share. Ignore transactions costs.
A. Calculate the percentage return from dividends.
B. Calculate the percentage return from capital gains or losses.
C. Calculate the total return.

2-4.   *Total return.* Following a hot tip, Brenda bought 100 shares of common stock of Brittany's Brands, Inc., at $12 per share. The expected annual dividend is $.60 per share. The hot tip said she could expect a total return of 30 percent over the next year. To what price will the stock have to rise in order for Brenda to realize this total return?

Answers to Chapter Summary

1. stock price
2. supply and demand
3. sole proprietorship
4. partnership
5. corporation
6. 80
7. corporations
8. easily established
9. tight control
10. not doubly taxed
11. unlimited liability
12. limited access to outside financing
13. specialization of labor
14. limited liability
15. unlimited life
16. good access to outside financing
17. owners can lose control
18. double taxation
19. more difficult to establish
20. savings surplus units
21. savings deficit units
22. households
23. businesses
24. deposit institutions
25. investment companies
26. contractual institutions
27. indirect
28. primary
29. facilitating the acquisition and investment of money
30. encouraging capital formation

31. establishing market prices
32. bonds
33. bank
34. stocks
35. proprietorship
36. real rate of interest
37. expected rate of inflation
38. risk premium
39. money market
40. capital market
41. primary market
42. secondary market
43. registered exchange
44. auction
45. National Association of Securities Dealers
46. state
47. federal
48. Securities Act of 1933
49. Securities Exchange Act of 1934
50. Securities and Exchange Commission
51. amount
52. timing
53. future
54. risk
55. 10.3
56. 5.2

Chapter 2: The Role of Financial Markets

Problem Solutions

2-1. *Interest rates.*
A. The risk-free rate of return is the sum of the real rate and the expected inflation rate. Use equation 2-2.

$$RF = RR + EI = 0.5 + 3.1 = 3.6\%$$

B. The nominal rate is the sum of the real rate plus the expected inflation rate plus the risk premium. Use equation 2-1.

$$NIR = RR + EI + RP = 0.5 + 3.1 + 1.6 = 5.2\%$$

C. The risk premium is the difference between the nominal rate and the risk-free rate. Using equation 2-1, solve for RP.

$$NIR = RR + EI + RP$$

$$10.3 = 0.5 + 3.1 + RP$$
$$RP = 10.3 - 0.5 - 3.1 = 6.7\%$$

2-2. *Interest rates.*
A. The expected rate of inflation is the nominal rate minus the real rate and the risk premium. Use equation 2-1 and solve for EI.

$$NIR = RR + EI + RP$$

$$15 = 1 + EI + 10$$

$$EI = 15 - 1 - 10 = 4\%$$

2-3. *Total return.*
A.   The return from dividends is the dollar amount of the dividend divided by the purchase price and expressed as a percentage.
Use only the relevant part of equation 2-3.

$$\frac{\text{Cash dividends}}{\text{Purchase price}} = \frac{1.50}{30.00} = .05 \text{ or } 5\%$$

12

Chapter 2: The Role of Financial Markets

B. The return from capital gains or losses is the change in price divided by the purchase price and expressed as a percentage. Use the relevant part of equation 2-3.

$$\frac{\text{Sale price - purchase price}}{\text{Purchase price}} = \frac{28.50 - 30.00}{30.00} = \frac{-1.50}{30.00} = -0.05 \text{ or } -5\%$$

C. The total return is the sum of the return from dividends and the return from capital gains or losses. Use equation 2-3.

$$TR = \frac{\text{cash dividends}}{\text{purchase price}} + \frac{\text{sale price - purchase price}}{\text{purchase price}}$$

$$= \frac{1.50}{30.00} + \frac{28.50 - 30.00}{30.00}$$

$$= 0 \text{ or } 0\%$$

2-4. *Total Return.*
Use equation 2-3 and solve for the sale price.

$$TR = \frac{\text{cash dividends}}{\text{purchase price}} + \frac{\text{sale price - purchase price}}{\text{purchase price}}$$

$$.30 = \frac{.60}{12} + \frac{\text{sale price - 12}}{12}$$

Simplifying, 3.60 = sale price - 11.40

And sale price = $15

CHAPTER 3
ACCOUNTING AND CASH FLOW CONCEPTS

Concepts You Should Understand

*   Management reports the financial condition of the company to stockholders and the world through four main financial statements: the balance sheet, income statement, statement of changes in stockholders equity, and statement of cash flows.

*   Accounting statements present historical data on an accrual basis. Financial management uses these statements as a report card of past performance and a guide to projecting future data on a cash flow basis.

*   Management's goal is to maximize the market value of owners' equity (i.e. stock price). The equity section of the balance sheet reports the book value, not the market value, of stockholders' equity.

*   Ratios concentrate on measuring five major aspects of financial performance: liquidity, activity, leverage, profitability, and market reaction.

*   A firm's ratios are most meaningful if compared to industry norms with attention given to changes over time.

*   Ratios help the analyst spot trouble; ratios do not recommend management action to correct the trouble.

*   Ratios are fraught with limitations in calculations, comparisons, international complications, and interpretation, and are valuable only if they are valid under the circumstances.

A Second Look

Financial statements are management's report to the world and are primarily aimed at stockholders, financial analysts, creditors, and employees. These statements are invaluable to financial managers of the firm but have certain limitations. The balance sheet, income statement, and statement of changes in stockholders' equity are compiled on the accrual basis and for the most part show book values instead of market values.

14

Chapter 3: Accounting and Cash Flow Concepts

The statement of cash flows looks beyond the accrual-based income to report cash inflows and outflows.

Accounting values depend on the method of calculation. Often, more than one method is acceptable under generally accepted accounting principles. This fact can lead to differences in the financial results reported by similar companies, and ratios may be distorted by accounting practices. Comparisons among companies are more difficult because of differing accounting practices. When a company changes an accounting method (such as inventory valuation), the change may cause a sudden change in certain ratios, further complicating the analyst's job.

Consider a ship that sets sail from New York to London. As the ship sails, the captain relies on navigational readings to keep the ship on course toward its destination. If the navigational readings indicate that the ship is getting off course, the captain can take corrective action before the ship bumps into an iceberg or runs aground on a tropical island. The readings do not, however, tell why the ship is off course or what the captain needs to do to get back on course. Financial ratios are much like the navigational readings for the captain. They help spot trouble but do not explain how the trouble began or what steps management should take to correct the problem.

A ratio by itself is of little use. Ratios need to be compared to ratios of other companies in the same industry, and the trends of both the company and the industry need to be considered. Some analysts emphasize period-to-period changes in ratios and think that industry norms are of limited significance. Interpretation of ratios is still a judgment call to some extent.

The basic ratios for a manufacturing firm are presented in the text. Specialized ratios are used in various industries such as electric utilities or banking.

Cash flow is important to the financial manager and is not the same as income or profits. The most straightforward way to calculate basic cash flow from the income statement is to use the equation: cash flow = net income + noncash charges. Add the changes in current assets and current liabilities to the basic cash flow to get operating cash flow. Then determine the long-term investments and long-term financing undertaken by the firm. The final item to be added is the change in the cash account to get the overall cash flow for the firm.

Chapter Summary

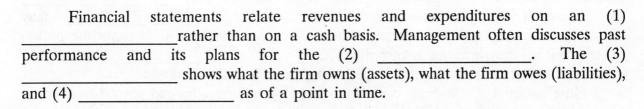

Financial statements relate revenues and expenditures on an (1) _____ rather than on a cash basis. Management often discusses past performance and its plans for the (2) _____. The (3) _____ shows what the firm owns (assets), what the firm owes (liabilities), and (4) _____ as of a point in time.

The five main categories on the balance sheet are (5)_____, (6) _____, (7)_____, (8) _____, and stockholders' equity. The balance sheet shows the (9)_____ of stockholders' equity, while the stock price, which is not on the balance sheet, reflects the (10)_____.

The (11) _____ shows the revenues and expenses over a given time period. When a firm earns money, it can either pay dividends or invest the money in more assets. If the firm invests in more assets, the balance sheet account which shows where the funds came from is called (12) _____. Retained earnings is not the same as cash; in fact, cash is an (13) _____ account, while retained earnings is a liability account.

In addition to the balance sheet and income statement, there are two other major statements: the (14) _____ and the (15)_____.

The relationships among various balance sheet and income statement accounts is shown through (16) _____. Ratios for a company being analyzed should be compared to (17) _____ over time in a (18) _____. Ratios are categorized into five major groups: (19) _____, (20) _____, (21) _____, (22)_____, and (23) _____ ratios.

Liquidity ratios access the ability of the firm to pay its bills on time and meet other cash needs. How well the firm's assets are utilized is indicated by the (24) _____ ratios. All of the ratios with "turnover" as part of their name relate an asset to (25) _____. (26) _____ ratios have to do with the extent of debt financing used by the firm. The profitability ratios relate (27) _____ to certain income statement and balance sheet items. Market ratios attempt to directly access management's success at maximizing the market value of owners' equity.

The (28) _____ system explores the relationships among the ratios themselves. This system helps the analyst trace the profitability (or lack thereof) back to the contributing accounts.

Financial statement analysis is limited by numerous factors. One of these is that the firm's cash flow situation may not be accurately reflected by accrual data. Different firms use different (29) _____ methods, which may make comparisons of ratios inaccurate and inappropriate. Often times companies do business is several different industries, which makes it impossible to find one (30) _____ for comparison. A problem in trend analysis is that (31) _____ may distort ratios over time. Management action taken near the end of a reporting period to temporarily improve ratios is known as (32) _____. In spite of these limitations, ratios are useful to both management and outside analysts.

International operations account for a large part of the sales and purchases of many United States corporations. SFAS #52 deals with the reporting of foreign operations and the translation of (33) _____ Gains or losses from translation are reported on the United States parent's balance sheet in the (34) _____ section.

Cash flow includes both the (35) _____ and (36) _____ of cash during a period. Cash flow is different from accounting income because some accounting expenses are not out-of-pocket cash outlays and are referred to as (37) _____. Two major noncash charges are (38) _____ and (39) _____. The "basic" cash flow is defined as (40) _____. Total cash flow also includes changes in currents assets and current liabilities, the purchase of and sale of fixed assets, and financing activities such as the sale or repayment of bonds. Cash flow will be used throughout the textbook for management decision making.

Acronyms and Notation You Should Know

AICPA	American Institute of Certified Public Accountants
FASB	Financial Accounting Standards Board
GAAP	Generally Accepted Accounting Principles
SFAS	Statements of Financial Accounting Standards
D&B	Dun & Bradstreet
ROA	Return on Assets
ROE	Return on Equity
EPS	Earnings per Share
DPS	Dividends per Share
P-E	Price-Earnings Ratio

Equations You Should Know

Liquidity ratios.

Current ratio = Current assets/current liabilities   (3-1)

Quick ratio = (current assets-inventory)/current liabilities   (3-2)

Activity ratios.

Inventory turnover = sales/inventory   (3-3)

17

Chapter 3: Accounting and Cash Flow Concepts

Collection period = [(receivables)(365)]/sales$\hspace{3cm}$(3-4)

Fixed-asset turnover = sales/fixed assets$\hspace{3cm}$(3-5)

Total-asset turnover = sales/total assets$\hspace{3cm}$(3-6)

Leverage ratios.

Debt-equity ratio = debt/equity$\hspace{3cm}$(3-7)

Debt to total assets = total debt/total assets$\hspace{3cm}$(3-8)

Times interest earned = net operating income/interest expense$\hspace{1cm}$(3-9)

Profitability ratios.

Profit margin = net income after tax/sales$\hspace{3cm}$(3-10)

Return on assets = net income after tax/total assets$\hspace{2cm}$(3-11)

Return on equity = net income after tax/equity$\hspace{2.5cm}$(3-12)

Market ratios.

Earnings per share = net income after tax/common shares outstanding

Dividends per share = cash dividends to common/common shares outstanding

Dividend yield = dividends per share/market price of common

Dividend payout = dividends per share/earnings per share

Price-earnings ratio = market price of common/earnings per share

DuPont System

Equity multiplier$\quad$=$\quad$Total assets/Equity$\hspace{3cm}$(3-13)

ROE$\quad$=$\quad$(ROA)(Equity multiplier)$\hspace{3cm}$(3-14)

18

Problems

3-1. *Liquidity ratios.* A novice analyst for Cee-Cee Enterprises has gathered the following account balances for the end of the fiscal year:

Cash and Equivalents	$800	Accounts Receivable	$3,200
Inventory	$2,800	Accounts Payable	$2,000
Deferred Income Taxes	$600	Plant and Equipment	$8,000
Wages Payable	$200	Short-term Debt	$1,200

A. Calculate the current ratio.
B. Calculate the quick ratio.
C. Are these two ratios enough information to make a definitive statement about the liquidity of the firm? What additional information would you need?
D. Suppose you had the additional information that Cee-Cee's credit terms are net 30, the average collection period is 72 days, and the industry average collection period is 33 days. Would this alter your view of the firm's liquidity?

3-2. *Inventory turnover.* Brenda's Boutique has annual sales of $40 million and an average inventory of $20 million. The average inventory turnover for other similar boutiques in the city is 4 times.
A. Calculate Brenda's Boutique's average inventory turnover.
B. Does Brenda seem to have an inventory management problem?
C. Brenda thinks she could raise her store's inventory turnover to the average of similar stores without reducing sales. If she could accomplish this feat, what would be the boutique's new inventory level?
D. Do these calculations tell Brenda what specific steps she should take to reduce the inventory?

3-3. *Average collection period.* Madd Manufacturing has annual credit sales of $3.65 million and an average accounts receivable balance of $500,000. The industry average collection period is 30 days.
A. Calculate Madd's average collection period.
B. Does Madd appear to have a credit policy problem?
C. If Madd could reduce its average collection period to the industry average without losing sales, what would its new receivables level have to be?
D. Do these calculations tell Madd exactly what policies should be followed to reach the new average collection period?

Chapter 3: Accounting and Cash Flow Concepts

3-4. *Asset turnover.* Chris' Cycle Shop has the following balance sheet:

Chris' Cycle Shop
Balance Sheet
March 31, 1991

Current assets	$150,000	Current Liabilities	$80,000
Fixed Assets	100,000	Stockholders' Equity	170,000
Total	$250,000	Total	$250,000

Chris' sales are $800,000 per year. Industry averages for a few ratios follow:

	Industry Average
Fixed asset turnover	7.5
Total asset turnover	5.0

A. Calculate Chris' fixed asset turnover. Does his investment in fixed assets appear to be excessive of the level of sales?
B. Calculate Chris' total asset turnover. Does his total investment appear to be excessive?
C. If you had additional information, what ratios would you calculate next in order to further analyze Chris' problem?

3-5. *Leverage ratios.* Susan's Specialty Steel Products, Inc., has the following balance sheet:

Susan's Specialty Steel Products
Balance Sheet
March 31, 1991
($millions)

Current Assets	$300	Current Liabilities	$150
		Long-term Debt	350
		Preferred Stock	100
Fixed Assets	500	Common Equity	300
Total	$900	Total	$900

Interest on the long-term debt is 12 percent per year, and the principal is not currently being repaid. There is no explicit interest paid on the current liabilities. The firm's sales are $3,700 million, and its net operating income is $210 million. The preferred stock pays

a nine percent dividend annually.
A. Calculate the debt-equity ratio.
B. Calculate the debt to total assets ratio.
C. Calculate the times interest earned ratio.

3-6. *Profitability ratios.* Use the information for Susan's Specialty Steel Products, Inc., in the previous problem. The firm's average income tax rate is 34 percent.
A. Calculate the net income after tax.
B. Calculate the profit margin.
C. Calculate the return on assets.
D. Calculate the return on equity.

3-7. *Market ratios.* The following common stockholders' equity section is taken from the balance sheet of Jennifer's Manufacturing Company:

Common stock (15 million shares)	$15,000,000
Capital in excess of par value	135,000,000
Retained earnings	450,000,000
Total	$600,000,000

Jennifer's sales are $2.5 billion, and the profit margin is three percent. Total dividends amount to $30 million. Stock is trading on the New York Stock Exchange for $72 per share.
A. Calculate the earnings per share.
B. Calculate the dividends per share.
C. Calculate the dividend yield.
D. Calculate the dividend payout ratio.
E. Calculate the price-earnings ratio.

3-8. *Ratios and Accounting practices.* Consider two separate companies, Adams Company and Barnes Company. They are competitors in the same industry. They buy product Y from the same supplier and resell it. Their physical and fiscal operations are identical except for their accounting for inventory. Adams uses first-in, first-out (FIFO) and Barnes uses last-in , first-out (LIFO) inventory valuation. Both methods are acceptable accounting practices. Each company has a beginning inventory of 500 units, which cost $2 each. Each company buys 2,000 units during the year at a cost of $3 per unit. Each company sells 2,000 units at a price of $5 per unit.
A.   Calculate the inventory turnover for each company, using ending inventory.
B.   Was there a difference in the physical units bought and sold by each company?
C.   What were the cash receipts and cash payments made by each company?
D.   What caused the difference in their ending inventory turnovers?

Answers to Chapter Summary

1. accrual
2. future
3. balance sheet
4. stockholders'
5. current assets
6. fixed assets
7. current liabilities
8. long-term debt
9. book value
10. market value
11. income statement
12. retained earnings
13. asset
14. statement of changes in stockholders' equity
15. statement of cash flows
16. ratio analysis
17. industry average
18. trend analysis
19. liquidity
20. activity

21. leverage
22. profitability
23. market
24. activity
25. sales
26. leverage
27. net income after taxes
28. DuPont
29. accounting
30. industry average
31. inflation
32. window dressing
33. currency
34. stockholders' equity
35. inflows
36. outflows
37. noncash charges
38. depreciation
39. deferred taxes
40. net income after taxes plus non cash charges

Problem Solutions

General Hint: One of the difficulties in calculating ratios is determining *exactly* which figures to use. Balance sheet figures often vary significantly from period to period (quarterly, for example) because of factors such as seasonality and a firm's operating cycle. Activity ratios are particularly vulnerable to this problem because they combine balance sheet figures, representing a *point* in time, with income statement figures, representing a *period* of time. The analyst may determine average figures, such as average inventory, to be more appropriate than end-of-period figures, such as end-of-year inventory, for calculating ratios. If averages are chosen, the method of averaging over the relevant time period needs to be considered with care. At times the analyst is hampered by lack of data; this is particularly true of the outside analyst.

In the ensuing problems you must refer to the data and the language in the problem to determine whether to use average or end-of-period balance sheet figures. The equations themselves make no reference to which figures to use. The general forms of the equations are flexible and open to your interpretation. The problems are stated so that it should be clear whether to use average or end-of-period figures.

3-1. *Liquidity ratios.*

The first thing to do is to separate the current assets and current liabilities from the other accounts. Some of these accounts are just extraneous information. But, then, a Wall Street analyst has all the information in the world and has to figure out what is relevant to the problem at hand.

Cash and equivalents	$ 800	Short-term debt	$1,200
Accounts receivable	3,200	Accounts payable	2,000
Inventory	2,800	Wages payable	200
Current assets	$6,800	Current liabilities	$3,400

A. Use equation 3-1:

Current ratio = current assets/current liabilities
= $6,800/$3,400
= 2

B. Use equation 3-2:

Quick ratio = (current assets - inventory)/current liabilities
= ($6,800 - $2,800)/$3,400
= 1.18

C. In order to make an informed judgment about the liquidity of this firm we would like to compare these ratios to industry averages and see how both the company and the industry compared in historical trends. We would also like to know more about the nature of the receivables, since they are considered to be quite liquid in both ratios.

D. If Cee-Cee's credit terms of net 30 seem to be in line with the industry which, on the average, collects its receivables in 33 days. Since Cee-Cee's average collection period is 72 days, there seems to be a problem somewhere in their credit and collections area. This would make an analyst wonder whether or not many of the receivables would ever be collected. This certainly casts a doubt on their liquidity.

3-2. *Inventory turnover.*

A. Use equation 3-3 with the average inventory figures given:

$$\text{Inventory turnover} = \text{sales/inventory}$$
$$= \$40/\$20$$
$$= 2 \text{ times}$$

B. Brenda's sales are only two times inventory compared to the industry average of four times. She seems to have a problem of too much inventory for the level of sales.

C. Use equation 3-3 again, only solve for a different variable:

$$\text{Inventory turnover} = \text{sales/inventory}$$
$$4 = \$40/\text{inventory}$$
$$\text{Inventory} = \$10 \text{ million}$$

D. The above calculation only tells Brenda what the new inventory level would have to be. It does not tell Brenda how to achieve the desired level.

3-3. *Average collection period.*

A. Use equation 3-4:

$$\text{Average collection period} = (\text{receivables})(365)/\text{sales}$$
$$= (\$500)(365)/\$3,650$$
$$= 50 \text{ days}$$

Note: Three zeroes are left off the dollar figures to make the arithmetic shorter.

B. Madd does appear to have a credit and collections problem since the industry average is only 30 days compared to Madd's 50 days.

C. Use equation 3-4 again, only solve for a different variable.

$$\text{Average collection period} = (\text{receivables})(365)/\text{sales}$$
$$30 = (\text{receivables})(365)/\$3,650$$
$$\text{Receivables} = \$300 \text{ thousand}$$

Chapter 3: Accounting and Cash Flow Concepts

3-4. *Asset turnover.*

A. Use equation 3-5:

Fixed-assets turnover = sales/fixed assets
                       = $800/$100
                       = 8 times

Compared to the industry average of 7.5 times, Chris' investment appears quite reasonable. In fact, Chris' ratio is a little better than average.

B. Use equation 3-6:

Total-assets turnover = sales/total assets
                       = $800/$250
                       = 3.2 times

Chris' total asset turnover appears excessive compared to the industry average of 5.0.

C. Let's think a little. If the fixed-asset turnover is OK, but the total asset turnover is poor, then the problem must be in current assets. The first things that come to mind to investigate the current assets are the liquidity ratios, inventory turnover, and average collection period.

3-5. *Leverage ratios.*
Remember that debt means total short-term and long-term debt, and equity means total preferred and common equity.

Total debt   = $150 + $350 = $500 million
Total equity = $100 + $300 = $400 million

A. Use equation 3-7:

Debt-equity ratio = debt/equity
                   = $500/$400
                   = 1.25

Chapter 3: Accounting and Cash Flow Concepts

B. Use equation 3-8:

Debt ratio   = total debt/total assets
               = \$500/\$900
               = 0.5556

This ratio is often expressed as a percentage, so you might also say this is 55.56 percent.

C. Before we can calculate the time interest earned, we must calculate the interest expense. Since we are working with annual figures and the principal balance is not declining during the year, the interest expense is the rate times the principal.

Interest expense   = (interest rate)(principal)
                    = (.12)(\$350)
                    = \$42 million

Now we can use equation 3-9:

Times interest earned   = net operating income/interest expense
                        = \$210/\$42
                        = 5 times

3-6. Profitability ratios.

A. Let's set up a partial income statement to work this problem.

Net operating income	$210
Interest expense	42
Net income before taxes	$168
Income taxes (.34)(168)	57 (rounded)
Net income	$111

B. Use equation 3-10:

Profit margin = net income after tax/sales
               = \$111/\$3,700
               = .03 or 3%

Chapter 3: Accounting and Cash Flow Concepts

C. Use equation 3-11:

$$\begin{aligned}
\text{ROA} &= \text{net income after tax/total assets} \\
&= \$111/\$900 \\
&= .1233 \text{ or } 12.33\%
\end{aligned}$$

D. Use equation 3-12. Equity means preferred equity and common equity. First calculate total equity.

$$\begin{aligned}
\text{Equity} &= \text{preferred equity} + \text{common equity} \\
&= \$100 + \$300 \\
&= \$400 \text{ million}
\end{aligned}$$

Now calculate ROE.

$$\begin{aligned}
\text{ROE} &= \text{net income after tax/equity} \\
&= \$111/\$400 \\
&= 0.2775 \text{ or } 27.75\%
\end{aligned}$$

3-7. *Market ratios.*

A. With the data given we have two ways to calculate EPS. So we'll do them both. First calculate the earnings or net income after tax.

$$\begin{aligned}
\text{Net income after tax} &= (\text{profit margin})(\text{sales}) \\
&= (.03)(\$2,500) \\
&= \$75 \text{ million dollars}
\end{aligned}$$

Now,

$$\begin{aligned}
\text{EPS} &= \text{net income after tax/number of common shares} \\
&= \$75 \text{ million/15 million shares} \\
&= \$5 \text{ per share}
\end{aligned}$$

The second method is to use equation 3-15. But to do that, we have to calculate both the ROE and the book value per share of common equity.

$$\begin{aligned}
\text{ROE} &= \text{net income after tax/stockholders' equity} \\
&= \$75/\$600 \\
&= .125 \text{ or } 12.5\%
\end{aligned}$$

$$\text{Book value per share} = \text{stockholders' equity/common shares}$$
$$= \$600 \text{ million/15 million shares}$$
$$= \$40 \text{ per share}$$

Now we can use equation 3-15:

$$\text{EPS} = (\text{ROE})(\text{book value per share})$$
$$= (.125)(\$40)$$
$$= \$5 \text{ per share}$$

Either way we got $5.00 per share.

B. Dividends per share is the total dividends divided by the number of shares outstanding.

$$\text{DPS} = \text{total dividends/number of common shares}$$
$$= \$30 \text{ million/15 million shares}$$
$$= \$2.00 \text{ per share}$$

C. The dividend yield is calculated as follows:

$$\text{Dividend yield} = \text{DPS/market price of common stock}$$
$$= \$2/\$72$$
$$= 0.0278 \text{ or } 2.78\%$$

D. The dividend payout ratio is calculated as follows:

$$\text{Dividend payout} = \text{DPS/EPS}$$
$$= \$2/\$5$$
$$= .40 \text{ or } 40\%$$

E. The price-earnings ratio is calculated as follows:

$$\text{Price-earnings ratio} = \text{market price/EPS}$$
$$= \$72/\$5$$
$$= 14.4 \text{ times}$$

3-8. *How accounting practices affect ratios.*

A.   To work this problem, let's decide to use ending inventories in the calculation of inventory turnover (as opposed to average inventory). Then we need to think back to principles of accounting and figure out ending inventory for each company. Remember that FIFO means that the company sells the first units that it purchased, so Able would have sold its original inventory and have only newly purchased units in its ending inventory. Barnes, on the other hand, using LIFO, would sell the last units it purchased first, leaving its original inventory in stock as its ending inventory, too.

	Able Company			Barnes Company		
	Units	Cost	Total	Units	Cost	Total
Beginning inventory	500	$2	$1,000	500	$2	$1,000
Purchases	2,000	$3	6,000	2,000	$3	6,000
Total available	2,500		$7,000	2,500		$7,000
Ending inventory-FIFO	500	$3	$1,500			
Ending inventory-LIFO				500	$2	$1,000

Note that sales is the same for each company in terms of units and dollars.

	Units	Cost	Total	Units	Cost	Total
Sales	2,000	$5	$10,000	2,000	$5	$10,000

Now let's use equation 3-3 to calculate ending inventory turnover:

		Able Company	Barnes Company
Inventory turnover	=	sales/inventory	sales/inventory
	=	$10,000/$1,500	$10,000/$1,000
	=	6.67 times	10.00 times

B.   These inventory turnover figures are drastically different, *even though* the companies began with the same number of units in inventory at the same cost, purchased the same number of units at the same cost, and sold the same number of units at the same price.

C.   The cash receipts ($10,000) and payments ($6,000) were the same for both companies.

D.   The difference in the ratios is caused by the accounting practices, which certainly makes it difficult for analysts to compare ratios with confidence.

CHAPTER 4
TIME VALUE OF MONEY

Concepts You Should Understand

*   Money has time value because it can be invested at a positive rate of return, which may include both a change in the amount of capital and interest income.

*   Compounding occurs when interest is added to the principal and both principal and interest then earn more interest to reach a future value.

*   Discounting is basically working the compounding problem backwards to reach a present value.

*   An annuity is a series of equal payments at equal intervals over time.

*   A future value is an amount of money to be received or paid at some time in the future; whereas, a present value is an amount of money to be received or paid today.

*   The interest factor tables have the complex part of the mathematical computations already done for you.

A Second Look

Let's take a brief second look at the present value-future value problem. Suppose you invest $1,000, for example, in a money market mutual fund that pays 10 percent compounded annually. You leave your investment in the fund for three years. Here's what happens:

Time	Activity	Balance
0	Initial investment	$1,000
1	During the first year you earn (10%)($1,000) = $100 interest. Your new balance = $1,000 + $100.	$1,100

Time	Activity	Balance
2	During the second year you earn (10%)($1,100) = $110 interest. Your new balance = $1,100 + $110.	$1,210
3	During the third year you earn (10%)($1,210) = $121 interest. Your new balance = $1,210 + $121.	$1,331

These calculations are simple enough, so let's relate them to the terminology used with time value of money problems. We shall work this problem two ways using the interest factor tables. The $1,000 is the *present value*. The $1,331 is the *future value*.

Question number 1. If you are given that the investment is $1,000, then the question is "What is the future value?" Since we start at the present and work toward the future, we talk about a *compound rate* of 10 percent and use the *FVIF* Table A-1.

$$FV_n = (PV)(FVIF_{k,n}) = (PV)(FVIF_{.10,3}) = (\$1,000)(1.331) = \$1,331$$

Question number 2. If you are given that you expect to receive $1,331 three years from now, then the question is "What is the present value?" Since we start in the future and work back to the present, we talk about a *discount rate* of 10 percent and use the *PVIF* Table A-2.

$$PV = (FV_n)(PVIF_{k,n}) = (FV_3)(PVIF_{.10,3}) = (\$1,331)(0.751) = \$1,000$$

This example used a single payment. Problems with annuities are similar.

Future value and present value problems can be solved by five approaches: (1) mathematical formulas, (2) interest factor tables, (3) financial calculators, (4) Lotus 1-2-3[1] or similar spreadsheets, and (5) software specifically designed for these problems. The first three approaches are explained in the text. This *Study Guide* emphasizes solutions with the tables. Solutions using a Lotus 1-2-3 spreadsheet are explained in "Lotus Notes."

Chapter Summary

Because money can be invested and earn interest over time, it is said to have a (1) _____. If one invests an amount of money today, this beginning

---

[1] Lotus 1-2-3 is the copyrighted trademark of Lotus Development Corporation.

amount is referred to as the (2) _____. If this amount earns interest, and the interest is added to the principal so that the interest also earns interest, the process is called (3) _____. The interest rate is then a (4) _____ rate. The amount, including interest, at the end of the compounding period is the (5) _____.

If one takes future values as given and calculates the present value, the process is called (6) _____, and the interest rate is then called the (7) _____.

A series of equal payments over time is an (8) _____. If the first payment is of the series is at the end of the first period, it is an (9) _____. If the payment is at the beginning of the first period, it is an (10) _____. An annuity with an infinite life is a (11) _____.

A loan that is paid back with a fixed number of payments, all of the same amount, is said to be (12) _____. Each payment includes both (13) _____ and (14) _____. The (15) _____ portion of each payment increases with each payment, but the (16) _____ portion of each payment decreases. To calculate the constant payment amount, one needs to use the (17) _____ table.

If an annuity is designed to provide a particular future value, then the future amount is called a (18) _____. A problem of this nature would require the (19) _____ table.

The stated annual interest rate is (20) _____ than the effective annual interest rate because of the number of (21) _____. The length of the compounding periods can be shortened and shortened until the compounding is said to be (22) _____.

Acronyms and Notation You Should Know

FV_n	Future value at the end of n periods
PV	Present value
FVA_n	Future value of an annuity of n periods
PVA_n	Present value of an annuity of n periods
$FVIF_{k,n}$	Future value interest factor for k percent and n periods
$PVIF_{k,n}$	Present value interest factor for k percent and n periods
$FVIFA_{k,n}$	Future value interest factor for an annuity for k percent and n periods
$PVIFA_{k,n}$	Present value interest factor for an annuity for k percent and n periods
C	Constant annuity payment
k	The rate of return or rate of interest
n	The number of compounding or discounting periods

Equations You Should Know

$$FV_n = (PV)(FVIF_{k,n}) \tag{4-5}$$

$$FV_n = (C_1)(FVIF_{k,n-1}) + (C_2)(FVIF_{k,n-2}) + \ldots + (C_{n-1})(FVIF_{k,1}) + C_n \tag{4-6}$$

$$FVA_n = (C)(FVIFA_{k,n}) \tag{4-7}$$

$$PV = (FV_n)(PVIF_{k,n}) \tag{4-10}$$

$$PV = \sum_{t=1}^{n} (C_t)(PVIF_{k,t}) \tag{4-13}$$

$$PVA_n = (C)(PVIFA_{k,n}) \tag{4-15}$$

$$PVA = \frac{C}{k} \tag{4-17}$$

$$\text{Effective annual interest rate} = (1 + k/m)^m - 1 \tag{4-22}$$

$$\text{Continuous compounding rate} = e^k - 1.0 \tag{4-23}$$

$$FV_n = (PV)(e^{kn}) \tag{4-27}$$

$$FV_n = (C)(1 + k/m)^{mn} \tag{4-25}$$

$$PVIF_{k,n} = 1/FVIF_{k,n}$$

Lotus Notes

Lotus 1-2-3 contains a set of eight financial functions to perform calculations required with compound interest problems. There are three functions in the financial group for calculating depreciation. Other calculations may be easily done by entering the necessary formula in the spreadsheet. Complete descriptions are found in the *Lotus 1-2-3 User's Manual*. Lotus 1-2-3 answers will differ slightly from answers calculated with the tables because of rounding in the tables.

Chapter 4: Time Value of Money

The following definitions apply for use in the functions:
interest - the periodic interest rate expressed as a decimal
payment - an annuity
term - the number of years or periods
range - the range on the spreadsheet where the data are contained

The financial functions are summarized here:

@CTERM(interest,future value,present value)
This function calculates the number of compounding periods required for the present value to grow to the future value at the rate specified.

@FV(payment,interest,term)
This function calculates the future value of an ordinary annuity (payment) at the interest rate and number of periods specified.

@IRR(guess,range)
This function calculates the discount rate that equates the present value of a series of future payments to the initial investment. The discount rate is called the internal rate of return or IRR. The range contains the data. The guess is an estimate of the answer.

@NPV(interest, range)
This function calculates the present value of data contained in the range discounted at the interest (discount) rate specified. A word of caution: Although the acronym NPV is for net present value, this function calculates only a present value, not a *net* present value as described in Chapter 12 of the text.

@PMT(principal,interest,term)
This function calculates the payment necessary to amortize a loan of the amount, principal.

@PV(payment,interest,term)
This function calculates the present value of an ordinary annuity, discounted at the rate for the term specified.

@RATE(future value,present value,term)
This function calculates the interest rate required for the present value to increase to the future value during the term specified.

@TERM(payment,interest,future value)
This function calculates the number of periods required for a sinking fund to reach a future value, given the size of the payments and the interest rate.

Chapter 4: Time Value of Money

Problems

4-1. *Future value - single payment.* Suppose your parents had deposited $1,000 in a savings account for you the day you were born. The account pays six percent interest compounded annually. How much would this account be worth on your 18th birthday?

4-2. *Future value - uneven payments.* You decided to invest in a money market mutual fund which pays eight percent interest compounded annually. Your first payment into the fund will be one year from today. Subsequent payments will be each year after that for five years total. Each payment into the fund is a different amount as given below.
A. How much will you have at the end of the fifth year?
B. Will any of the five payments *not* earn interest? Is so, which one?

Year	End of year payment
1	$5,000
2	$1,000
3	$4,000
4	$2,000
5	$3,000

4-3. *Future value - ordinary annuity.* You are 22 years old and plan to retire a millionaire at age 40. You feel confident you can land a job as senior vice president and invest $30,000 at the end of each of the next 18 years.
A. Will you reach your goal by the end of the 18th year if the investment earns six percent compounded annually?
B. Will you reach your goal by the end of the 18th year if the investment pays eight percent compounded annually?

4-4. *Future value - ordinary annuity.* You have decided to save for a down payment on a house. Your goal is to save $10,000 in five years. You plan contribute an equal amount each year to a savings account that pays six percent compounded annually. Your first deposit will be one year from today. How much will each deposit have to be in order to reach your goal?

4-5. *Present value - single payment.* Suppose you want to have a lump sum of $50,000 available in twelve years.
A. How much will you have to invest today if you can earn 12 percent compounded annually?
B. How much will you have to invest today if you can earn six percent compounded annually?

4-6.   *Present value - series of uneven payments.* Suppose you want to invest some money today and make withdrawals at the end of each of the next four years. You have an account that pays eight percent compounded annually. How much will you have to invest in order to withdraw the following amounts?

Year	End of year withdrawal
1	$500
2	$1,000
3	$1,500
4	$2,000

4-7.   *Present value - annuity.* You want to invest some money today and make withdrawals of $1,000 at the end of each of the next four years. You have an account that pays 10 percent compounded annually. How much will you have to invest?

4-8.   *Present value - perpetuity.* Now that you are rich and famous, you want to establish a scholarship for students just like you were back when. You want the lucky student to receive $5,000 each year. When you discuss this with the financial aid office at your alma mater, you learn that they average nine percent compounded annually on their investments. You want the scholarship to continue paying $5,000 per year as long as the university exists. How much will you have to donate if the first scholarship is to be given one year from your donation?

4-9.   *Present value - series of payments, part uneven, part annuity.*
Calculate the present value of the following series of payments. Use a discount rate of 20 percent.
A. Use Table A-2 only.
B. Use Table A-2 and Table A-3.

Year	Payment
1	$10,000
2	$50,000
3	$50,000
4	$50,000
5	$50,000
6	$50,000
7	$20,000

4-10.   *Present value - annuity: loan amortization.* Pete's Pizza Palace is planning to invest in some new kitchen equipment at a cost of $80,000. They can borrow the entire amount at 16 percent compounded annually. The loan will be amortized in three equal annual

36

payments beginning one year from the loan date. How much is each annual payment?

4-11. *Future value - annuity: sinking fund.* The Acme Corporation needs to provide for $100 million to be available 15 years from now. The treasurer intends to make 15 annual, year-end deposits starting one year hence. The money will be invested at six percent. How much must be deposited each year?

4-12. *Future value, present value: discount rate.* Your good buddy wants to borrow $1,013.20 for a trip to the beach over spring break. He says he will pay you back $2,000 as soon as he finishes his master's degree. Of course, that will be at the end of six years, since he is a freshman now. What annual compound rate of interest is he promising you?
A. Work this problem using the future value Table A-1.
B. Work this problem using the present value Table A-2.

4-13. *Present value - annuity: discount rate.* Pete's Pizza Palace is going to by a new turbo delivery truck, complete with pin stripes and racing slicks, for only $24,000. The bank will lend them $20,000 with three annual payments of $8,327.09 or with five annual payments of $5,966.23.
A. Calculate the interest rate on the three-year loan.
B. Calculate the interest rate on the five-year loan.

4-14. *Present value - uneven payments: discount rate.* Sam just got a hot tip on a new gold mining technique. His source says that on a $6,150 investment, he could expect to receive $4,000 at the end of the first year, $3,000 at the end of the second year, and $1,000 at the end of the third year. What rate of return will Sam receive if his expectations are met?

4-15. *Effective annual interest rates.* Calculate the effective annual interest rate for a nominal 12 percent investment if the compounding is done on the following intervals: annually, semiannually, quarterly, monthly, daily, continuously.

4-16. *Present value - monthly compounding.* You have decided to trade in the old pickup truck on a new one. Well, at least a newer one. After a lot of hard bargaining with the used car salesman and astute dealing with the credit union, you owe $16,000 at 12 percent interest with 40 monthly payments. How much are your monthly payments?

4-17. *Present value - quarterly compounding: discount rate.* Blaze Torch Company has the opportunity to invest $750,000. Blaze will receive quarterly payments of $55,186.42 for five years. Calculate the annual rate of return.

Answers to Chapter Summary

1. time value
2. present value
3. compounding
4. future value
5. future value
6. discounting
7. discount rate
8. annuity
9. ordinary annuity
10. annuity due
11. perpetuity

12. amortized
13. interest
14. principal
15. principal
16. interest
17. $PVIFA_{k,n}$
18. sinking fund
19. $FVIFA_{k,n}$
20. smaller
21. compounding periods
22. continuous

Problem Solutions

General hint: Most of these problems are to be worked with the interest factor tables. There are four tables, so you have to figure out which one to use. If in doubt, ask yourself two questions. First, am I looking for an amount to be accumulated by some time in the future or for an amount today? And second, is a single payment or an annuity involved? The combined answers should tell you which table to use.

Combined Answers	Table
Future value, single payment	A-1
Present value, single payment	A-2
Present value, annuity	A-3
Future value, annuity	A-4

Lotus 1-2-3 cell entries and answers are given for comparison on certain problems.

4-1. *Future value - single payment.* The money is deposited, and interest is added to it every year. The present value is $1,000; k is six percent; and n is 18 years. We are looking for a future amount, so this is a future value, single payment problem. Use equation 4-5 and Table A-1.

$$
\begin{aligned}
FV_{18} &= (PV)(FVIF_{.06,18}) \\
&= (\$1,000)(2.854) \\
&= \$2,854
\end{aligned}
$$

Chapter 4: Time Value of Money

4-2. *Future value - uneven payments.*
A. We are looking for a future amount, so it is a future value problem. The series of payments is *not* an annuity, though, because each payment is different. We have to use the future value, single payment table again. Use equation 4-6 and Table A-1.

$$FV_5 = (C_1)(FVIF_{.08,4}) + (C_2)(FVIF_{.08,3}) + (C_3)(FVIF_{.08,2}) + (C_4)(FVIF_{.08,1}) + C_5$$
$$= (\$5,000)(1.361) + (\$1,000)(1.260) + (\$4,000)(1.166) + (\$2,000)(1.080) + \$3,000$$
$$= \$17,889$$

B. The fifth payment does not earn interest because it is made on the last day of the annuity. The fourth payment earns one year's interest, and so on.

4-3. *Future value - ordinary annuity.* We are looking for a future sum, and the payments are an annuity. Use equation 4-7 and Table A-4.

A. FVA_{18} = (C)(FVIFA$_{.06,18}$)   Lotus function: @FV(payment,interest,term)
    = (\$30,000)(30.906)   Lotus entry: @FV(30000,0.06,18)
    = \$927,180   Lotus answer: \$927,169.50

B. FVA_{18} = (C)(FVIFA$_{.08,18}$)   Lotus function: @FV(payment,interest,term)
    = (\$30,000)(37.450)   Lotus entry: @FV(30000,0.08,18)
    = \$1,123,500   Lotus answer: \$1,123,507.00

4-4. *Future value - ordinary annuity.* We are looking for the future amount of an annuity. We have to use the future value of an annuity Table A-4 and equation 4-7. In this case the payment, C, is the unknown, because we know the desired amount at the end and we can look up the interest factor in the table.

FVA_5 = (C)(FVIFA$_{.06,5}$)
\$10,000 = (C)(5.637)

Solving for C, this becomes equation 4-19.

C = \$10,000/5.637
    = \$1,773.99

4-5. *Present value - single payment.* We want to find an amount today, so this is a present value problem. It is a single payment problem because there is no annuity involved. Use equation 4-10 and Table A-2.

A. PV = $(FV_{12})(PVIF_{.12,12})$
   = $(\$50,000)(0.257)$
   = $\$12,850$

B. PV = $(FV_{12})(PVIF_{.06,12})$
   = $(\$50,000)(0.497)$
   = $\$24,850$

4-6. *Present value - uneven payments.* We are trying to figure out an amount today, so this is a present value problem. There is no annuity because the payments are not equal. Each payment must be treated as a single payment. Use equation 4-13 and Table A-2.

PV = $(C_1)(PVIF_{.08,1}) + (C_2)(PVIF_{.08,2}) + (C_3)(PVIF_{.08,3}) + (C_4)(PVIF_{.08,4})$
   = $(\$500)(0.926) + (\$1,000)(0.857) + (\$1,500)(0.794) + (\$2,000)(0.735)$
   = $\$3,981$

4-7. *Present value - annuity.* We are trying to find an amount to invest today, so this is a present value problem. The series of payments is an annuity. Use equation 4-15 and Table A-3.

PVA_4 = $(C)(PVIFA_{.10,4})$ Lotus function: @PV(payment,interest,term)
   = $(\$1,000)(3.170)$ Lotus entry: @PV(1000,0.1,4)
   = $\$3,170$ Lotus answer: $\$3,169.87$

4-8. *Present value - perpetuity.* This is a present value problem because we are looking for an amount to donate today. It is a perpetuity because it is an unending series of equal payments. Use equation 4-17. A table is not needed.

PVA = C/k
   = $\$5,000/.09$
   = $\$55,555$

4-9. *Present value - uneven payments and annuity.* In this problem we have a single payment of $10,000 at the end of the first year, an annuity of $50,000 in years two through six, an a single payment of $20,000 at the end of the seventh year.

A. Let us set this up in table form so that we can see what we are doing. Use Table A-2 for the present value interest factors.

Year	Payment	$PVIF_{.20,n}$	Present Value $(Payment)(PVIF_{.20,n})$
1	$10,000	.833	$ 8,330
2	$50,000	.694	34,700
3	$50,000	.579	28,950
4	$50,000	.482	24,100
5	$50,000	.402	20,100
6	$50,000	.335	16,750
7	$20,000	.279	5,580
			Total $138,510

B. We shall work this problem again, using the tables in a different manner. We shall use Table A-2 on years one and seven, and Table A-3 on years two through six. We should get the same answer, except maybe for rounding errors.

Year	Payment	$PVIF_{.20,n}$	Present Value $(Payment)(PVIF_{.20,n})$
1	$10,000	.833	$ 8,330
2-6	$50,000	2.493	124,650
7	$20,000	.279	5,580
			Total $138,560

The interest factor for years 2-6 is derived from Table A-3:

$$PVIFA_{.20,6} - PVIFA_{.20,1} = 3.326 - .833 = 2.493$$

This calculation takes the interest factor for years 1-6 and subtracts out year 1, leaving only years 2-6. To check another way, look at part A and add the PVIFs for years 2-6:

$$.694 + .589 + .482 + .402 + .335 = 2.502$$

This factor differs from 2.493 only because of rounding in three-place tables, it causes the $50 difference in the answers in parts A and B.

The cell entry for a Lotus 1-2-3 spreadsheet solution follows.

        Lotus function: @NPV(interest,range)
        Lotus entry: @NPV(0.2,range)
        Lotus answer: $138,523.80

The Lotus answer is close to the solution in part A above.

Note: See the *Lotus 1-2-3 Reference Manual* for information about ranges.

4-10. *Present value - annuity: loan amortization.* In a loan problem the amount of the loan is the present value and the future payments are the annuity. Use Table A-3 and equation 4-15, which can be rearranged to equation 4-18.

$$PVA_3 \quad = \quad (C)(PVIFA_{.16,3}) \qquad\qquad (4\text{-}15)$$
$$\$80,000 \quad = \quad (C)(2.246)$$

Solving for C, this becomes equation 4-18.

$$C \quad = \quad PVA_3/PVIFA_{.16,3}$$
$$= \quad \$80,000/2.246$$
$$= \quad \$35,618.88$$

Lotus function: @PMT(principal,interest,term)
Lotus entry: @PMT(80000,0.16,3)
Lotus answer: $35,620.62

4-11. *Future value - annuity: sinking fund.* We need to accumulate a future amount with an annuity. Use equation 4-7, which rearranges to equation 4-19, and Table A-4.

$$FVA_{15} \quad = \quad (C)(FVIFA_{.06,15}) \qquad\qquad (4\text{-}7)$$
$$\$100,000 \quad = \quad (C)(23.276)$$

Solving for C, this becomes equation 4-19.

$$C \quad = \quad FVA_{15}/FVIFA_{.06,15} \qquad\qquad (4\text{-}19)$$
$$= \quad \$100,000/23.276$$
$$= \quad \$4,296.27$$

Chapter 4: Time Value of Money

4-12. *Future value, present value: discount rate.* This is a single payment problem with one future value and one present value. We shall work it two ways.

A. Use equation 4-5 and Table A-1. Notice that the $FVIF_{k,6}$ is the unknown in this instance. We cannot look up the FVIF without knowing the rate, and the rate is what the problem asks us to calculate.

FV_6	=	$(PV)(FVIF_{k,6})$	Lotus function: @Rate(FV,PV,term)
$2,000	=	$1,013.20(FVIF_{k,6})$	Lotus entry: @Rate(2000,1013.20,6)
$FVIF_{k,6}$	=	$2,000/$1,013.20	Lotus answer: .120011 or 12%
	=	1.974	

Now, 1.974 is an interest *factor*, not an interest *rate*. So we must look in Table A-1 under six periods, until we find an interest factor close to 1.974. Then look at the top of the column to find the interest rate. In this case it is 12 percent.

$$k \quad = \quad 12\%$$

B. We can also work this as a present value problem, using equations 4-10 and 4-20 and Table A-2.

$$PV \quad = \quad (FV_6)(PVIF_{k,6}) \qquad\qquad (4\text{-}10)$$
$$\$1,013.20 \quad = \quad (\$2,000)(PVIF_{k,6})$$

Solving for $PVIF_{k,6}$, this becomes equation 4-20.

$PVIF_{k,6}$	=	PV/FV_6
	=	$1,013.20/$2,000
	=	.507

Again, .507 is an interest *factor*, not an interest *rate*. We must look up the rate in Table A-2. Of course we get the same answer.

$$k \quad = \quad 12\%$$

4-13. *Present value - annuity: discount rate.* In a loan problem the amount borrowed is the present value and the payments are the future annuity. Use equation 4-15 and Table A-3.

A. We have to solve for the interest factor and look up the corresponding rate in the table.

$$PVA_3 = (C)(PVIFA_{k,3})$$
$$\$20,000 = (\$8,327.09)(PVIFA_{k,3})$$
$$PVIFA_{k,3} = \$20,000/\$8,327.09$$
$$= 2.402$$

Look in Table A-3 under three periods until you find a value near 2.402. Look at the top of the column and find k = 12 percent.

B. Repeat the process with the five-year loan.

$$PVA_5 = (C)(PVIFA_{k,5})$$
$$\$20,000 = (\$5,966.23)(PVIFA_{k,5})$$
$$PVIFA_{k,5} = \$20,000/\$5,966.23$$
$$= 3.352$$

Look in Table A-3 under five periods until you find a value near 3.352. Look at the top of the column and find k = 15 percent.

4-14. *Present value - uneven payments: discount rate.* Finding the discount rate with uneven payments is a little more tedious than with an annuity or a single payment, but the idea is the same. We must find the discount rate that makes the present value of the future payments equal to the amount of the investment.

We shall have to treat each payment as a single payment and use Table A-2. We shall use a *trial and error* technique. We shall try different discount rates until we get the present value equal to $6,150. Let us set this one up in a table for convenience.

We have to start somewhere, so let us try 16 percent. If the present value does not equal $6,150, then we shall try another rate.

Trial #1: 16%

Year	Payment	$PVIF_{.16,n}$	$(Payment)(PVIF_{.16,n})$
1	$4,000	.862	$3,448
2	$3,000	.743	2,229
3	$1,000	.641	641
			Total $6,381

We were trying to get $6,150, but we got $6,381. Let's try again to see if we can get closer. Do we need to try a higher or lower rate? The relationship between the discount rate and the present value is inverse. Since we need a *lower* present value, we need to try a *higher* discount rate. Let's try 20 percent.

Trial #2: 20%

Year	Payment	PVIF$_{.20,n}$	(Payment)(PVIF$_{.20,n}$)
1	$4,000	.833	$3,332
2	$3,000	.694	2,082
3	$1,000	.579	579
			Total $5,993

Oops! We went a little too far. The total of $5,993 is now *below* our target of $6,150. The correct answer must be between 16 percent and 20 percent. Let's try 18 percent.

Trial #3: 18%

Year	Payment	PVIF$_{.18,n}$	(Payment)(PVIF$_{.18,n}$)
1	$4,000	.848	$3,392
2	$3,000	.718	2,154
3	$1,000	.607	607
			Total $6,153

There we have it! Using tables, $6,153 is close enough to $6,150. The answer is 18 percent.

4-15. *Effective annual interest rates.* Use equation 4-22 for all the periodic compounding, and equation 4-23 for continuous compounding. A financial calculator or spreadsheet are convenient for doing the mathematics on the daily and continuous compounding.

Period	$(1 + k/m)^m - 1$	Effective rate
Annual	$(1 + .12/1)^1 - 1$	.12
Semiannual	$(1 + .12/2)^2 - 1$	.1236
Quarter	$(1 + .12/4)^4 - 1$	.1255
Month	$(1 + .12/12)^{12} - 1$	.1268
Day	$(1 + .12/365)^{365} - 1$	.1275
Continuous	$e^{.12} - 1$	.1275

Notice that the more frequent the compounding, the higher the effective rate.

4-16. *Present value - annuity: monthly compounding.* The loan amount is the present value, and the payments are the annuity. The only trick is to adjust <u>both</u> the discount rate and the number of periods to show that the periods are months, not years. We have to divide the rate by 12 and use the number of months, not years.

Since the annual interest rate is 12 percent or .12, the monthly rate is .12/12 = .01 per month for 40 months. Use equation 4-15 and Table A-3.

$$
\begin{aligned}
PVA_{40} &= (C)(PVIFA_{.01,40}) \\
\$16,000 &= (C)(32.835) \\
C &= \$16,000/32.835 \\
&= \$487.28
\end{aligned}
$$

4-17. *Present value - annuity: quarterly compounding.* Use equation 4-15 and Table A-3. Adjust the rate and periods for quarters. The number of periods is:

(5 years)(4 quarters per year) = 20 quarters.

$$
\begin{aligned}
PVA_{20} &= (C)(PVIFA_{k,20}) \\
\$750,000 &= (\$55,186.42)(PVIFA_{k,20}) \\
PVIFA_{k,20} &= \$750,000/\$55,186.42 \\
&= 13.590
\end{aligned}
$$

Now that we have calculated the interest *factor*, we must look up the *rate* in Table A-3. Look on the 20 periods line for a value near 13.590. When you find it, look at the top of the column to find the rate of 4 percent. But wait! We are not through yet. Four percent is a *quarterly* rate. Convert it to an *annual* rate by multiplying by 4 quarters per year:

(4%)(4 quarters per year) = 16% per year.

Do not forget this last step; it can mess you up on an exam or cause a bad investment decision.

CHAPTER 5
RISK CONCEPTS

Concepts You Should Understand

*   Expected return and risk for a single asset and for a portfolio is explained through probability theory.

*   The expected return-risk tradeoff means that investors accept higher risk only in expectation of higher return.

*   For an asset in a portfolio, the asset's covariance with the rest of the portfolio is the most important measure of risk, as long as that asset's weight in the portfolio is small.

*   Some risk is caused by factors that affect only the individual asset, while some risk is caused by factors that affect all assets within the same market.

*   Required return, as defined by the Capital Asset Pricing Model, consists of a risk-free return plus a single market-related risk premium for the asset.

*   Required return, as defined by the Arbitrage Pricing Model, consists of a risk-free return plus risk premiums related to a number of economic variables.

*   The risk that firm may fail, failure risk, is not adequately measured by covariance and should be considered separately.

A Second Look

When a business decision is made, the amount of money that will be realized from it in the future is not for sure. A businessman does, of course, have expectations about the future results of his decision. The chance that the actual results will not be the same as his expectations is known as risk or uncertainty.

Some business ventures involve more risk than others. The reason that managers take on more risky investments is that they have expectations of higher returns. This concept is called the expected return-risk tradeoff. It is easy enough to talk about risk and return but measuring them is a more demanding task.

The statistical concept of probability distributions is used to measure both risk and return. A probability distribution of the likelihoods of investment returns gives a manager the basis for calculating the expected return and the related risk measure, the standard deviation. These are appropriate for use by someone with only one investment or asset, but a portfolio of assets requires additional analysis.

A manager with a portfolio of investments is more concerned with the riskiness of the entire portfolio than with the riskiness of individual projects or securities within the portfolio. The expected return and standard deviation of the portfolio are somewhat more complex to calculate than for an individual asset. The portfolio's risk depends heavily upon the covariance among the various assets comprising the portfolio. An individual asset's risk in a well-diversified portfolio is measured by its covariance with the rest of the portfolio as long as the asset's weight in the portfolio is small.

Considering that a small weight within a portfolio is similar to a small weight within the market place in general, a manager can use covariance with a market index as a practical measure of risk. The Capital Asset Pricing Model (CAPM) develops beta as a measure of an asset's risk relative to the market. The Arbitrage Pricing Theory (APT) is an alternative to the CAPM. The APT is more complex in that it takes into account the asset's risk relative to any number of economic variables, not just to market movement. The final measure of risk is the probability of failure, that is, the probability that the firm will not be able to make payments on time to its creditors.

This chapter has defined expected return and risk in statistical terms for both an individual asset and a portfolio of assets. Probability theory, the CAPM, the APT, and probability of failure all have their usefulness to the financial manager.

Chapter Summary

(1)_____ and (2)_____ are key concepts throughout financial decision making. The mean of a probability of returns is the (3)_____. Risk is the chance that the (4)_____ will not equal the expected outcome. The (5)_____ is a risk measure that gives a numerical value to the dispersion of returns in the probability distribution. The expected return and standard deviation are appropriate expected return-risk measures when an investor owns (6)_____.

When a number of assets, such as stocks and bonds, are owned, the investor is said to have a (7)_____. The standard deviation of a portfolio depends heavily upon the (8)_____ among securities in the portfolio. When an investor is considering the risk of an asset within a (9)_____ portfolio, the most important measure of risk is that asset's (10)_____ with the rest of the portfolio.

For investors in general, the relevant measure of risk for an asset is the asset's covariance with a (11)_____. (12)_____ is an alternative way to measure risk by relating an asset's returns to the market returns. Beta can be estimated with (13)_____ and is the (14)_____ of the resultant equation.

The expected return-risk tradeoff means that financial managers accept higher risk only in expectation of (15)_____. The (16)_____ is the minimum expected return that would be acceptable to an investor for a particular level of risk. This return is composed of (17)_____, (18)_____, and (19)_____.

The (20)_____ explains the required rate of return on an asset in terms of a risk-free rate, the expected rate of return on the (21)_____, and the asset's (22)_____. The resultant equation is a (23)_____ relationship known as the (24)_____.

The (25)_____ employs a more general model than the Capital Asset Pricing Model (CAPM), relating an asset's expected return to several variables instead of to only one. The APT is a newer model than the CAPM, and there is still a great deal of testing and refining to be done before it becomes readily usable as a measure of an asset's required rate of return.

If an asset has a large (26)_____, many managers will find it unacceptable as an investment regardless of its standard deviation of expected returns or its beta.

In summary, the mean of a probability distribution of possible returns is called the (27)_____ and is a suitable measure of return for an individual asset or for a portfolio. The risk of an individual asset or a portfolio can be measured by the (28)_____; however, the relevant risk measure for an asset in a well-diversified portfolio is (29)_____.

Equations You Should Know

$$E(R_x) \quad = \quad \sum_{j=1}^{n} \text{Prob}_j X_j \qquad\qquad (5\text{-}1)$$

$$\sigma_x \quad = \quad [\sum_{j=1}^{n} \text{Prob}_j (X_j - E(R_x))^2]^{1/2} \qquad\qquad (5\text{-}2)$$

$$E(R_p) \quad = \quad \sum_{j=1}^{n} W_j E(R_j) \qquad\qquad (5\text{-}3)$$

$$Cov_{XY} = Corr_{XY}\sigma_X\sigma_Y \tag{5-4}$$

$$SD(R_p) = [\sum_{j=1}^{n} W_j^2 Var(R_j) + \sum_{j=1}^{n} \sum_{k=1}^{n} W_j W_k Cov_{j,k}]^{1/2} \tag{5-5}$$

$$\text{where } j = k$$

$$B_X = Cov_{XM}/\sigma_m^2 \tag{5-8}$$

Required rate of return = real rate of return +
$$\text{expected inflation premium +}$$
$$\text{risk premium} \tag{5-9}$$

$$k_X = RF + (E(R_m) - RF)B_X \tag{5-13}$$

$$k_X = RF + (F_1)(B_{X1}) + (F_2)(B_{X2}) + (F_3)(B_{X3}) \tag{5-15}$$

Problems

5-1. *Expected returns and standard deviations.*   (Note: This problem results in a risk-return tradeoff that is contrary to the typical situation and would not exist long in an efficient market.)

Big River Excursions, Inc., has the following probability distribution:

State of Economy	Prob	Expected Returns
Boom	0.10	30.00%
Good	0.40	20.00%
Bad	0.40	0.00%
Ugly	0.10	-10.00%
	1.00	

A.   Calculate the expected rate of return, $E(R)$, for Big River Excursion.
B.   Calculate the standard deviation, σ_x, for Big River Excursion.

Big River Electric Power, Inc., has the following probability distribution:

State of Economy	Prob	Expected Returns
Boom	0.10	17.00%
Good	0.40	15.00%
Bad	0.40	12.00%
Ugly	0.10	10.00%
	1.00	

C.   Calculate the expected rate of return, E(R) for Big River Electric.

D.   Calculate the standard deviation, σ_x, for Big River Electric.

E.   Would you rather invest in Big River Excursions or in Big River Electric? Explain you answer in terms of their relative risk and expected return.

F.   Calculate the expected return of a portfolio with 35 percent of its funds invested in Big River Excursions stock and 65 percent in Big River Electric Stock.

G.   Calculate the standard deviation of a portfolio with 35 percent of its funds invested in Big River Excursions stock and 65 percent in Big River Electric stock. The correlation coefficient between the stocks is 0.6.

5-2.   *Expected portfolio returns and portfolio betas.*   Calculate the expected portfolio return and portfolio beta for a portfolio consisting of the following common stocks:

Stock	$ Amount	$E(R_j)$	$Beta_j$
CNB	$8,000	15%	.95
BCB	20,000	22%	1.30
LAR	12,000	12%	.80
LAV	4,000	19%	1.15
DEF	50,000	14%	.90
ABC	24,000	20%	1.20
ZYX	41,000	16%	1.00
HAL	17,000	15%	.95
AGO	36,000	10%	.70
XT	11,000	18%	1.10

5-3.   *Covariance.*   Fast Motor Cars, Inc., has a standard deviation of 5 percent, and the market's standard deviation is 9 percent. The correlation coefficient between FMCI and the market is +0.9. Calculate the covariance between the company and the market.

5-4. *Required rate of return.*   The real rate of return is 2 percent; expected inflation is 4 percent; and the risk premium for Adams Finance Company is 8 percent. What is the approximate rate of return required for Adams?

5-5. *Required rate of return.*   The historical real rate of return is 3 percent; a survey reveals that business leaders expect 5 percent inflation on the average during the next year. Wildcat Drilling Company's stock is priced so that investors will make 27 percent if their expectations are met. What risk premium is implied for Wildcat?

5-6. *Beta.*   The S&Q 800 stock market index has a standard deviation of 12 percent. Onion Creek Manufacturing and Mining, Inc., has a covariance with the market of +0.015. Calculate Onion Creek's beta.

5-7. *Security Market line.*   The risk-free rate of return is 12 percent, while the rate of return on Standard and Poor's index of 500 stocks is 18 percent. The beta of Hi-Phi Sounds, Inc., a New York Stock Exchange traded stock, is 1.10.
A.   Calculate the risk premium for the market.
B.   Calculate the risk premium for the stock.
C.   Calculate the rate of return required by the market place for stock of this risk.
D.   If the risk-free rate were to increase by one percentage point, and the entire security market line shifted upward, what would be the new rate of return on the stock?
E.   If the original SML (with the risk-free rate of 12 percent) were to remain unchanged, but the stock's beta were to change to 1.20, what would be the new required rate of return on the stock?

5-8. *Security Market Line.*   The risk-free rate is 8 percent, and the market return is 17 percent. Ed's Electronics stock has a beta of 0.85.
A.   Calculate Ed's required rate of return.
B.   The risk-free rate does not change, but the market return falls to 16 percent. Calculate Ed's new required rate of return. What might cause this type of shift in the SML?

5-9. *Probability of Failure.*   A firm has the following probability distribution of returns:

Probability	Returns
.05	35%
.15	25%
.30	15%
.30	0%
.15	-10%
.05	-20%

If failure is defined as any return less than 0 percent, then what is the probability of failure?

Answers to Chapter Summary

1.	Expected return		16.	required rate of return
2.	risk		17.	the real rate of return
3.	expected return		18.	an inflation premium
4.	actual outcome		19.	a risk premium
5.	standard deviation		20.	CAPM
6.	only one asset		21.	market index
7.	portfolio		22.	beta
8.	covariances		23.	linear
9.	well-diversified		24.	SML
10.	covariance		25.	APT
11.	market index		26.	risk of failure
12.	Beta		27.	expected return
13.	regression analysis		28.	standard deviation
14.	slope		29.	beta
15.	higher returns			

Problem Solutions

5-1. *Expected returns and standard deviations.* Big River Excursions has a given probability distribution of expected returns.

A. The first step is to calculate the expected return using equation 5-1. Plug in the probability figures for $Prob_j$ and the returns for X_j.

$$E(R_x) = \sum_{j=1}^{n} Prob_j X_j \tag{5-1}$$
$$= (.10)(40) + (.40)(25) + (.40)(10) + (.10)(-5)$$
$$= \underline{17.5\%}$$

B. The second step is to calculate the standard deviation using equation 5-2. We have to use $E(R_x) = 17.5$ percent calculated in part A.

$$\sigma_x = \left[\sum_{j=1}^{n} Prob_j (X_j - E(R_x))^2 \right]^{1/2} \tag{5-2}$$
$$= [.10(40-17.5)^2 + .40(25-17.5)^2 + .40(10-17.5)^2 + .10(-5-17.5)^2]^{1/2}$$
$$= [50.625 + 22.500 + 22.500 + 50.625]^{1/2}$$
$$= [146.250]^{1/2}$$
$$= \underline{12.093\%}$$

We have now calculated both expected return and risk.

An alternative method to use equation 5-1 is to setup a table and do the calculations step by step. This might be a convenient format if you were using an electronic spreadsheet. In the first step the table appears as follows:

State of Economy	Probability	(X) Returns	(Prob)(X)	(Prob)(X-E(R))²
Boom	0.10	40%	(0.10)(40)	
Good	0.40	25%	(0.40)(25)	
Bad	0.40	10%	(0.40)(10)	
Ugly	0.10	-5%	(0.10)(-5)	
Totals	1.00			

Let's complete this step of the arithmetic and then fill in the last column.

Chapter 5: Risk Concepts

State of Economy	Probability	(X) Returns	(Prob)(X)	(Prob)(X-E(R))^2
Boom	0.10	40%	4.00%	$(.10)(40-17.5)^2$
Good	0.40	25%	10.00	$(.40)(25-17.5)^2$
Bad	0.40	10%	4.00	$(.40)(10-17.5)^2$
Ugly	0.10	-5%	-0.50	$(.10)(-5-17.5)^2$
Totals	1.00		E(R) = 17.50%	

Now we can complete the standard deviation arithmetic. The sum of the last column is called the variance. The square root of the variance is the standard deviation.

State of Economy	Probability	(X) Returns	(Prob)(X)	(Prob)(X-E(R))^2
Boom	0.10	40%	4.00%	50.625%
Good	0.40	25%	10.00	22.500
Bad	0.40	10%	4.00	22.500
Ugly	0.10	-5%	-0.50	50.625
Totals	1.00		E(R) = 17.50%	σ_x^2 = 146.250%
				σ_x = 12.093%

We have done exactly the same arithmetic in two different formats and have arrived at exactly the same answers.

C. We'll repeat the process for Big River Electric Power.

$$E(R_x) = \sum_{j=1}^{n} Prob_j X_j \tag{5-1}$$
$$= (.10)(17) + (.40)(15) + (.40)(12) + (.10)(10)$$
$$= \underline{13.5\%}$$

D. We'll repeat the standard deviation calculations for Big River Electric.

$$\sigma_x = \left[\sum_{j=1}^{n} Prob_j (X_j - E(R_x))^2 \right]^{1/2} \tag{5-2}$$
$$= [.10(17-13.5)^2 + .40(15-13.5)^2 + .40(12-13.5)^2 + .10(10-13.5)^2]^{1/2}$$
$$= [1.225 + 2.250 + 2.250 + 1.225]^{1/2}$$
$$= [4.250]^{1/2}$$
$$= \underline{2.062\%}$$

E. There is no right answer as to which *you* would rather invest in because that depends upon your individual expected return-risk preferences. We can, however, try to understand what you are getting with each company. Big River Excursions offers a expected return of 17.5 percent compared to Big River Electric's 13.5 percent. But Excursions also has higher risk as indicated by the standard deviation of 12.09 percent compared to 2.06 percent for Electric.

Remember from statistics class that the outcome falls within plus or minus one standard deviation of the expected returns approximately 68 percent of the time, if certain assumptions about the normality of the distribution are met. You could expect, then, that 68 percent of the time Excursion's return would fall within the range 5.41 percent to 29.59 percent. Compare that to Electric's range of 11.44 percent to 15.56 percent.

F. The expected return of the portfolio is the weighted average of the individual securities' returns. Use equation 5-3.

$$E(R_p) = \sum_{j=1}^{n} W_j E(R_j) \tag{5-3}$$
$$= (.35)(.175) + (.65)(.135)$$
$$= .149 \text{ or } \underline{14.9\%}$$

G. Since we have only two assets in the portfolio, the portfolio's standard deviation can be calculated with equation 5-6.
But first, we must calculate the covariance between the returns of Big River Excursions and Big River Electric, using equation 5-4.

$$Cov_{xy} = Cov_{xy} \, \sigma_x \sigma_y$$
$$= (0.6)(.12093)(.02062)$$
$$= .001496$$

Now we can use equation 5-6.

$$SD(R_p) = [W_x^2 \sigma_x^2 + W_y^2 \sigma_y^2 + 2W_x W_x Cov_{xy}]^{1/2} \tag{5-6}$$
$$= [(.35)^2(.12093)^2 + (.65)^2(.02062)^2 + (2)(.35)(.65)(.001496)]^{1/2}$$
$$= 0.051495 \text{ or } \underline{5.15\%}$$

5-2. *Expected portfolio returns and portfolio betas.* The expected returns and beta of a portfolio are the weighted average of the individual securities' expected returns and betas. This problem is easy to work with in columnar format.

The first step is to calculate the weight of each stock based on its dollar amount in portfolio. Add the amounts of the stocks to get a total portfolio value of $223,000. Then divide each individual amount by the portfolio total. CNB stock, for example, comprises 3.59 percent of the portfolio ($8000/$223,000 = 0.0359). Note that the weights must add to 1.00 or 100 percent.

The second step is to multiply the weights by the expected returns using equation 5-3. The sum is 15.38 percent. The third step is to multiply the weights by the betas and sum the products to get a portfolio beta of 0.97 as shown below.

Stock	$ Amount	$E(R_j)$	Beta	Weights	$W_j E(R_j)$	$W_j B_j$
CNB	$8,000	15%	0.95	0.0359	0.54%	0.03
BCB	20,000	22%	1.30	0.0897	1.97%	0.12
LAR	12,000	12%	0.80	0.0538	0.65%	0.04
LAV	4,000	19%	1.15	0.0179	0.34%	0.02
DEF	50,000	14%	0.90	0.2242	3.14%	0.20
ABC	24,000	20%	1.20	0.1076	2.15%	0.13
ZYX	41,000	16%	1.00	0.1839	2.94%	0.18
HAL	17,000	15%	0.95	0.0762	1.14%	0.07
AGO	36,000	10%	0.70	0.1614	1.61%	0.11
XT	11,000	18%	1.10	0.0493	0.89%	0.05
	$223,000			1.0000	15.38%	0.97

5-3. *Covariance*   Use equation 5-4.

$$\text{Cov}_{xy} = \text{Corr}_{xy}\, \sigma_x \sigma_y \qquad (5\text{-}4)$$
$$= (.9)(5\%)(9\%)$$
$$= \underline{0.405\%}$$

5-4. *Required rate of return*   Use equation 5-9.

Required rate of return = real rate of return +
expected inflation premium +
risk premium   (5-9)
$$= \quad 2\% + 4\% + 8\%$$
$$= \quad \underline{14\%}$$

Chapter 5: Risk Concepts

5-5. *Required rate of return*   Plug into equation 5-9 and solve for the risk premium.

Required rate of return = real rate of return +

$$\begin{aligned}
&\text{expected inflation premium +} \\
&\qquad\text{risk premium} \qquad\qquad\qquad\qquad (5\text{-}9) \\
27\% \;=\;\; &3\% + 5\% + \text{risk premium} \\
\text{risk premium} =\;\; &\underline{19\%}
\end{aligned}$$

5-6. *Beta*   Use equation 5-8.

$$\begin{aligned}
B_x \;&=\; \text{Cov}_{xm}/\sigma_m^2 \qquad\qquad\qquad\qquad\qquad (5\text{-}8) \\
&=\; .015/(.12)^2 \\
&=\; \underline{1.04}
\end{aligned}$$

5-7. *Security Market Line.*

A.   The market risk premium is the difference between the expected return on the market and the fisk=free rate.

$$\begin{aligned}
\text{Market risk premium} \;&=\; E(R_m) - RF \\
&=\; 18\% - 12\% \\
&=\; \underline{6\%}
\end{aligned}$$

B.   The risk premium for the security is the product of the market's risk premium and the security's beta.

$$\begin{aligned}
\text{Stock risk premium} \;&=\; (E(R_m) - RF)\text{Beta}_x \\
&=\; (18\% - 12\%)(1.10) \\
&=\; \underline{6.6\%}
\end{aligned}$$

C.   The equation for the SML is 5-13. In words this equation says that the return required on security X by the market is a risk-free rate plus a risk premium for that security.

$$\begin{aligned}
k_x \;&=\; RF + (E(R_m) - RF)\text{Beta}_x \qquad\qquad (5\text{-}13) \\
&=\; 12\% + (18\% - 12\%)(1.10) \\
&=\; 12\% + 6.6\% \\
&=\; \underline{18.6\%}
\end{aligned}$$

D.   If the SML shifts upward by one percentage point, then the risk-free rate is 13% and the market rate is 19%. Use equation 5-13 with these new rates.

$$k_x \quad = \quad RF + (E(R_m) - RF)Beta_x \qquad\qquad (5\text{-}13)$$
$$= \quad 13\% + (19\% - 13\%)(1.10)$$
$$= \quad \underline{19.6\%}$$

E.   Use equation 5-13 with beta equal to 1.20.

$$k_x \quad = \quad RF + (E(R_m) - RF)Beta_x \qquad\qquad (5\text{-}13)$$
$$= \quad 12\% + (18\% - 12\%)(1.20)$$
$$= \quad \underline{19.2\%}$$

5-8. *Security Market Line.*

A.   The required rate of return is the risk-free rate plus a risk premium for Ed's stock. Use equation 5-13.

$$k_{Ed} \quad = \quad RF + (E(R_m) - RF)Beta_{Ed} \qquad\qquad (5\text{-}13)$$
$$= \quad 8 + (17 - 8)(.85)$$
$$= \quad \underline{15.65\%}$$

B.   Use equation 5-13 with the new market return.

$$k_{Ed} \quad = \quad RF + (E(R_m) - RF)Beta_{Ed} \qquad\qquad (5\text{-}13)$$
$$= \quad 8 + (16 - 8)(.85)$$
$$= \quad \underline{14.80\%}$$

This type of shift, which is a change in slope, would be caused by investor psychology. A shift to a lower slope means that investors are willing to accept a smaller increase in expected return for a given increase in risk.

5-9. *Probability of failure.*   Since only return *less than* zero percent, not zero itself, are defined as failure, the two negative returns (-10 percent and -20 percent) would constitute failure. Add the probabilities associated with these negative returns.

$$\text{Probability of failure} \quad = \quad .15 + .05$$
$$= \quad .20 \text{ or } \underline{20\%}$$

CHAPTER 6
VALUATION AND FINANCIAL MANAGEMENT

Concepts You Should Understand

*   The value of an asset is the present value of cash flows the owners expect to receive in the future, discounted at a rate of return required by the owners to compensate them for the risk involved.

*   The valuation models are based on investors' expectations about the future.

*   The cash flow expected from common stock is a continuously growing stream of dividends.

*   The cash flow expected from bonds is a stream of fixed interest payments and a return of principal at maturity.

*   The cash flow expected from perpetual bonds and preferred stock, is a perpetual stream of fixed interest or fixed dividend payments, respectively.

*   The discount rate compensates the owner for the risk involved in the investment.

*   The valuation models can be used to calculate either the price of the asset or the return expected from the asset.

A Second Look

In order for management to go about maximizing owners' wealth, they must understand what causes stock prices to behave as they do. The value of any earning asset is the present value of cash flows the owner expects to receive in the future, discounted at a rate of return required by the owner to compensate him for the risk involved. Valuation of physical assets is presented in later chapters. Here, the valuation of securities is considered from the owners' point of view.

To employ the principal that the value of an asset is the present value of its expected future cash flows, one must estimate the cash flows, establish a discount rate, and do the calculations. We shall study the cash flows of bonds, perpetuities, common stock, and preferred stocks.

Chapter 6: Valuation and Financial Management

The general valuation model is given mathematically as equation 6-1:

$$V_0 = \sum_{t=1}^{n} C_t/(1+k)^t \qquad (6\text{-}1)$$

Note the general nature of the notation: V for value, C for expected cash flow, and k for the required rate of return. The subsequent models in this chapter are adaptations of the general model to specific securities. For each of the specific securities, more descriptive notation is adopted, as summarized below.

Security	Cash Flows	Required return	Used in equation
General	Cash flow, C_t	k	(6-1)
Common stock	Dividends, D_t, Price, P_n	k_e	(6-4) (6-8)
Bonds	Interest, I_t, Par value, B_n	k_i	(6-13)
Perpetual bonds	Interest, I_t	k_i	(6-15)
Preferred stock	Dividends, d	k_p	(6-18)

The first security addressed is common stock. Investors who buy common stock expect to receive dividends and growth. The growth can be realized as dividends increase over time and as the stock price increases. The model that is useful from the viewpoint of buying a stock, holding it for a few years, then selling it, is equation 6-4. It provides for future dividends and a future price as cash flows to the investor.

$$P_0 = \sum_{t=1}^{n} D_t/(1+k_e)^t + P_n/(1+k_e)^n \qquad (6\text{-}4)$$

A second model for common stock takes into account the fact the stock has an indefinite life and should continue to pay dividends forever or at least far into the future. This model assumes that dividends grow at a constant rate, g. Only the next expected dividend, D_1, is used in equation 6-8.

$$P_0 = D_1/(k_e\text{-}g) = \frac{D_1}{k_e - g} \qquad (6\text{-}8)$$

Using the above format, we are trying to calculate price, taking the other variables as known values. This same equation can be used to estimate the expected return, simply by solving for k_e and taking price as given. The result is equation 6-9.

$$k_e = D_1/P_0 + g = \frac{D_1}{P_0} + g \qquad (6\text{-}9)$$

In words, equation 6-9 says that investors expect a return consisting of a dividend yield plus growth. Compare this to the Capital Asset Pricing Model in Chapter 5, repeated in Chapter 6 as equations 6-11 and 6-12. It says that investors require a return consisting of a risk-free rate plus a risk premium.

To adapt the general model to bonds, we must understand that the cash flow an investor expects from a bond with a finite life is annual or semiannual interest payments and repayment of the principal at the end of the bond's life. The amount of the principal goes by several names, including the par value, the maturity value, and the face value. The value of an annual bond is given by equation 6-13.

$$B_0 = \sum_{t=1}^{n} I_t/(1+k_i)^t + B_n/(1+k_i)^n \qquad (6\text{-}13)$$

The interest payments are an annuity, and the par value is a single payment. Equation 6-13 can be rewritten for use with the tables as follows:

$$B_0 = I(PVIFA_{k,n}) + B_n(PVIF_{k,n})$$

Many bonds pay interest semiannually. This requires the above equation to be modified with respect to the interest payment, the discount rate, and the number of periods. The semiannual interest payment is one-half of the annual payment. The discount rate is one-half of the annual rate. The number of discounting periods is twice the number of years.

Perpetual bonds and preferred stocks have the same type cash flow: a fixed payment, *ad infinitum*. The models, equations 6-15 and 6-18, are mathematically similar. Only the notation is changed to differentiate between interest, I_t, dividends, d, the return required on bonds, k_i, and the return required on preferred stock, k_p. These equations can be used to calculate prices or returns, depending on the desired usage.

It is worthwhile to note that the value of both bonds and stocks consists of the present value of two components: income and capital gains. The income for bonds is interest and for stocks is dividends. Capital gains or losses are realized through price appreciation or depreciation for both bonds and stocks.

Chapter Summary

A financial manager must understand the variables and relationships that affect the price of securities if he/she is to attempt to maximize owners' wealth. This area of study is known as (1)_____. The underlying concept is that an asset's value is the (2)_____ of (3)_____ discounted at a rate commensurate with the (4)_____.

Individual investors use this discounted cash flow method to calculate an (5)_____ of a security, which is how much they think it is worth. The buying and selling among investors establishes the (6)_____ of the security. The risk/return tradeoff is at the heart of the investors' (7)_____ which is used as the discount rate in valuation models.

The (8)_____ holds that market prices reflect all information that is known by the market about assets. Generally speaking, (9)_____ are not very efficient; whereas, the markets for (10)_____ are quite efficient. Realistically, then, securities are traded at prices that are (11)_____, considering the level of risk involved.

In the common stock valuation model for n periods, the cash flows expected by an investor are expected future (12)_____ and the (13)_____ expected at the end of the last period.

The dividend growth model for calculating stock prices assumes the future dividends continue (14)_____. The case where the future dividends are not expected to grow is equivalent to the valuation models for (15)_____ and preferred stocks. A frequently used form of the model is for (16)_____ growth, and another form accommodates variable growth.

The constant dividend growth model is often rearranged to calculate the (17)_____. One limitation of the constant growth model is that (18)_____. The stock price calculated by this model will increase if dividends (19)_____; whereas, the price will (20)_____ if the required rate of return increases.

The required rate of return on equity is the return that investors require in order to get them to buy the company's stock. This required rate is the sum of a risk-free rate and a (21)_____. The aggregate market required rate of return on equity can be calculated using the (22)_____, which can then be used in the dividend growth model to calculate the stock price.

The cash flows an investor expects from corporate (and most other) bonds consists of periodic (23)_____ and the (24)_____ at maturity. The par value and the (25)_____ do not change over the life of a bond, but the price of a bond and its (26)_____ do change. The par value of most corporate bonds is (27)_____, and interest payments are made (28)_____. The relationship between bond prices and yield-to-maturity

Chapter 6: Valuation and Financial Management

is (29)_____. That is, if market interest rates increase, bond prices (30)_____.

Acronyms and Notation You Should Know

B_0	Market price of a bond today
B_n	Par value of a bond to be received at the end of period n
C_t	Cash flow during period t
CAPM	Capital asset pricing model
D_t	Common stock dividends in dollars during period t
d	Fixed preferred stock dividends in dollars
I_t	Interest payment in dollars during period t
k	Percentage required return on an asset
k_e	Percentage required return on equity (common stock)
k_i	Percentage required return on bonds (perpetual or finite)
k_p	Percentage required return on preferred stock
P_t	Price of common or preferred stock at time t
P_0	Price of common or preferred stock today
V_0	Value (price) of an asset

Equations You Should Know

$$V_0 = \sum_{t=1}^{n} C_t/(1+k)^t \qquad (6\text{-}1)$$

$$P_0 = \sum_{t=1}^{n} D_t/(1+k_e)^t + P_n/(1+k_e)^n \qquad (6\text{-}4)$$

$$P_0 = D_1/(k_e-g) \qquad (6\text{-}8)$$

$$k_e = D_1/P_0 + g \qquad (6\text{-}9)$$

$$B_0 = \sum_{t=1}^{n} I_t/(1+k_i)^t + B_n/(1+k_i)^n \qquad (6\text{-}13)$$

$$\text{Annual interest} = (\text{Coupon rate})(\text{Par value}) \qquad (6\text{-}14)$$

64

$$B_0 \quad = \quad I/k_i \qquad\qquad\qquad (6\text{-}15)$$

$$P_0 \quad = \quad d/k_p \qquad\qquad\qquad (6\text{-}18)$$

Problems

6-1. *General valuation.* An apartment building has projected future cash flow of $120,000 each year for at least five years. A prospective buyer plans to purchase the building, keep it for five years, then sell it to realize a terminal cash flow of $1,250,000. If she will accept a 10 percent rate of return, what is the value of the building today?

6-2. *Stock price.* Celia's stock broker expects Phabulous Phurniture Phactory, Inc., common stock to be selling for $60 per share three years from now. Its last dividend was $0.25 per share. The broker thinks there is good reason to believe that the board of directors will increase the dividend by a nickel a share in each of the next three years. Celia thinks the furniture industry in general, and this company in particular, is quite risky during uncertain economic times. What price is Celia willing to pay for this stock if she requires a return of 20 percent?

6-3. *Stock price.* The common stock of Blaze Torch Company just paid a dividend of $1.89 per share. The growth rate of six percent is expected to continue indefinitely. What is the price of Blaze's stock if investors require a 16 percent return on securities of similar risk?

6-4. *Expected return.* Midnite Supply, Inc., has a current price of $18 per share and an expected dividend of $2. The dividends are expected to grow indefinitely at four percent per year. An investor apparently expects what rate of return from this stock?

6-5. *Stock price and CAPM.* The dividend paid today on Super Software Stores common stock was $2.75. This dividend is expected to grow at an annual rate of 5.5 percent indefinitely. SSS's beta is 1.15. U. S. Treasury bills yield eight percent, and the market index's return is 17 percent. Calculate the price of SSS's stock, assuming market equilibrium.

6-6. *Bond price-annual interest.* A $1,000 par value bond with 15 years to maturity has a coupon rate of 15 percent. The market yield on bonds of similar risk is 12 percent. Calculate the bond's current price.

Chapter 6: Valuation and Financial Management

6-7. *Bond price-semiannual interest.* A $1,000 par value bond with 11 years to maturity and a nine percent coupon rate makes semiannual interest payments. The current market rate on bonds with similar risk is 10 percent. Calculate the price of this bond.

6-8. *Bond yield-to-maturity.* A $1,000 par value bond with a 10 percent coupon rate and eight years to maturity sells for $811.35. Interest is paid semiannually. What is the yield-to-maturity?

6-9. *Perpetual bond price.* A perpetual bond has an annual interest payment of $35. If securities of similar risk yield 8 3/4 percent, what is the price of this bond?

6-10. *Preferred stock price.* A preferred stock has an annual dividend of $5.40. Similar preferred stocks offer a yield of 12 percent. Calculate the price.

6-11. *Market equilibrium.* Jones and Jones, Inc., a large international investment banking house, has a beta of 1.20. U. S. Treasury bills offer safety conscious investors a return of seven percent, while the market index return is 18 percent. Jones and Jones' expected dividend is $12 per share with a growth rate of three percent. Their current price is $69.77.
A.   Calculate the return required by the market place for J&J stock. Use the CAPM.
B.   Calculate the return expected by J&J stockholders. Use the constant dividend growth model.
C.   Based on your answers in A and B, is the market in equilibrium?
D.   Suppose Miss Jones announces a new global strategy that is expected to increase the next dividend to $12.06 and the future growth rate to 3.5 percent. Assuming no changes in risk (beta), calculate the new stock price.

Answers to Chapter Summary

1.	valuation	16.	constant
2.	present value	17.	return on equity
3.	expected future cash flow	18.	$k_e > g$
4.	risk	19.	increase
5.	intrinsic value	20.	decrease
6.	market value	21.	risk premium
7.	required rate of return	22.	CAPM
8.	Efficient Market Hypothesis	23.	interest payments
9.	real asset markets	24.	par value
10.	financial assets	25.	coupon rate
11.	fair	26.	yield-to-maturity
12.	dividends	27.	$1000
13.	expected future stock price	28.	semiannually
14.	indefinitely	29.	inverse
15.	perpetuities	30.	decrease

Problem Solutions

6-1. *General valuation.*

The cash flows are given, so all we have to do is discount them at 10 percent for five years. The relevant equation is 6-1, but we may use the tables as follows:

$$V_0 = \$120,000(PVIFA_{10\%,5}) + \$1,250,000(PVIF_{10\%,5}) \qquad (6\text{-}1)$$
$$= \$120,000(3.791) + \$1,250,000(.621)$$
$$= \$1,234,691$$

6-2. *Stock price.*

The cash flow in this case is the dividend for three years and the price at the end of the third year. Since dividends are expected to grow by five cents each year, the next three dividends should be $0.30, $0.35, and $0.40. The relevant equation is 6-4, used with the present value table for a single payment at 20 percent.

$$P_0 = D_1(PVIF_{20\%,1}) + D_2(PVIF_{20\%,2}) + D_3(PVIF_{20\%,3}) + P_3(PVIF_{20\%,3}) \quad (6\text{-}4)$$
$$= \$.30(.833) + \$.35(.694) + \$.40(.579) + \$60(.579)$$
$$= \$35.46$$

6-3. *Stock price.*

This problem calls for the constant dividend growth model, equation 6-8. Looking at this equation carefully, we note that the expected dividend, D_1, is subscripted with a one. This means that the relevant dividend is the *next* dividend, not the last one. Investors buy stock for the dividends they expect to be paid in the future, not for dividends paid to the previous owner of the stock. The first step is to calculate the next expected dividend. Equation 4-1 from Chapter 4 can be used here. In terms of dividends and growth, the expected dividend is the future value and the current dividend is the present value:

$$
\begin{aligned}
FV_1 &= PV_0(1+k) \\
D_1 &= D_0(1+g) \\
&= \$1.89(1 + .06) \\
&= \$2.00
\end{aligned}
\qquad (4\text{-}1)
$$

Now we are ready to use equation 6-8.

$$
\begin{aligned}
P_0 &= D_1/(k_e\text{-}g) \\
&= \$2.00/(.16 - .06) \\
&= \$20
\end{aligned}
\qquad (6\text{-}8)
$$

6-4. *Expected return.*

In this case we are given the expected dividend, so the data are ready for equation 6-9.

$$
\begin{aligned}
k_e &= D_1/P_0 + g \\
&= \$2/\$18 + .040 \\
&= .151 \text{ or } 15.1\%
\end{aligned}
\qquad (6\text{-}9)
$$

6-5. *Stock price and CAPM.*

We are going to use the dividend growth model, equation 6-8, to calculate the price, but first we have to calculate the expected dividend and the required return on equity. The next dividend can be calculated using equation 4-1 from Chapter 4. In terms of dividends and growth, the expected dividend is the future value and the current dividend is the present value:

$$
\begin{aligned}
FV_1 &= PV_0(1+k) \\
D_1 &= D_0(1+g) \\
&= \$2.75(1 + .055) \\
&= \$2.90
\end{aligned}
\qquad (4\text{-}1)
$$

Chapter 6: Valuation and Financial Management

The next step is to calculate the required rate of return using equation 6-12.

$$k_e = R_F + (E(R_M) - RF)Beta \qquad (6-12)$$
$$= .08 + (.17 - .08)(1.15)$$
$$= .1835 \text{ or } 18.35\%$$

At this point we are ready to plug into equation 6-8.

$$P_0 = D_1/(k_e - g) \qquad (6-8)$$
$$= \$2.90/(.1835 - .055)$$
$$= \$22.57$$

6-6. *Bond price-annual interest.*

The first step to calculating a bond price is to calculate the annual interest payment using equation 6-14.

$$\text{Annual interest} = (\text{Coupon rate})(\text{Par value}) \qquad (6-14)$$
$$= (.15)(\$1,000)$$
$$= \$150$$

The basic bond valuation model is equation 6-13.

$$B_0 = \sum_{t=1}^{n} I_t/(1+k_i)^t + B_n/(1+k_i)^n \qquad (6-13)$$

We use the market interest rate for the discount rate because we are trying to calculate the market price of the bond. For use with the present value tables this can be rewritten as:

$$B_0 = \$150(PVIFA_{.12,15}) + \$1,000(PVIF_{.12,15})$$
$$= \$150(6.811) + \$1,000(.183)$$
$$= \$1,204.65$$

When this bond was issued, interest rates were about 15 percent or management would not have agreed to a 15 percent coupon rate. Over the life of the bond, the par value, the coupon rate, and the periodic interest payments stay the same. The price of the bond and the yield-to-maturity change frequently. Since this bond was issued, interest rates have fallen to 12 percent, and the price has risen to $1,204.65.

6-7. *Bond price-semiannual interest.*

This bond pays interest twice a year instead of once a year. Most bonds are like this. The semiannual interest payment is half of the annual interest payment. Use equation 6-14 to calculate the annual interest, then divide by two.

$$
\begin{aligned}
\text{Annual interest} \quad &= \quad \text{(Coupon rate)(Par value)} &\text{(6-14)}\\
&= \quad (.09)(\$1,000)\\
&= \quad \$90
\end{aligned}
$$

$$
\begin{aligned}
\text{Semiannual interest} &= \quad \$90/2\\
&= \quad \$45
\end{aligned}
$$

Since we are using half-year periods, we must use half the market rate and twice the number of periods for compounding. Thus, the discount rate is five percent $(10/2 = 5)$, and the number of compounding periods is 22 $(11 \times 2 = 22)$. The present value can be found as follows:

$$
\begin{aligned}
B_0 \quad &= \quad \$45(\text{PVIFA}_{.05,22}) + \$1,000(\text{PVIF}_{.05,22})\\
&= \quad \$45(13.163) + \$1,000(.342)\\
&= \quad \$934.34
\end{aligned}
$$

Does this price of $934 seem reasonable? Yes, because the market rate of interest, 10 percent, is above the coupon rate, nine percent. This means the price of the bond is lower than the par value.

6-8. *Bond yield-to-maturity.*

This problem uses the same equation used for the calculating the bond price, except that we solve for a different variable. We shall set this problem up to be solved algebraically and find that it is a complex problem. We shall then abandon trying an algebraic solution and solve it by trial and error.

Since this problem has semiannual interest payments, we must find the annual interest payment using equation 6-14 and divide by two.

$$
\begin{aligned}
\text{Annual interest} \quad &= \quad \text{(Coupon rate)(Par value)} &\text{(6-14)}\\
&= \quad (.10)(\$1,000)\\
&= \quad \$100
\end{aligned}
$$

$$
\begin{aligned}
\text{Semiannual interest} \quad &= \quad \$100/2\\
&= \quad \$50
\end{aligned}
$$

Chapter 6: Valuation and Financial Management

We have 16 compounding periods (8 x 2 = 16). We plug in the price and the semiannual interest payment in equation 6-13. The discount rate, k_i, will be a six-month rate instead of an annual rate, so we shall have to multiply our answer by two to convert it to an annual rate.

$$\$811.35 \quad = \quad \$50/(1 + k_i)^1 + \$50/(1 + k_i)^2 + \ldots +$$
$$\$50/(1 + k_i)^{16} + \$1,000/(1 + k_i)^{16} \quad \text{(6-13)}$$

As you can see, it would take an algebra expert to solve this for k_i. Let's try another approach: trial and error using the present value tables. In present value interest factor terms, we have:

$$\$811.35 \quad = \quad \$50(PVIFA_{k,16}) + \$1,000(PVIF_{k,16})$$

Notice that the $50 is an annuity, but the $1,000 is a single payment. This means that we have to use two tables. Since PVIFA and PVIF are both unknown, we have one equation with two unknowns, which cannot be solved directly. So we go to trial and error.

The object of trial and error is to try different interest rates until we get one that results in a price of $811.35. Where do we begin? The coupon rate is 10 percent, and the price is less than par value. Remembering the inverse relationship between discount rates and present value, we know that the yield-to-maturity must be greater than 10 percent. Let's try 12 percent, since it is greater than 10 percent.

Trial #1: The semiannual rate is six percent (12/2), and the number of periods is 16 (8 x 2). Look up interest factors for six percent and 16 periods and calculate the trial price.

$$\begin{aligned} \text{Trial \#1 price} \quad &= \quad \$50(10.106) + \$1,000(.394) \\ &= \quad \$899.30 \end{aligned}$$

The trial price of $899.30 does not equal the actual price of $811.35, so we erred and must try again.

Trial #2: The first trial of 12 percent was not high enough, so let's try 14 percent. Look up interest factors for seven percent and 16 periods.

$$\begin{aligned} \text{Trial \#2 price} \quad &= \quad \$50(9.447) + \$1,000(.339) \\ &= \quad \$811.35 \end{aligned}$$

Hooray! We got the right answer this time. The yield to maturity of this bond is 14 percent.

Chapter 6: Valuation and Financial Management

Lotus Hint: The yield-to-maturity on a bond is mathematically equivalent to the internal rate of return on any asset investment. The Lotus 1-2-3 function, @IRR(guess,range), will solve this problem. The "guess" value can be a rate such as 0.1. The range must contain the market price as a negative value in the first cell and the remaining semiannual interest payments in the following cells. The final cell must contain the sum of the final interest payment and the par value. The answer will be more exact than is usually obtained by the trial and error method using tables.

6-9. *Perpetual bond price.*

A perpetual bond price can be determined by equation 6-15.

$$
\begin{aligned}
B_0 &= I/k_i & \text{(6-15)} \\
&= \$35/.0875 \\
&= \$400
\end{aligned}
$$

6-10. *Preferred stock price.*

A preferred stock price can be determined by equation 6-18.

$$
\begin{aligned}
P_0 &= d/k_p & \text{(6-18)} \\
&= \$5.40/.12 \\
&= \$45
\end{aligned}
$$

6-11. *Market equilibrium.*

This problem involves calculating the stock returns with two models and comparing them. The first is the return required by the market for any security with the stated risk level (beta = 1.20), and the second is the dividend growth model.

A. To calculate the required return we plug into equation 6-12.

$$
\begin{aligned}
k_e &= R_F + (E(R_M) - RF)Beta & \text{(6-12)} \\
&= .07 + (.18 - .07)(1.20) \\
&= .202 \text{ or } 20.2\%
\end{aligned}
$$

Investors require a return of 20.2 percent for any security with a beta of 1.20.

B. The return expected by investors is revealed by the price they are willing to pay for the stock. Thus the dividend growth model can be used to calculate the expected return by taking the price as a given input. Use equation 6-9.

$$k_e = D_1/P_0 + g \tag{6-9}$$
$$= \$12/\$69.77 + .03$$
$$= .202 \text{ or } 20.2\%$$

Investors willing to pay \$69.77 for this stock apparently expect a return of 20.2 percent.

C. Comparing answers in parts A and B, Jones & Jones stock is in equilibrium, because the return required by the market equals the return expected by investors.

D. We can use the dividend growth model to evaluate the effect of Miss Jones' announcement. Since the risk is unchanged, the required return calculated in part A is not affected. Use equation 6-8.

$$P_0 = D_1/(k_e-g) \tag{6-8}$$
$$= \$12.06/(.202 - .035)$$
$$= \$72.22$$

The change in investor expectations causes the intrinsic value of the stock to rise to \$72.22. In a fairly efficient market the price will react very quickly as investors hear the news and bid up the price of the stock. If investors pay \$72.22 and receive a dividend of \$12.06, which continues to grow at 3.5 percent per year, they will make 20.2 percent.

CHAPTER 7
WORKING-CAPITAL
MANAGEMENT

Concepts You Should Understand

*   Working capital management is critical to the survival of the firm.

*   The cash-conversion cycle refers to the sequence of turning cash into inventory, inventory into receivables, and receivables back into cash.

*   When dealing with working capital, cost minimization is the approach usually taken to maximize stockholders' wealth.

*   For a given level of sales, the more current assets relative to total assets, the less risk and the less expected return.

*   For a given level of financing, the less current liabilities relative to total financing, the less risk and the less expected return.

*   Marginal analysis is the principle underlying the decision as to how much to invest in current assets.

A Second Look

Management of short-term assets and short-term liabilities is critical to the financial survival of the firm. A business must be able to pay its bills on time, collect the money that is owed to it, and carry enough inventory to satisfy its customers' needs. If a firm cannot handle these day-to-day activities in a timely and efficient manner, it will soon be added to the statistics of bankrupts.

Working capital is another term for current assets, and net working capital (NWC) is defined as current assets (CA) minus current liabilities (CL). An alternative definition of net working capital is that NWC is the amount of current assets financed by long-term financing.

The operating cycle and cash-conversion cycle zero in on the problem of using and collecting cash. The cash-conversion cycle is the time period between the day when cash is paid out for inventory and the day when the receivables arising from the sale of the finished product are collected.

Because current assets are by definition expected to be turned into cash within one operating period, the label "permanent current assets" at first appears to be a contradiction of terms. On any day that one looks at the balance sheet, however, there will be some level of current assets. The minimum level is referred to as permanent to emphasize the need for continuing financing, which is called permanent financing.

Temporary current assets are those in excess of the permanent or minimum level. Temporary current assets are normally financed by temporary current liabilities that will be paid off as these assets are converted into cash in the normal course of business.

Working capital is tied into maximizing the value of the firm in that the net present value (NPV) of expected future cash flows increases the firm's value, if the NPV is positive. In practice minimizing costs is often more useful with current assets and liabilities because of the short-term nature of both.

Two ratios are important in analyzing the risk/return posture of the firm's net working capital position. The ratios are current assets to total assets (CA/TA) and current liabilities to total financing (CL/TF). Remembering that the balance sheet must balance, total assets must equal total financing.

Having a larger proportion of current assets (higher CA/TA) means having plenty of cash on hand to pay debts on time, carrying lots of receivables, and keeping plenty of inventory to meet all needs. This higher CA/TA provides safety but also implies lower returns. The lower returns are a result of the larger investment in current assets, which does not provide any additional income.

Having a larger proportion of current liabilities (higher CL/TF) means more risk of not being able to pay short-term debts when due. It also means lower overall costs because current liabilities typically have lower costs than long-term financing.

The risk/return tradeoff is at work on both sides of the balance sheet. A higher CA/TA means lower risk and lower expected return; whereas, a higher CL/TF means higher risk and higher expected return. Conservative management is willing to accept lower returns in trade for safety, while aggressive management is seeks higher returns in spite of the higher risk involved. Management can be aggressive or conservative on both sides of the balance sheet or aggressive on one side and conservative on the other.

Management decides on CA/TA and CL/TF levels either by design or by accident. Hopefully they adopt optimal investment and financing policies that will maximize the market value of owners' equity. The chief analytical tool for this decision is marginal analysis. Management should invest in additional current assets until the marginal benefit just equals the marginal cost.

Chapter Summary

Current assets, mainly cash, accounts receivable, and inventory, are necessary for a business to function. Part of the current assets are financed by current liabilities, namely accounts payable, notes payable, and accruals. Net working capital is defined as (1)_____ minus (2)_____.

The operating cycle is the sum of the (3)_____ and the (4)_____. The time period between when cash is paid out to begin producing a product and the time when the firm finally collects from customers who bought the product is the (5)_____. The cash cycle is calculated as the operating cycle minus the (6)_____.

(7)_____ are a minimum level of short-term assets required for the firm's operation. Additional current assets are sometimes required due to seasonal or other factors and are referred to as (8)_____.

The importance of current assets varies according to the industry and the size of the firm. Current assets constitute about (9)_____ percent of the total assets of all manufacturing firms and about (10)_____ percent of the total assets of small manufacturing firms.

Two analytical tools for making decisions to maximize owners' wealth are (11) _____ and (12) _____. A ratio that is useful in analyzing the investment in and cost of current assets is the (13) _____ ratio. The larger the current asset investment relative to total assets, the (14) _____ this ratio, the (15) _____ the risk, the (16) _____ the costs, and the (17) _____ the profitability.

A useful ratio for analyzing the financing side of the balance sheet is the (18) _____ ratio. The more financing provided by short-term funds, the (19) _____ this ratio, the (20) _____ the risk, the (21) _____ the costs, and the (22) _____ the profitability.

Conservative working-capital management would have a (23) _____ CA/TA and a (24) _____ CL/TF compared to aggressive management. Management can mix strategies, being more aggressive on one side of the balance sheet and more conservative on the other.

A useful tool for determining the optimal investment in current assets is (25) _____. Two costs are relevant: the costs of (26) _____ and of (27) _____. The optimal amount of current assets would minimize the total of these two costs. Three factors involved in the balancing of costs and the level of current assets are the level of (28) _____ and operating expenses, company (29) _____, and (30) _____.

Turning now to the financing side of the balance, we are faced with a risk/return tradeoff. Current liabilities are (31) _____ than long-term financing because they must be repaid or renewed in a shorter period of time. They usually have

(32) _____ than long-term financing, which contributes to a higher return.
Short-term financing (current liabilities) can be either (33) _____
or (34) _____. Accounts payable and accruals are examples of (35)
_____; whereas, short-term bank loans and commercial paper are
examples of (36) _____.

One approach to determining the mix of short-term and long-term financing is to
match the maturity of the financing to the asset maturity. (37) _____
debt would be used to finance all fixed assets and (38) _____, while (39)
_____ financing would be used for temporary needs. Aggressive financing
would be to use more (40) _____; whereas, the use of more (41)
_____ is conservative.

Acronyms and Notation You Should Know

CA	Current assets
FA	Fixed assets
TA	Total assets
CL	Current liabilities
TF	Total financing
NWC	Net Working capital

Equations You Should Know

Current assets/Total assets	=	CA/TA	(7-1)
Current liabilities/Total financing	=	CL/TF	(7-2)

Lotus Notes

Lotus 1-2-3[1] or a similar spreadsheet is an excellent tool for analyzing balance sheet
relationships and the resultant profitability. The analyst must specify the relationships
thought to exist and enter appropriate formulas. Sensitivity analysis can be accomplished
by changing various input data and observing the resultant changes in the ratios and
profitability. The visual impact of graphs can be readily added using the graph feature
of the spreadsheet.

---

[1]Lotus 1-2-3 is a registered trademark of Lotus Development Corporation.

Problems

7-1. *Cost of liquidity.* As an analyst in the Treasury Department of a large corporation, you have come up with the estimates of costs of liquidity and illiquidity given in the table below. Use a minimum total cost approach to determine the optimal CA/TA ratio.

CA/TA	Cost of Liquidity	Cost of Illiquidity
0.1	$50,000	$93,000
0.2	54,000	80,000
0.3	59,000	70,000
0.4	66,000	62,000
0.5	75,000	54,000
0.6	86,000	48,000
0.7	99,000	41,000

7-2. *NWC, CA/TA, and CL/TF.* Calculate Net working capital (NWC), and the ratios of CA/TA and CL/TF for companies A, B, and C. Rank the companies as conservative or aggressive for CA/TA, CL/TF, and overall.

	A	B	C
Current Assets	$300	$467	$700
Fixed Assets	700	700	700
Total Assets	$1,000	$1,167	$1,400
Current Liabilities	$200	$350	$560
Long-term Debt	300	317	340
Common Equity	500	500	500
Total funds	$1,000	$1,167	$1,400

7-3. *Financing alternatives.* Three companies have identical asset structures as shown below. Accounts payable are 60 percent of each companies' current liabilities, which consist only of accounts payable and notes payable. They each have $325 million in equity. Each company finances all of its fixed assets and some proportion of its permanent current assets by equity and long-term debt. The proportions are 100 percent for A, 50 percent for B, and 125 percent for C.
A. Which company uses a matching plan? Which is conservative? Which is aggressive?
B. Compile the financing side of the balance sheet for each company.

Chapter 7: Working-Capital Management

The data for the three companies in problem 7-3 are given here:

	A	B	C
Temporary current Assets	$ 80	$ 80	$ 80
Permanent current assets	120	120	120
Total current assets	$200	$200	$200
Fixed assets	300	300	300
Total assets	$500	$500	$500

7-4. *Integrated NWC and profitability.* Balance sheet data are given for companies A, B, C, and D below. Each company has a fixed asset turnover of eight times. Each company experiences an operating profit margin (to sales) of four percent. The interest rate on short-term notes payable is 10 percent, and the long-term interest rate is 15 percent. The average corporate income tax rate is 30 percent.

	A	B	C	D
Cash	$60,000	$50,000	$40,000	$35,000
Accounts receivable	210,000	200,000	160,000	150,000
Inventory	260,000	250,000	200,000	160,000
Current assets	$530,000	$500,000	$400,000	$345,000
Fixed assets	800,000	800,000	800,000	800,000
Total assets	$1,330,000	$1,300,000	$1,200,000	$1,145,000
Accounts payable	$150,000	$150,000	$120,000	$150,000
Notes payable	30,000	50,000	40,000	60,000
Accruals	25,000	50,000	40,000	50,000
Current liabilities	$205,000	$250,000	$200,000	$260,000
Long-term debt	325,000	250,000	200,000	85,000
Common Equity	800,000	800,000	800,000	800,000
Total Funds	$1,330,000	$1,300,000	$1,200,000	$1,145,000

A.   Calculate the NWC, CA/TA, CL/TF, current ratio, and quick ratio for each company.

B.   Rank the companies from most conservative to most aggressive based on CA/TA.

C.   Rank the companies from most conservative to most aggressive based on CL/TF.

D.   Rank from most liquid to least liquid based on current ratio and quick ratio.

E.   Do NWC and CA/TA add information to the current and quick ratios?

F.   Use the fixed asset turnover to calculate sales for each company. Then complete the income statements and calculate the rate of return on equity.

G.   Rank the companies according to ROE. Is this ranking what you would expect according to the risk/return tradeoff observed in the working capital management?

Answers to Chapter Summary

1. current assets
2. current liabilities
3. inventory-conversion period
4. receivables-conversion period
5. cash-conversion period
6. payables deferral period
7. permanent current assets
8. temporary current assets
9. 40
10. 65
11. net present value
12. cost minimization
13. CA/TA
14. higher
15. lower
16. higher
17. lower
18. CL/TF
19. higher
20. higher
21. lower
22. higher
23. high
24. low
25. marginal analysis
26. liquidity
27. illiquidity
28. sales
29. policies
30. technology
31. more risky
32. lower cost
33. spontaneous
34. negotiated
35. spontaneous financing
36. negotiated financing
37. long-term
38. permanent current assets
39. short-term
40. current liabilities

Answers to Problems

7-1. *Cost of liquidity.*

The idea here is to get the lowest *total* cost, since one cost is increasing and the other is decreasing. The method is to add the two costs at each CA/TA level and choose the lowest one. This is shown in the following table.

CA/TA	Cost of Liquidity	Cost of Illiquidity	Total Cost	
0.1	$50,000	$93,000	$144,000	
0.2	54,000	80,000	134,000	
0.3	59,000	70,000	129,000	
0.4	66,000	62,000	128,000	Minimum
0.5	75,000	54,000	129,000	
0.6	86,000	48,000	134,000	
0.7	99,000	41,000	140,000	

The optimal CA/TA ratio if 0.4 or 40 percent, because total cost is minimized at this point.

7-2. *NWC, CA/TA, and CL/TF.*

This problem is a matter of calculating the required ratios and ranking the companies according to each set of ratios. The results of the calculations are given below. Detailed calculations for company A follow.

	A	B	C
NWC	$100	$117	$140
CA/TA	0.30	0.40	0.50
CL/TF	0.20	0.30	0.40

On the asset side of the balance sheet, company A is the most aggressive and C the most conservative, because the higher the proportion of CA to TA, the safer the situation, other things the same. On the liability side, A is the most conservative and C the most aggressive, because the more permanent funding used, the safer the situation, other things the same. Since these are contradicting stances, what can be said about them overall? There is not anything really conclusive revealed by these limited figures; but notice that NWC is 10 percent of total assets in each case. This suggests that their overall working capital management risk is similar.

Here are the calculations for company A.

NWC	=	CA - CL
	=	$300 - $200
	=	$100
CA/TA	=	$300/$1,000
	=	0.30 or 30%
CL/TF	=	$200/$1,000
	=	0.20 or 20%

Calculations for the other companies are similar.

7-3.   *Financing alternatives.*
    This problem focuses on the matching of maturities of assets and financing. We begin by framing the liability and capital side of the balance sheet and filling in the given numbers. The two figures that we know are total funds (because it must equal total assets) and equity (because it is stated in the problem). This first step takes us to the following:

	A	B	C
Accounts payable			
Notes payable			
Total current liabilities			
Long-term debt			
Equity	325	325	325
Total Financing	$500	$500	$500

Now we have to figure out how much more long-term financing is required for each financing plan. Each company requires $300 for fixed assets. Company A requires $120 for financing 100 percent of permanent current assets. Company B requires $60 to finance 50 percent of the $120 of permanent current assets. Company C requires $150 to finance 125 percent of permanent current assets. Company C actually finances $30 of the temporary current assets with permanent financing.

We have to back into the answers, so let's make a table to show the process.

	A	B	C
Fixed assets requiring long-term financing	$300	$300	$300
Current assets requiring long-term financing	120	60	150
Total long-term financing required	$420	$360	$450
Minus financing provided by equity	325	325	325
Funds to be provided by long-term debt	$ 95	$ 35	$125

Fill in the liability side of the balance sheet with these new numbers.

	A	B	C
Accounts payable			
Notes payable			
Total current liabilities			
Long-term debt	$ 95	$ 35	$125
Equity	325	325	325
Total financing	$500	$500	$500

We know that current liabilities must equal total funds minus long-term debt minus equity. The problem states that accounts payable are 60 percent of each companies' current liabilities, so we can calculate accounts payable. The last figure is notes payable, which is the other 40 percent of current liabilities. The completed financing side of the balance sheet follows:

	A	B	C
Accounts payable	$48	$84	$30
Notes payable	32	56	20
Total current liabilities	$80	$140	$50
Long-term debt	95	35	125
Equity	325	325	325
Total financing	$500	$500	$500

Chapter 7: Working-Capital Management

7-4. *Integrated NWC and profitability.*
We'll take this long problem figure-by-figure, and it will be quite easy. We shall show the results for all the companies here, then do detailed calculations for company A as required in parts A and F. We'll answer the remaining questions as we get to them.

	A	B	C	D
NWC	$325,000	$250,000	$200,000	$85,000
CA/TA	0.40	0.38	0.33	0.30
CL/TF	0.15	0.19	0.17	0.23
CA/CL	2.59	2.00	2.00	1.33
Quick ratio	1.32	1.00	1.00	0.71
Sales	$6,400,000	$6,400,000	$6,400,000	$6,400,000
Operating profit	256,000	256,000	256,000	256,000
Interest-short term	3,000	5,000	4,000	6,000
Interest-long term	48,750	37,500	30,000	12,750
Profit before taxes	$204,250	$213,500	$222,000	$237,250
Taxes	61,275	64,050	66,600	71,175
Net profit	$142,795	$149,450	$155,400	$166,075
ROE	17.87%	18.68%	19.43%	20.76%

A. Item-by-item calculations of NWC, CA/TA, CL/TF, CA/CL, and the quick ratio follow for company A only. Calculations for companies B, C, and D are similar. Results for all four companies are given above.

$$NWC = CA - CL$$
$$= \$530,000 - \$205,000$$
$$= \$325,000$$

$$CA/TA = \$530,000/\$1,330,000 \tag{7-1}$$
$$= 0.40 \text{ or } 40\%$$

$$CL/TF = \$205,000/\$1,330,000 \tag{7-2}$$
$$= 0.15 \text{ or } 15\%$$

$$CA/CL = \$530,000/\$205,000 \tag{3-1}$$
$$= 2.59$$

$$Quick\ ratio = (CA - Inventory)/CL \tag{3-2}$$
$$= (\$530,000 - \$260,000)/\$205,000$$
$$= 1.32$$

B.   To rank these companies we need to remember that conservative on the asset side means a higher CA/TA ratio. The companies rank A-B-C-D, with A having the most conservative CA/TA of 0.40, and D having the least conservative CA/TA of 0.30.

C.   To rank these companies we need to remember that conservative on the liability side means a lower CL/TF ratio. The companies rank A-B-C-D, with A having the most conservative CL/TF of 0.15, and D having the least conservative CL/TF of 0.23.

D.   The higher the current ratio and the higher the quick ratio, the more liquid the company. These ratios indicate that A is most liquid and D least liquid. They show B and C having the same liquidity, since their ratios are identical.

E.   NWC and CA/TA do add information to that provided by the current ratio and quick ratio alone. The larger NWC and CA/TA of company B suggest that it is more liquid than company C, in spite of the fact that their current and quick ratios are the same.

F.   An item-by-item calculation of income statement items follow for company A only. Calculations for companies B, C, and D are similar. Results for all four companies are given above.

Sales	=	(Fixed asset turnover)(Fixed assets)
	=	(8)($800,000)
	=	$6,400,000
Operating profit	=	(Sales)(Operating profit margin)
	=	($6,400,000)(0.04)
	=	$256,000
Interest-short term	=	(Interest rate)(Notes payable)
	=	(0.10)($30,000)
	=	$3,000
Interest-long term	=	(Interest rate)(Long-term debt)
	=	(0.15)($325,000)
	=	$48,750
Profit before taxes	=	Operating profit - short-term interest - long-term interest
	=	$256,000 - $3,000 - $48,750
	=	$204,250

Taxes	=	(Profit before taxes)(Tax rate)
	=	($204,750)(0.30)
	=	$61,275

Net profit	=	Profit before taxes - taxes
	=	$204,250 - $61,275
	=	$142,795

ROE	=	Net profit/equity
	=	$142,795/$800,000
	=	0.1787 or 17.87%

G.   From lowest to highest ROE, the companies rank A-B-C-D. This is the expected ranking, since the lowest profitability should go with the most conservative company.

CHAPTER 8
CASH AND MARKETABLE SECURITIES

Concepts You Should Understand

*   Two main reasons for a firm to hold cash are for transactions and compensating balances.

*   The objective of cash management is to contribute to the maximization of owners' wealth by minimizing the level of cash and marketable securities while providing liquidity for the operation of the firm.

*   Cash flow management requires speeding up cash collections and controlling cash payments.

*   The optimal level of cash minimizes the total of opportunity costs from holding too much cash and the transfer costs incurred by not holding enough cash.

*   Marketable securities are short-term investments that a firm purchases when it has extra cash or has a need for cash in the near future.

*   The optimal level of marketable securities minimizes the total opportunity costs and stockout costs.

*   Marketable securities must have minimal risk and maximum marketability.

A Second Look

To the business, the terms "cash" and "near cash" mean primarily a checking account but also include currency and coins. Even on the retail level many transactions are concluded with checks. The analysis of cash management, then, centers on managing checking account balances. The firm's cash account is an investment just as any other asset.

Checking accounts that are available to businesses pay no interest on the balances and, consequently, cash is called a non-earning asset. A business must have cash, nonetheless, for two major reasons: (1) to conduct daily business transactions and (2) to satisfy the bank's compensating balance requirements, which are often written into loan agreements. The third and fourth reasons to hold cash, (3) precautionary motives and (4) speculative motives, have been largely replaced by investments in marketable securities and lines of credit. The less cash the firm can get by with the better, since it does not earn a return.

The management problem hinges on understanding that a firm collects cash from customers and pays cash to creditors. The object is twofold: (1) to collect your money as fast as you can and (2) to pay your bills on time, but not early. The methods for speeding up collections focus on the firm's depositing customer checks in the bank as quickly as possible. Lockboxes, concentration banking, electronic funds transfer, and depository transfer checks are among the available collection techniques. The second aspect, controlling disbursements, involves avoidance of early payments, remote disbursing, zero-balance accounts, and bank drafts.

Cash budgeting is the planning phase of cash management. It requires estimating the amount and timing of future cash inflows and outflows. With this information management is able to provide for the company's needs without keeping excess cash.

Marketable securities are short-term investments that a company's cash manager can buy instead of keeping large cash balances. This way a firm can turn a non-earning asset into an earning asset until it is needed. "Short-term" in this context means a maturity ranging from one day to one year. The market for these investments is called the "money market," and the securities are generically called "money market instruments."

All money market instruments are debt instruments, which means that when you buy one you are really loaning money to the issuer. Common issuers are the U.S. Treasury, various federal agencies, large corporations, large banks, and securities dealers.

Marketable securities must meet three criteria to be appropriate for cash management needs. They must have very low default risk (also called credit risk); they must have very short-term maturities to reduce interest-rate risk; and there must be a substantial market for them so they can be bought and sold quickly without significantly affecting the price.

The cash manager balances the firm's need for cash against the opportunity costs of keeping cash and invests in marketable securities as an alternative to cash.

Chapter Summary

There are two primary reasons for a firm to keep cash: (1) _____ and (2) _____. Two secondary reasons for holding cash are (3) _____ and (4) _____. Cash management activities fall into four categories: (5) _____ while controlling disbursements, (6) _____, (7) _____, and (8) _____ excess cash effectively.

Cash management should contribute to shareholder wealth maximization. Since cash is a non-earning asset and marketable securities earn less than fixed assets, management attempts to (9) _____ the firm's investment in cash and marketable securities, while providing sufficient (10) _____ for the firm's financial activities.

Speeding up cash collections requires methods to reduce (11) _____ float, which is composed of (12) _____ float, (13) _____ float, and (14) _____ float. One method of reducing float is to optimize collection points, which includes using a (15) _____ system or a (16) _____ system.

When a firm's customers mail their payments to a post office box, and the firm's bank picks up the checks out of the post office box, the firm is utilizing a (17) _____. When the firm, itself, collects its customers' checks at regional offices, deposits them in a local (depository) bank, then transfers the funds to another bank, the firm is using (18) _____.

Electronic funds transfer systems move funds without having to physically transfer pieces of paper, such as checks. Three forms of EFT are (19) _____, (20) _____, and (21) _____. EFT virtually eliminates float and is resisted by many businesses which feel that they benefit from disbursement float.

One aspect of controlling disbursements is to pay creditors on time to maintain a good credit rating, but to avoid paying prior to the due date. When company A writes a check to company B on a bank that is located far away from company B, in order to increase disbursement float, company A is said to be using (22) _____. A (23) _____ is a type of checking account that goes negative as checks are presented, and then is replenished by a transfer of funds from a central control account. A bank draft is presented by the bank to the (24) _____ for approval, thus adding a measure of control.

A worksheet showing inflows, outflows, and balances of cash over a six-to-twelve month time horizon is called a (25) _____. Its three parts are (26) _____, which requires an estimate of the collection of receivables, (27) _____, cash outflows, which requires a schedule for payment of payables, and the (28) _____ section. Management must make decisions as to how to balance the cash budget, which may require long-run and well as short-run solutions.

An optimal cash balance will minimize the total costs of having a cash account, which consist of (29) _____ and transactions costs from buying and selling marketable securities or borrowing funds as needed. The (30) _____ is a mathematical approach to determining the optimal cash balance and maintaining the cash account within control limits.

Instead of keeping excess cash in the checking account, the cash manager can invest in (31) _____ and earn interest. Investing large sums of money is often worthwhile even for one or two days, because the interest earned more than offsets the transactions costs incurred. If company A buys commercial paper (a marketable security) issued by company B, the paper is A's (32) _____ and B's (33)

_____.

A treasurer or cash manager requires securities that have extremely low (34) _____, because the firm will need to sell the securities and use the cash in the very near future. Short-term (35) _____ contribute to price stability as market rates of interest fluctuate. In order for a security to be bought and sold readily, there must be an active (36) _____. Commonly used marketable securities are debt instruments issued by various borrowers for different maturities and face amounts.   U. S. Treasury bills are issued by the Treasury, negotiable CD's by (37) _____, and (38) _____ by large corporations. Time drafts guaranteed by a bank and used in international trade are (39) _____. When a government-bond dealer sells securities to an investor with an agreement to buy them back at a later date, the deal is a (40) _____. All of these securities are appropriate substitutes for cash to be used by the corporate cash manager.

Acronyms You Should Know

ACH	Automated Clearing House
CD	Certificate of Deposit
CHIPS	Clearing House Interbank System
DTC	Depository Transfer Check
EFT	Electronic Funds Transfer
EFTS	Electronic Funds Transfer System
Repo	Repurchase Agreement

Equations You Should Know

Yield = (Interest/market price)(365/days to maturity) (8-1)

Discount = Face value - Market price (8-2)

Problems

1.   *Cash budget.* A manufacturing firm's sales for the prior three months and their sales projections for the next four months are given below. Eighty percent of the sales are credit sales; the rest are cash sales. Seventy-five percent of the credit sales are collected during the first month after the sales are made. Fifteen percent are collected during the second month, and nine percent during the third month. One percent are never collected.

Payables during any month are 40 percent of the prior month's sales, and other variable expense is 10 percent of prior month's sales. Fixed expenses are $135,000 per month. Project the company's cash flow for the months of June through September.

	March	April	May
Previous sales	$500,000	$450,000	$420,000

	June	July	August	September
Projected sales	$480,000	$520,000	$550,000	$580,000

2.   *Lockbox system.* Phillips, Inc., is considering replacing its existing cash collection system with a lockbox system. Both systems are described below.

Existing system. Phillips has five sales offices nationwide, located in New York, Detroit, Chicago, Los Angeles, and Houston. The corporate headquarters are in Kansas City. Each office is responsible for shipping to and invoicing customers within its geographical region. Customers mail their checks to the invoicing office. The regional office marks the customers' records paid and notifies the Accounting Department in the home office.

The checks are deposited daily at noon in a local bank near each office. The funds sit idly in non-interest bearing accounts until Friday of each week, when they are transferred by wire to a central account in a Kansas City bank. The sales offices do not use the local banks for any services other than as a temporary depository.

Proposed lockbox system. Each sales office will still ship to and invoice its own customers. The customers will receive a new mailing address to which to remit their payments. The address will be a Post Office box in Kansas City. When the bank picks up the checks, it will immediately deposit them in an account that can be used by Phillips. The bank will notify Phillips' Accounting Department, which will notify the sales offices which payments have been made. The deposit account earns 7.5 percent per annum compounded daily. Added costs for bank fees, administration, and communication are expected to be $75,000 per year.

General information. Each office deposits approximately $300,000 each working day (five days per week, 52 weeks per year). Mail float between the customers and the

Chapter 8:   Cash and Marketable Securities

Kansas City bank will be the same as to the regional sales offices.
A. Should Phillips proceed with the new system?
B. Are there any potential problems with customers relations that might arise from the lockbox system?

Answers to Chapter Summary

1.	transactions purposes	21.	DTCs
2.	compensating balances	22.	remote disbursing
3.	precautionary motives	23.	zero-balance account
4.	speculative motives	24.	paying company
5.	speeding collections	25.	cash budget
6.	determining cash needs	26.	cash inflows
7.	making cash forecasts	27.	cash outflows
8.	investing	28.	surplus or shortage
9.	minimize	29.	opportunity costs
10.	liquidity	30.	Miller-Orr Model
11.	collection float	31.	marketable securities
12.	mail	32.	asset
13.	processing	33.	liability
14.	availability	34.	default risk
15.	lockbox	35.	maturities
16.	concentration banking	36.	secondary market
17.	lockbox	37.	banks
18.	concentration banking	38.	commercial paper
19.	wire payments	39.	bankers' acceptances
20.	ACHs	40.	repurchase agreements

Problem Solutions

1. *Cash budget.* We must project the cash collections and payments during each of the future four months. The first step is to determine the credit sales each month. We multiply the total sales by 80 percent, the proportion of credit sales.

Chapter 8: Cash and Marketable Securities

	March	April	May
Previous sales	$500,000	$450,000	$420,000
Credit sales	$400,000	$360,000	$336,000

	June	July	August	September
Projected sales	$480,000	$520,000	$550,000	$580,000
Projected credit sales	$384,000	$416,000	$440,000	$464,000
Projected cash sales	$96,000	$104,000	$110,000	$116,000

The cash inflows during June will be the sum of the following: cash sales during June, 75 percent of credit sales during May, 15 percent of credit sales during April, and nine percent of credit sales during March. The cash outflows during June will be the sum of the following: payables, which is 40 percent of total May sales (not just credit sales), other variable expense, which is 10 percent of total May sales, and fixed expense. Net cash flow is the difference between inflows and outflows. The subsequent months follow the same pattern.

	June	July	August	September
Projected cash inflows				
Cash sales	$96,000	$104,000	$110,000	$116,000
1st month collections (75%)	252,000	288,000	312,000	330,000
2nd month collections (15%)	54,000	50,400	57,600	62,400
3rd month collections	36,000	32,400	30,840	34,560
Projected cash inflow	$438,000	$474,800	$509,840	$542,960
Projected cash outflows				
Payables (40%)	$168,000	$192,000	$208,000	$220,000
Variable expense (10%)	42,000	48,000	52,000	55,000
Fixed expenses	135,000	135,000	135,000	135,000
Total cash outflow	$345,000	$375,000	$395,000	$410,000
Net cash flow	$93,000	$99,800	$114,840	$132,960

2. *Lockbox system.* The problem is that the cash collected is sitting in non-interest bearing accounts in regional banks instead of earning interest in a centralized bank.

A. Since the offices are all the same size, let's set up a table for one office to determine how much interest is lost and, therefore could be gained by utilizing the lockbox system. Then we can multiply by five for a total for all offices.

Daily interest rate	=	Annual rate/365
	=	0.075/365
	=	0.000205479452

For Monday's deposit:

Interest gained	=	(Deposit)(Days)(Daily interest rate)
	=	($300,000)(4)(0.000205479452)
	=	$246.58

Calculations for the other days are similar and are summarized below.

	Deposit	Days Interest Gained	Interest Gained
Monday	$300,000	4	$246.58
Tuesday	$300,000	3	184.93
Wednesday	$300,000	2	123.29
Thursday	$300,000	1	61.64
Friday	$300,000	0	0.00
Total			$616.44 interest gained per week per office

| Interest gained for five offices | = | (5)($616.44) |
| | = | $3,082.20 per week |

| Annual benefit for five offices | = | (52)($3,082.20) |
| | = | $160,274.40 per year |

Net annual benefit	=	Annual benefit - annual cost
	=	$160,274.40 - $75,000.00
	=	$85,274.40

B.   A potential problem with customer relations exists in that the sales office will no longer know as rapidly when a customer has paid through the lockbox system. Under the old system, the sales office knew the day when the check arrived in the mail. With the lockbox system, the Kansas City bank will notify the home office Accounting Department, which will record the transactions and notify the sales office. At best there will be several days' delay. This delay will not be a problem with most customers. Marginal customers, who operate near their credit limit, have been known to make a payment right before they need another shipment. In such a case a customer could have a shipment delayed until the sales office can receive verification of payment from the home office.

CHAPTER 9
ACCOUNTS RECEIVABLE
AND INVENTORY

Concepts You Should Understand

*   Sound investment decisions compare marginal benefits to marginal costs in order to achieve the ultimate goal of owners' wealth maximization.

*   Both accounts receivable and inventory are investments and should be treated as such.

*   Management of accounts receivable focuses on credit policy.

*   Credit policy decisions fall into four categories: credit standards, credit terms, evaluation of receivables management, and collection policies.

*   Management of inventory must balance having sufficient inventory to maintain a smooth production process and to serve customers well against minimizing costs.

*   The economic order quantity model is a classic, cost-minimizing inventory model.

A Second Look

Two really important investments for many firms are accounts receivable and inventory. Both are necessary to the operation of most businesses. The question, then, is not whether to invest, but how much to invest. This chapter considers the characteristics of receivables and inventory, analytical approaches for value maximizing and cost minimizing, and the evaluation of management of both assets.

If management is to control the size of the investment in receivables, it needs to determine what factors affect it. Rearranging equation 9-6, we see that

accounts receivable = (collection period)(sales/365).

Analyzing this equation, we note that there is nothing we can do about the number of days in the year, and we would not want to reduce sales as a method to reduce

95

receivables. The only variable left under the influence of management is the collection period. So we turn our attention to it.

One factor that affects how long our customers take to pay is how long we agree to give them. This is the credit terms. The credit period is the maximum time in which they may pay within our terms. If they pay within the discount period, they may take a cash discount. The length of these periods and the amount of the discount, if any, has a lot to do with when the customers pay. Competition within the industry often forces management to offer competitive credit terms, preempting part of their discretionary decision making.

Regardless of our credit terms, some customers will pay early, some on time, some late, and some never. In an attempt to weed out the "nevers" before selling to them, we establish credit standards and separate customers into risk classifications. The incremental benefits and costs of selling to each risk class can be estimated as the basis of a decision. When a new customer applies for credit, we apply our standards and assign him to a risk class. If we sell to that risk class, we have a new customer. Otherwise, we don't.

How can upper management tell whether or not the credit manager is doing a good job? The collection period, an aging schedule, and a collection experience matrix help answer this question.

To determine what factors affect the inventory investment decision, let's rearrange equation 9-12. We see that

inventory = sales/inventory turnover.

Average inventory turnover would normally be used here to capture the overall level of inventory investment. We don't want to adjust sales to adjust inventory, so we are left with only one variable to consider: inventory turnover.

Inventory turnover is a complex problem requiring consideration of numerous variables, such as the product itself, the production process, and the product markets. The economic order quantity (EOQ) model minimizes the combined costs of ordering and carrying the inventory. The EOQ can be used along with a safety stock, delivery times, and sales patterns to get a good grasp of the inventory requirements of the company.

The inventory turnover tells us how many dollars of sales our firm is making for every dollar of inventory. Comparing our inventory turnover to that of other companies within the same industry over several years gives upper management a tool for evaluating inventory management.

Chapter Summary

Accounts receivable and inventory represent a huge investment for many companies. For manufacturing firms approximately (1) _____ percent of current assets and (2) _____ of total assets are made up of accounts receivable, notes receivable, and inventory.

When one firm sells to another without collecting payment immediately, the type credit granted is called (3) _____. The resulting documents are an (4) _____ to the purchasing firm and an (5) _____ to the selling company. The selling company is able to control, although imperfectly, its investment in receivables within the constraints of (6) _____ and (7) _____.

Since the amount of funds invested in receivables is the product of the credit sales per day times the (8) _____, management decisions must focus on (9) _____. These policy decisions fall into four major categories: (10) _____, (11) _____, evaluating (12) _____, and establishing a (13) _____.

Setting credit standards involves deciding which customers will be granted credit and what their limits will be. To determine a potential customer's creditworthiness, management considers the three "Cs" of credit: (14) _____, (15) _____, and (16) _____. The credit manager garners information from (17) _____, such as Dun & Bradstreet, from the customers' own (18) _____, and from the customer's bank. After careful scrutiny, each potential customer is put into a risk class. The entire risk class is either accepted or rejected on the basis of a (19) _____ analysis.

Credit terms consist of the (20) _____ and (21) _____. In addition to considering a firm's own goals and financial strength when setting credit terms, management is heavily influenced by (22) _____ and (23) _____. Credit terms are part of the firm's competitive package used in marketing its products. Other things the same, a company's investment in receivables will be increased by a (24) _____ credit period, a (25) _____ cash discount, and a (26) _____ discount period.
Generally speaking, a firm's sales could be increased by a (27) _____ credit period and a (28) _____ cash discount.

The costs of extending trade credit include (29) _____, (30) _____, (31) _____, (32) _____, and (33) _____. These costs must be weighed against the benefits to make a decision to grant credit to a particular risk class of customers. A net present value framework using (34) _____ production, selling, and administrative costs per day as the (35) _____ is suitable for the analysis.

Receivables management must balance the contribution of credit policy to the sales effort against the cost of the investment in receivables in the context of maximizing owners' wealth. Three particularly useful analytical tools for evaluating credit management are the (36) _____, the (37) _____, and the (38) _____.

Establishing a collection policy is a matter of walking a tightrope between being

97

Chapter 9: Accounts Receivable and Inventory

so lenient that costs become prohibitive and being so stringent that customers are driven away.

The three major types of inventory are (39) _____, (40) _____, and (41) _____. Inventories allow (42) _____, (43) _____, and (44) _____ to be carried out independently of one another, thereby providing the opportunity for efficiencies in each area. Three types of costs associated with inventories are (45) _____, (46) _____, and (47) _____.

The (48) _____ model minimizes the total of two costs: (49) _____ and (50) _____. A system to reduce inventory levels and the operating cycle while increasing efficiency is the (51) _____ inventory management system.

A widely used method of evaluating inventory management is to compare the firm's (52) _____ to that ratio of similar firms in the same industry.

Acronyms and Notation You Should Know

A	Cost to place one order for inventory ($ per order)
C	Carrying cost per unit ($ per unit per period)
D	Total demand for product (units per period)
EOQ	Economic Order Quantity
JIT	Just-In-Time
PS&A	Production, Selling, and Administrative
Q	Quantity ordered (units)

Equations You Should Know

Taxes $=$ Tax rate(Sales - PS&A - Cash discounts - bad-debt losses) (9-1)

$$k_{daily} = k_{annual}/365 \quad (9-2)$$

Approximate discount factor $= 1/(1 + kt)$ (9-3)

Initial investment $=$ PS&A costs (9-4)

Benefit $=$ Sales - Cash discount - Bad-debt losses - Taxes (9-5)

Chapter 9: Accounts Receivable and Inventory

Collection period = (Accounts receivable)(365)/Sales (9-6)

Total inventory cost = QC/2 + DA/Q (9-10)

EOQ = $(2DA/C)^{1/2}$ (9-11)

Inventory turnover = Sales/Inventory (9-12)

Problems

9-1. *Approximate discount factors.* Calculate the daily required rate of return and the approximate discount factors for the annual rates and periods given.

Annual rate	Days
6.00%	45
10.00%	7
15.00%	15
18.00%	30

9-2. *NPV analysis of risk classes.* You have estimated the data below for five risk classes of customers of your manufacturing firm. Costs of production, selling, and administration are expected to be 82 percent of sales. The marginal corporate tax rate is 40 percent. The credit terms are 3/15, net 45. The required rate of return is 12 percent.
A. Do a NPV analysis of each class.
B. To which classes will your firm sell?

Risk class	Sales $/day	Bad debt losses % of sales	Collection period days
I	$40,000	0.50%	16
II	$50,000	2.50%	26
III	$60,000	5.00%	37
IV	$75,000	10.00%	63
V	$100,000	20.00%	98

9-3. *Collection period.* A corporation has annual sales of $5 billion, and an accounts receivable balance of $500 million. Calculate the collection period.

9-4.   *Collection period.* Big Tyme, Inc., has annual sales of $2.5 billion, and an accounts receivable balance of $192 million. The industry average collection period is 25 days.

A.   What is Big Tyme's collection period? Round answer to the nearest whole day.

B.   If Big Tyme could reduce its collection period to the industry average without losing sales, what would its new receivables be? Round answer to the nearest million.

C.   If Big Tyme has a cost of capital equal to 11.5 percent per year, how many dollars can it save per year by reducing the collection period to industry average? Round answer to nearest one-hundred thousand dollars.

9-5.   *Collection period with discount period.* The firm sells on terms of 3/15, net 60. Management has categorized its customers into risk classes as shown below. The columns show the sales per day to each class and the percent of customers who take the discount. The column labeled "Days late" shows how many days past the final credit period that the remainder, who do not take the discount, pay. For example, in risk class II, 80 percent of the customers take the discount and pay on day 15, while the other 20 percent pay on day 65 (60 + 5).

Risk Class	Sales/day	% who take Discount	Days late
I	$200,000	95%	0
II	$250,000	80%	5
III	$350,000	75%	15
IV	$500,000	40%	30
V	$750,000	25%	60

A.   Use a weighted average to calculate the collection period of each risk class. Round to two decimal places.

B.   Use the collection period of each class to calculate the receivables balance associated with each risk class.

C.   What is the total receivables balance for all five risk classes?

9-6.   *EOQ.* Harlow's Wholesale House, Inc., purchases 540,000 units of Item 06AU22 annually. Because of the technical nature of the product, each order incurs costs of $750. Since the item is small and light, the annual carrying cost is only $0.40 per unit. Harlow maintains a safety stock equivalent to 10 percent of annual usage.

A.   Calculate the EOQ.

B.   Calculate the total annual inventory cost.

C.   How many orders will Harlow place each year?

D.   Calculate the average inventory, assuming constant usage.

Answers to Chapter Summary

1.	80	27.	longer
2.	30	28.	larger
3.	trade credit	29.	PS&A costs
4.	accounts payable	30.	cash discounts
5.	accounts receivable	31.	bad debts losses
6.	economic activity	32.	taxes
7.	industry practice	33.	required rate of return
8.	collection period	34.	incremental
9.	credit policy	35.	initial investment
10.	setting credit standards	36.	collection period
11.	developing credit terms	37.	aging schedule
12.	receivables management	38.	collection experience matrix
13.	collection policy	39.	raw materials
14.	character	40.	goods in process
15.	capacity	41.	finished goods
16.	conditions	42.	purchasing
17.	credit rating agencies	43.	production
18.	financial statements	44.	sales
19.	NPV	45.	ordering costs
20.	credit period	46.	carrying costs
21.	cash discount	47.	stockout costs
22.	economic conditions	48.	EOQ
23.	industry factors	49.	ordering costs
24.	longer	50.	carrying costs
25.	smaller	51.	just-in-time
26.	longer	52.	inventory turnover

Problem Solutions

9-1. *Approximate discount factors.*

Let's calculate the daily rate for 6.00 percent using equation 9-2:

$$k_{daily} = k_{annual}/365 \qquad (9\text{-}2)$$
$$= .06/365$$
$$= .00016438 \text{ or } 0.016438\%$$

Now let's calculate the approximate discount factor for six percent and 45 days

101

using equation 9-3:

$$\begin{aligned}
\text{Discount factor} \quad &= \quad 1/(1 + kt) \quad &(9\text{-}3)\\
&= \quad 1/[1 + (0.00016438)(45)]\\
&= \quad 1/1.0073971\\
&= \quad 0.992657
\end{aligned}$$

These two calculations complete the first row in the table below. The remaining rows require similar calculations with the differing rates and number of days.

Annual rate	Days	Daily rate	Approximate discount factor
6.00%	45	0.016438%	0.992657
10.00%	7	0.027397%	0.998086
15.00%	15	0.041096%	0.993873
18.00%	30	0.049315%	0.985421

9-2. *NPV analysis of risk classes.*
      This problem requires us to calculate the daily benefits, to discount the daily benefits, to calculate the initial investment, to calculate the NPV, and to make a decision based on the NPV for each risk class. The data from the problem is repeated here for convenience.

Risk class	Sales/day	Bad debt losses % of sales	Collection period days
I	$40,000	0.50%	16
II	$50,000	2.50%	26
III	$60,000	5.00%	37
IV	$75,000	10.00%	63
V	$100,000	20.00%	98

A.   We'll calculate each variable for risk class I. The calculations for the other risk classes are similar. The results for all classes are summarized in the table following these item-by-item calculations for risk class I.

$$\begin{aligned}
\text{Cash discount} \quad &= \quad (\text{Sales})(\% \text{ discount})\\
&= \quad (\$40,000)(0.03)\\
&= \quad \$1,200 \text{ per day}
\end{aligned}$$

Chapter 9: Accounts Receivable and Inventory

Bad debt losses	=	(Sales)(% bad debt losses)
	=	($40,000)(0.0050)
	=	$200 per day

PS&A expenses	=	(Sales)(%PS&A to sales)
	=	($40,000)(0.82)
	=	$32,800/day

Taxes	=	Tax rate(Sales - PS&A -	
		Cash discounts - bad-debt losses)	(9-1)
	=	0.40($40,000 - $32,800 - $1,200 - $200)	
	=	$2,320/day	

Benefits	=	Sales - cash discounts - bad debt losses - taxes	(9-5)
	=	$40,000 - $1,200 - $200 - $2,320	
	=	$36,280/day	

k_{daily}	=	$k_{annual}/365$	(9-2)
	=	0.12/365	
	=	0.00032877 or 0.032877% per day	

Approximate discount factor	=	1/(1 + kt)	(9-3)
	=	1/(1 + .12(16))	
	=	0.99476725	

PV of benefits	=	(Benefits)(discount factor)
	=	($36,280)(0.99476725)
	=	$36,090 per day

Initial investment	=	PS&A expenses
	=	$32,800 per day as calculated above

NPV	=	PV of benefits - initial investments
	=	$36,090 - $32,800
	=	$3,290 per day

Calculations for all five risk classes are given in the following tables.

Risk class	Sales $/day	Cash discount $/day	Bad debt losses $/day	Taxes $/day	Benefit $/day
I	$40,000	$1,200	$200	$2,320	$36,280
II	$50,000	$1,500	$1,250	$2,500	$44,750
III	$60,000	$1,800	$3,000	$2,400	$52,800
IV	$75,000	$2,250	$7,500	$1,500	$63,750
V	$100,000	$3,000	$20,000	($2,000)	$79,000

Risk class	Approximate discount factor	PV of benefit $/day	PS&A $/day	NPV $/day
I	0.99476725	$36,090	$32,800	$3,290
II	0.99152450	$44,371	$41,000	$3,371
III	0.98798181	$52,165	$49,200	$2,965
IV	0.97970797	$62,456	$61,500	$956
V	0,96878650	$76,534	$82,000	($5,466)

B.   The decision is now easy. We sell to all customers in risk classes I through IV because the NPV is positive for them, and reject sales to risk class V because its NPV is negative.

9-3.   *Collection period.* We have to plug the figures into equation 9-6. Since this problem is dealing with millions of dollars, let's knock off six zeros when we do the calculations so we don't have to keep track of all the zeros.

$$\begin{aligned}
\text{Collection period} \quad &= \quad \text{(Accounts receivable)}(365)/\text{Sales} \quad &(9\text{-}6)\\
&= \quad (\$500)(365)/\$5,000\\
&= \quad 36.5 \text{ days}
\end{aligned}$$

9-4.   *Collection period.* We'll take this step-by-step.

A.   We need equation 9-6 to calculate the collection period. Let's drop the unnecessary zeros to keep the arithmetic easy.

$$\begin{aligned}
\text{Collection period} \quad &= \quad \text{(Accounts receivable)}(365)/\text{Sales} \quad &(9\text{-}6)\\
&= \quad (\$192)(365)/(\$2,500)\\
&= \quad 28 \text{ days}
\end{aligned}$$

B.   To calculate the receivables balance, given the collection period, we use equation 9-6, but solve for receivables instead of collection period. The rearranged equation is:

$$\begin{aligned} \text{Accounts receivable} &= \text{(collection period)(Sales)/365} \\ &= (25)(\$2,500)/365 \\ &= \$171 \text{ million} \end{aligned}$$

C.   The idea in this part is that if we can reduce the asset side of the balance sheet by reducing receivables, we can simultaneously reduce the financing side. We save the cost of capital on the funds no longer needed. We have to see how much the reduction would be, if management could accomplish it, and how much that would save us on an annual basis.

$$\begin{aligned} \text{Reduction in receivables} &= \text{Current receivables - target receivables} \\ &= \$192 - \$171 \\ &= \$21 \text{ million} \end{aligned}$$

$$\begin{aligned} \text{Capital costs saved} &= \text{(Reduction in receivables)(cost of capital)} \\ &= (\$21)(0.115) \\ &= \$2.4 \text{ million per year} \end{aligned}$$

9-5.   *Collection period with discount period.* We'll do the calculations for risk class I, then summarize the results for all five risk classes.

A.   This problem needs a different approach, since the number of days that the various customers take to pay are given. We need a average, weighted by the percent that take the discount and the percent who do not.

Weighted average
$$\begin{aligned} \text{collection period} &= \text{(discount period)(\% that take discount) +} \\ &\quad \text{(credit period + days late)(1 - \% that take discount)} \\ &= (15 \text{ days})(.95) + (60 \text{ days} + 0 \text{ days})(1 - .95) \\ &= 17.25 \text{ days} \end{aligned}$$

B.   We'll use equation 9-6, rearranged to solve for receivables. This calculation will have to be done for each class individually. Here is the calculation for risk class I.

$$\begin{aligned} \text{Accounts receivable} &= \text{(collection period)(sales per day)} \\ &= (17.25 \text{ days})(\$200,000) \\ &= \$3,450,000 \end{aligned}$$

C.   Now all that is left to do is add the receivables for each risk class. Below is a table giving the results for all categories and the total.

Risk Class	Sales/day	% who take Discount	Days late	Average Days	Balance for class
I	$200,000	95%	0	17.25	$3,450,000
II	$250,000	80%	5	25.00	6,250,000
III	$350,000	75%	15	30.00	10,500,000
IV	$500,000	40%	30	60.00	30,000,000
V	$750,000	25%	60	90.00	45,000,000
					$95,200,000

9-6. *EOQ*.

A.   EOQ $=$ $(2DA/C)^{1/2}$ (9-11)
$=$ $[(2)(540,000 \text{ units})(\$750)/\$.40]^{1/2}$ $=$ $(2,025,000,000)^{1/2}$
$=$ 45,000 units

B.   Total cost $=$ $QC/2 + DA/Q$ (9-10)
$=$ $(45,000 \text{ units})(\$.40)/2$ $+$ $(540,000 \text{ units})(\$750)/45,000 \text{ units}$
$=$ $18,000

C.   # orders $=$ Annual Usage/EOQ
$=$ 540,000 units/18,000 units/order
$=$ 30 orders per year

D.   Average inventory $=$ EOQ/2 + Safety Stock
$=$ 45,000 units/2 $+$ 54,000 units
$=$ 27,900 units

CHAPTER 10
SHORT-TERM FINANCING

Concepts You Should Understand

*   Working-capital management should contribute to the goal of maximizing owners' wealth. Management attempts to provide short-term financing for temporary current assets at minimum cost with maximum flexibility of repayment terms.

*   Temporary current assets are financed by short-term borrowing, which may be either spontaneous or negotiated.

*   Spontaneous sources of short-term financing include trade credit and accruals; whereas, negotiated sources include short-term bank loans and commercial paper.

*   Short-term loans are sometimes secured with the assets they are intended to finance: accounts receivable and inventory.

A Second Look

Temporary current assets require short-term financing, which means that the business borrows money to be repaid within one year. Some of this borrowing, such as trade credit and accruals, is automatic or spontaneous. Other types of borrowing, such as bank loans and commercial paper, must be negotiated for each loan. Management tries to use the lowest-cost form of short-term credit only for the period needed.

Trade credit is simply unpaid bills, usually for inventory. This is a type of financing because the purchaser would have had to pay on or before delivery if the supplier had not been willing to ship on credit. Trade credit is said to be spontaneous because as sales increase, purchases increase, and accounts payable (that is, trade credit) increase. An increase in sales, thus, causes an increase in payables without any management decisions or negotiations with the supplier. Small firms depend more heavily on trade credit as a source of short-term funds than large companies.

Trade credit has both visible and hidden costs, sometimes referred to as explicit and implicit costs, respectively. The visible costs are quantifiable costs such as forgoing cash discounts or paying late penalties. Hidden costs are less easy to quantify, and are paid in the price of the product, though not explicitly enumerated.

Accruals are also spontaneous in that an increase in sales leads to an increase in unpaid wages and unpaid taxes. Since these are not paid immediately when the service is performed or the tax liability incurred, they are a source of short-term financing. There are no visible costs associated with accruals.

Negotiated sources of short-term funds are mainly bank loans and commercial paper. These are not spontaneous because an increase in sales does not automatically lead to a new loan; a new loan must be negotiated between management and the lender.

When a company applies for a bank loan, the bank analyzes the company's potential for repaying the loan and the suitability of the loan for the bank's loan portfolio. The cost of a loan is the effective interest paid.

Commercial paper is a loan from one large business to another. The loan is a short-term investment to the company that supplies the funds and a form of financing to the other. The borrower sells the paper (that is, issues unsecured promissory notes) through a securities dealer to whomever will buy it.

A bank or finance company may require collateral on riskier loans. A loan with collateral is known as a secured loan. The life of the collateral is typically matched with the life of the loan. For short-term loans the security is often accounts receivable or inventory. The details of the security arrangements can be complex, which raises the cost of the financing.

Chapter Summary

Short-term sources of funds, which are used to finance temporary current assets, are classified as (1) _____ or (2) _____. The spontaneous sources are primarily (3) _____ and (4) _____. An account payable results from a purchase on (5) _____; whereas, a more formal promissory note results in a (6) _____. The advantages of trade credit include (7) _____, (8) _____, and (9) _____.

The cost of trade credit may include both (10) _____ and (11) _____ costs. When payment is (12) _____ there are no visible costs, but there are hidden costs, such as credit checking and bad-debt losses. These hidden costs are covered in the (13) _____ rather than as an explicit charge to the customer. If a payment is delayed, the visible costs may take the form of forgoing a (14) _____ or a (15) _____ charge. The hidden costs of delayed payments include potential repercussions related to the firm's lack of ethical behavior by not fulfilling its financial responsibilities and possible deterioration of the firm's (16) _____. In spite of these costs, trade credit is often considered to be an economical source of funds.

Accrued (17) _____ and accrued (18) _____ are sources of funds to practically every business. There is no visible or explicit cost to accruals, because there are no interest or penalty charges and no discounts to forgo.

One form of negotiated short-term financing used by small and large firms alike is (19) _____. Choosing a bank and nurturing the relationship between the company and the bank is often critical to the company's success.

When a firm applies for a loan, the bank carefully analyzes the firm's (20) _____, the (21) _____ of the loan, and the realistic expectations of (22) _____. Loans to increase short-term assets, such as receivables or inventory, are expected to pay themselves off as the inventory is sold and the receivables are collected. Such loans are called (23) _____ loans.

Common types of short-term bank loans are (24) _____, (25) _____, and (26) _____. A (27) _____ is for a specific amount to be repaid in a lump sum at the end of a fixed period of time. Sometimes this type loan my be renewed when it comes due.

A line of credit is for a (28) _____ amount, but the bank is not legally obligated to loan the entire amount. It may require that the borrower keep a minimum checking account balance known as a (29) _____, which raises the effective interest cost on the borrowed funds. A (30) _____ clause in a line-of-credit agreement requires a borrower to pay off the loan for at least a month (maybe more) once a year to prove that the firm is, indeed, using the short-term loan for temporary needs.

In a revolving credit agreement the borrower pays a (31) _____ on the unused portion of the maximum amount of credit under the agreement. The bank is legally obligated to make the funds available if the firm wishes to borrow them. The cost on such loans is often a (32) _____ pegged to the U. S. Treasury bill rate.

The effective interest cost for a loan depends on the (33) _____, the method used by the lender to (34) _____ the interest, and the firm's (35) _____. The (36) _____ is an often-quoted benchmark interest rate set by banks. Three factors to consider in the computation of the interest payments are the (37) _____, any (38) _____, and use of the (39) _____.

Two sources of short-term funds through the open market are (40) _____ and (41) _____. An unsecured promissory note maturing in three to 270 days is called (42) _____. Only large companies with sterling credit ratings can borrow through this market, because other companies are not willing to lend to a firm if substantial credit risk exists. Commercial paper is (43) _____, and the percentage cost is typically below prime rate.

Secured loans are often made by banks and finance companies. There are three types of the latter: (44) _____, (45) _____, and (46) _____ finance companies.

A firm can use accounts receivable for collateral for loans by either factoring or pledging the receivables. When a company sells its accounts receivable, it is said to be

(47) _____ its receivables. Factoring is a fairly costly source of credit, but, in addition to the financing, the borrower receives (48) _____ and passes on the
collection risk to the factor. When receivables are pledged, they remain the property of the borrower, who is still responsible for their collection.

A company can also use inventory as collateral for a loan. If the borrower continues to control the pledged inventory, the pledge may take the form of a blanket lien covering all inventory or a (49) _____ for one individual item.

The lender may require a third party to oversee the inventory to make sure that the borrower does not sell the collateral without paying back the loan. One system has the inventory stored in a terminal warehouse, whose management is responsible to the lender as well as to the owner of the inventory. Another arrangement has the goods remaining on the premises of the borrower under the supervision of an independent warehouseman. This latter setup is called a (50) _____.

Acronyms and Notation You Should Know

i	Nominal interest rate (%)
I	Interest payment ($)
L	Loan principal ($)
L_0	Loan proceeds ($)
m	Number of periods per year
N	Number of days between discount date and due date
N'	Number of days between discount date and date paid
r	Effective annual interest rate (%)

Equations You Should Know

$$\text{Visible annual cost of forgoing cash discount} = \frac{\% \text{ cash discount}}{100\% - \% \text{ cash discount}} \times \frac{365}{N} \qquad (10\text{-}1)$$

$$\text{Visible annual cost of penalty charge} = (\% \text{ penalty})(\# \text{ of periods/year}) \qquad (10\text{-}2)$$

$$\text{Visible annual cost of forgoing cash discount with late payment} = \frac{\% \text{ cash discount}}{100\% - \% \text{ cash discount}} \times \frac{365}{N'} \qquad (10\text{-}3)$$

Total cost of forgoing
cash discounts or $\quad=\quad$ Visible $\quad+\quad$ Hidden $\hspace{3cm}$ (10-4)
late payment penalties $\hspace{1.5cm}$ cost $\hspace{2cm}$ cost

$$I \quad = \quad (L)(i)(t) \hspace{4cm} (10\text{-}5)$$

$$r \quad = \quad (I/L_0)(m) \hspace{3.7cm} (10\text{-}6)$$

$$\text{Interest yield} \quad = \quad \frac{\text{Face value - Sale price}}{\text{Sale price}} \quad \text{x} \quad \frac{365}{\text{Days to maturity}} \quad (10\text{-}7)$$

Problems

10-1. *Forgoing cash discounts.* Discount City has purchased merchandise on open account with the terms 1/10, net 30.
A. Calculate the visible cost of forgoing the cash discount and making a delayed payment on the 30th day.
B. Calculate the visible cost of forgoing the cash discount and making a late payment on the 45th day.
C. What are possible hidden costs of making a late payment?

10-2. *Forgoing cash discounts.* Mammoth Manufacturing purchases raw materials on terms that take into account that the production process extends their cash cycle. The terms are 3/15, net 60.
A. Calculate the visible cost of forgoing the cash discount and making delayed payment on the 60th day.
B. Calculate the visible cost of forgoing the cash discount and stretching the payable to the 90th day.
C. Calculate the visible cost of forgoing the cash discount and making the payment on the 20th day instead of waiting until the 60th day.
D. What are possible hidden costs of stretching payables?

10-3. *Forgoing cash discounts.* Plastic Products, Inc., purchased $25,000 worth of resin on terms of 3/10, net 35. They will not have the cash for prompt payment to take the discount on the 10th day, but expect to have the funds by the 35th day. They could borrow money on their line of credit at the bank at 18 percent and take the discount, then repay the bank on the 35th day.
A. Compare the percentage cost of forgoing the cash discount and borrowing from the

bank.

B.   Compare the dollar cost of forgoing the cash discount and borrowing from the bank.

10-4. *Late payment penalty.* Your company purchases from a supplier who sells on terms of net 25 and charges a five percent late charge each month (or partial month) a payment is past due.

A.   Calculate the cost of paying two weeks after the due date. Base your calculations on 52 weeks per year.

B.   Calculate the cost of paying 45 days late, thereby incurring two penalty charges. Base your calculations on 365 days per year.

10-5. *Effective interest rates.* This problem asks you to do a number of calculations in order to compare the effects of discounts, compensating balances, and the banker's year on effective interest rates. Use a $100,000 single-payment loan for 90 days at a nominal interest rate of 12% per annum. Calculate the dollar amount of interest, the loan proceeds, and the effective rate for each of the combinations given below. Compare the results.

Discount	Compensating Balance	Banker's Year
No	0%	No
Yes	0%	No
No	15%	No
Yes	15%	No
No	0%	Yes
Yes	0%	Yes
No	15%	Yes
Yes	15%	Yes

10-6. *Effective interest rates.* Consider a $100,000 bank loan at 11.25 percent nominal rate for 270 days. The bank requires a 10 percent compensating balance, does not charge a discount, and does not use the banker's year.

A.   What is the effective rate?

B.   If the bank wants to raise the effective rate one-half of one percentage point without raising the nominal rate, how much will it have to increase the compensating balance requirement?

C.   If the bank uses the banker's year, how much will it have to increase the compensating balance to raise the effective rate one-half of one percentage point?

10-7. *Commercial paper yield.* Calculate the annualized yield for commercial paper for each of the cases below. What is the relationship between price, maturity, and yield?

Price	Maturity in days
$97.81	60
$96.75	90
$93.70	180

Answers to Chapter Summary

1.	spontaneous	26.	revolving credit
2.	negotiated	27.	single loan
3.	trade credit	28.	maximum
4.	accruals	29.	compensating balance
5.	open account	30.	clean-up
6.	trade note payable	31.	commitment fee
7.	availability	32.	floating interest rate
8.	flexibility	33.	nominal interest rate
9.	few restrictions	34.	compute
10.	visible	35.	tax rate
11.	hidden	36.	prime rate
12.	prompt	37.	discount
13.	price of the product	38.	compensating balance
14.	cash discount	39.	banker's year
15.	penalty	40.	commercial paper
16.	credit rating	41.	banker's acceptance
17.	wages	42.	commercial paper
18.	taxes	43.	discounted
19.	bank loans	44.	consumer
20.	integrity	45.	sales
21.	intended use	46.	business
22.	repayment	47.	factoring
23.	self-liquidating	48.	credit checking
24.	single loans	49.	trust receipts
25.	lines of credit	50.	field warehouse

Problem Solutions

10-1. *Forgoing cash discounts.*
A.   When a company forgoes a cash discount but makes the delayed payment on time, the company gets to use the amount they would have paid at the end of the discount period until the end of the credit period. In this case the amount due on the 10th day is 99 percent (100% - 1%) of the invoice amount. They get to use this amount for an extra 20 days (30 days - 10 days). The added cost is the one percent. The problem is to convert this cost to an annualized percentage basis. We use equation 10-1 to calculate the visible cost of forgoing a cash discount.

$$\text{Visible annual cost of forgoing cash discount} = \frac{\% \text{ cash discount}}{100\% - \% \text{ cash discount}} \times \frac{365}{N} \quad (10\text{-}1)$$

$$= \frac{1}{100 - 1} \times \frac{365}{20}$$

$$= 0.1229 \text{ or } 12.29\%$$

B. If the company pays late on the 45th day, they are getting more time at no extra visible cost, which lowers the annual percentage rate. In this case they get 35 extra days (45 days - 10 days) use of the funds before paying the bill. Use equation 10-3.

$$\text{Visible annual cost of forgoing cash discount with late payment} = \frac{\% \text{ cash discount}}{100\% - \% \text{ cash discount}} \times \frac{365}{N'} \quad (10\text{-}3)$$

$$= \frac{1}{100 - 1} \times \frac{365}{35}$$

$$= 0.0819 \text{ or } 8.19\%$$

This lower cost may tempt some business persons to stretch their payables in spite of possible hidden costs.

C.   Possible hidden costs of making late payments include a poor credit rating, a reputation as being a slow-paying customer, and possible loss of the privilege of purchasing on credit at all.

10-2. *Forgoing cash discounts.*

A.   By not taking the discount Mammoth can keep its payment an extra 45 days (60 days - 15 days) and pay the price of the discount. Use equation 10-1.

$$
\begin{aligned}
\text{Visible annual} & \\
\text{cost of forgoing} &= \frac{\% \text{ cash discount}}{100\% - \% \text{ cash discount}} \times \frac{365}{N} \qquad (10\text{-}1)\\
\text{cash discount} &
\end{aligned}
$$

$$
= \frac{3}{100 - 3} \times \frac{365}{45}
$$

$$
= \quad 0.1881 \text{ or } 18.81\%
$$

B.   If Mammoth stretches payment until the 90th day, it uses the funds for the payment 75 days (45 days + 30 days). Use equation 10-3.

$$
\begin{aligned}
\text{Visible annual} & \\
\text{cost of forgoing} &= \frac{\% \text{ cash discount}}{100\% - \% \text{ cash discount}} \times \frac{365}{N'} \qquad (10\text{-}3)\\
\text{cash discount} & \\
\text{with late payment} &
\end{aligned}
$$

$$
= \frac{3}{100 - 3} \times \frac{365}{75}
$$

$$
= \quad 0.1254 \text{ or } 12.54\%
$$

C.   If Mammoth fails to take the discount, it might as well wait until the end of the credit period to pay. In this case they pay the discount for using the funds only five extra days (20 days - 15 days), causing the annualized percentage cost to soar. Use equation 10-1.

$$
\begin{aligned}
\text{Visible annual} & \\
\text{cost of forgoing} &= \frac{\% \text{ cash discount}}{100\% - \% \text{ cash discount}} \times \frac{365}{N} \qquad (10\text{-}1)\\
\text{cash discount} &
\end{aligned}
$$

$$
= \frac{3}{100 - 3} \times \frac{365}{5}
$$

$$
= \quad 0.5644 \text{ or } 56.44\%
$$

D. Possible hidden costs of making late payments include a poor credit rating, a reputation as being a slow-paying customer, and possible loss of the privilege of purchasing on credit at all.

10-3. *Forgoing cash discounts.*

A.   We must calculate the annualized percentage cost of forgoing the cash discount and compare it to the interest rate at the bank. Use equation 10-1.

$$
\begin{array}{l}
\text{Visible annual} \\
\text{cost of forgoing} \\
\text{cash discount}
\end{array}
\; = \; \frac{\text{\% cash discount}}{100\% - \text{\% cash discount}} \; \times \; \frac{365}{N} \qquad (10\text{-}1)
$$

$$
= \; \frac{3}{100 - 3} \; \times \; \frac{365}{25}
$$

$$
= \; 0.3225 \text{ or } 32.25\%
$$

This cost of 32.25% is much higher than the bank rate of 18%. It would be cheaper to borrow from the bank and take the discount on the 10th day, then repay the bank on the 35th day.

B.   We have to calculate the dollar amount of the discount and compare it to the dollar amount of interest on a bank loan.

$$
\text{Discount} \; = \; (0.03)(\$25,000) \; = \; \$750
$$

If we borrow the money from the bank we have to borrow $24,250 ($25,000 minus the 750 discount) for 25 days (35 - 10 days). Use equation 10-5 for the interest amount.

$$
\begin{array}{ll}
I & = \quad (L)(i)(t) \qquad\qquad\qquad\qquad\qquad\qquad\qquad (10\text{-}5)\\
I & = \quad (\$24,250)(0.18)(25/365) \\
  & = \quad \$298.97
\end{array}
$$

The interest cost on the bank loan is much less than the discount which would be lost. This, of course, corresponds to the conclusion based on rates in part A.

10-4. *Late payment penalty.*
A.   In the case of a penalty, we simply have to annualize the percentage amount of the penalty. Since the payment is two weeks late, and there are 52 weeks in a year, we can use weeks to annualize. Use equation 10-2.

Visible annual cost
of penalty charge   =   (% penalty)(# of periods/year)   (10-2)
                                  =   (0.05)(52/2)
                                  =   1.30 or 130%

B.   Two five percent penalties are charged for being 45 days late. This time the number of days late is given, so let's annualize using 365 days per year in equation 10-2.

Visible annual cost
of penalty charge   =   (% penalty)(# of periods/year)   (10-2)
                                  =   (0.05 + 0.05)(365/45)
                                  =   0.8111 or 81.11%

10-5. *Effective interest rates.* In this problem we use equation 10-5 for the dollar amount of interest and equation 10-6 for the percentage cost. If the loan is discounted we must subtract the interest from the loan proceeds. If there is a compensating balance we must subtract the amount of the compensating balance from the loan proceeds. If the banker's year is used, we must use 360 days when calculating the interest payment, but switch to 365 days to annualize the effective rate. We shall go through the last case step-by-step, since it has all of these features. The results for all of the cases are then presented in tabular form.

The case in point follows: $100,000 loan for 90 days, discounted at 12 percent on a banker's year. First use equation 10-5 to calculate the dollar amount of interest.

$$ I \quad = \quad (L)(i)(t) \qquad\qquad (10\text{-}5) $$
$$ = \quad (\$100,000)(0.12)(90/360) $$
$$ = \quad \$3,000 \ \text{interest} $$

We also need to know the compensating balance.

Compensating balance   =   ($100,000)(0.15)
                                  = $15,000

The proceeds that the borrower receives are:

Proceeds   =   face amount - discount - compensating balance
               = $100,000 - $3,000 - $15,000
               = $82,000

To calculate the annualized effective rate, use equation 10-6.

$$r \quad = \quad (I/L_o)(m) \hspace{4cm} (10\text{-}6)$$
$$= \quad (\$3{,}000/\$82{,}000)(365/90)$$
$$= \quad 0.1484 \text{ or } 14.84\%$$

Results for all eight cases follow:

Common to all cases

Face amount	$100,000
Nominal interest rate	12%
Term	90 days

Discount	Comp Balance	Banker's year	Interest	Proceeds	Effective rate
No	0%	No	$2,958.90	$100,000.00	12.00%
Yes	0%	No	$2,958.90	$97,041.10	12.37%
No	15%	No	$2,958.90	$85,000.00	14.12%
Yes	15%	No	$2,958.90	$82,041.10	14.63%
No	0%	Yes	$3,000.00	$100,000.00	12.17%
Yes	0%	Yes	$3,000.00	$97,000.00	12.54%
No	15%	Yes	$3,000.00	$85,000.00	14.31%
Yes	15%	Yes	$3,000.00	$82,000.00	14.84%

Notice that the banker's year raises the effective rate in each case. Also notice that the effective rate rises with a discount and compensating balance because the effective loan proceeds are reduced, not because the dollar amount of interest increases.

10-6. *Effective interest rates.*
A.   To calculate the effective rate, we must calculate the amount of interest and the amount of the compensating balance.

Use equation 10-5 for the interest calculation.

$$I = (L)(i)(t) \qquad (10\text{-}5)$$
$$= (\$100,000)(.1125)(270/365)$$
$$= \$8,321.92$$

Compensating
balance $= $ (% compensating balance)(face)
$\quad = $ (.10)($100,000)
$\quad = $ $10,000

Loan proceeds $= $ face amount - compensating balance
$\quad = $ $100,000 - $10,000
$\quad = $ $90,000

Use equation 10-6 to calculate the effective rate.

$$r = (I/L_o)(m) \qquad (10\text{-}6)$$
$$= (\$8,321.92/\$90,000)(365/270)$$
$$= 0.1250 \text{ or } 12.50\%$$

B.   Now to raise the effective rate 0.5 percentage point would raise it 13.00 percent from the 12.50 percent calculated in part A. One way to go about this would be to set up an electronic spreadsheet like Lotus 1-2-3 and use the trial-and-error method or solve it directly. Whether we solve this electronically or with pencil and paper, we still have to figure it out algebraically. Let's set up the effective rate equation with compensating balance included.

$$\text{Effective rate} = \frac{(\text{Nominal rate})(\text{Face value})(\text{maturity}/365)}{(\text{Face value})(1 - \text{compensating balance})} \times \frac{365}{\text{Maturity}}$$

Simplifying,

Effective rate $= $ (Nominal rate)/(1 - compensating balance)

(1 - compensating balance) $= $ Nominal rate/Effective rate

Compensating balance $= $ 1 - (Nominal rate/Effective rate)

Now we can plug in the 13.00 percent effective rate and solve for the compensating balance.

Chapter 10: Short-Term Financing

Compensating
balance
$$\begin{aligned} &= \quad 1 \text{ - (Nominal rate/Effective rate)} \\ &= \quad 1 \text{ - } 0.1125/0.1300 \\ &= \quad 1 \text{ - } 0.8656 \\ &= \quad 0.1346 \text{ or } 13.46\% \end{aligned}$$

The bank is charging a nominal 11.25 percent interest, but is currently realizing an effective yield of 12.50 percent because of the 10 percent compensating balance. They could raise the effective yield to 13.00 percent by increasing the compensating balance to 13.46 percent, while still charging a nominal interest rate of 11.25 percent. You may want to calculate the effective rate using a 13.46 percent compensating balance to verify that the effective rate is, indeed, 13.00 percent.

The relationship we derived above, holds only for a nondiscounted, single loan using a 365-day year. It could be shown that this relationship for a nondiscounted, single loan on a banker's year is the following:

Compensating balance = 1 - (nominal rate/effective rate)(365/360).

10-7. *Commercial paper interest yield.*

We shall calculate the yield for the first case, then give the rest in tabular form. Because commercial paper is priced on the basis of $100 of face value, we do not even need to know the total amount sold. Use equation 10-7.

$$\text{Interest yield} \quad = \quad \frac{\text{Face value - Sale price}}{\text{Sale price}} \quad \text{x} \quad \frac{365}{\text{Days to maturity}} \quad (10\text{-}7)$$

$$= \quad \frac{100.00 \text{ - } 97.81}{97.81} \quad \text{x} \quad \frac{365}{60}$$

$$= \quad 0.1362 \text{ or } 13.62\%$$

The results for all three cases follow:

Price	Days	Yield
97.81	60	13.62%
96.75	90	13.62%
93.70	180	13.62%

Notice that as the maturity lengthens, the price must be lower to produce the same yield.

CHAPTER 11
CAPITAL BUDGETING AND CASH
FLOW PRINCIPLES

Concepts You Should Understand

*   Capital budgeting is the process of deciding whether or not to invest in particular fixed assets.

*   Any earning asset derives its value from its perceived ability to generate cash flows in the future.

*   Once a potential project has been identified, management must forecast future cash flows over the life of the asset.

*   The relevant cash flows for decision purposes are the cash flows added by the project and are called incremental cash flows.

*   Depreciation, a noncash expense, provides a tax shield by reducing the income taxes the company would have had to pay without the depreciation expense.

*   Management estimates a value for the asset by discounting the expected future cash flows.

*   Capital budgeting projects can often be categorized as either projects to replace existing assets with new ones or projects to expand the company's operations.

A Second Look

Capital budgeting is the decision framework for investing in new assets. We are dealing with investments that will add to the fixed asset section of the balance sheet. These investments are for large dollar amounts, and their lives are longer than one year.

These investments, called projects, will be financed by long-term funds. Management's job is to purchase assets that will earn sufficient return to keep the creditors, bondholders and preferred stockholders happy, while maximizing the common stockholders' wealth. Management forecasts future cash flows in dollars for a project under consideration, yet is faced with investors who state their return requirements in percentage terms. The tie-in is through the discount rate and is considered in more depth in the next two chapters.

This chapter concerns itself with projecting future cash flows. There are three major types of cash flows. The first cash flow associated with a project is an outflow representing the acquisition of the new asset. This initial investment includes all costs incurred by the firm because this project is undertaken. Typical of these outflows are the purchase price, delivery and installation costs, any permanent increase in net working capital, and relevant opportunity costs. The initial outflows may be partially offset by inflows if an existing asset is sold.

The second type is the operating cash flow which results from using the asset throughout its life. When a firm manufactures a product and sells it, the firm receives revenues, pays expenses, and pays taxes. What's left is the operating cash flow.

Termination cash flow is the third type. Any inflows or outflows occurring because the project has ended are included. Salvage of the equipment and recovery of working capital are examples.

A crucial concept is that the relevant cash flows are the incremental cash flows attributed to the project. These cash flows will not occur if the project is not undertaken. Because we are dealing with added income, the marginal tax rate is the appropriate tax rate to use.

Depreciation is a noncash expense because the company treasurer does not have to write a check for it each month. The accountants, on the other hand, deduct it as an expense when determining the firm's income taxes. Its importance, then, is as a tax shield.

Chapter Summary

Capital budgeting is the process of determining whether or not a company should invest in particular fixed assets. The overall process has four major steps: project development and (1) _____, estimation of (2) _____, applying (3) _____, and adjusting for (4) _____. Can budgeting projects can often be classified as (5) _____ projects or (6) _____ projects.

Any project undertaken by the firm should add to the stockholders' wealth. The value of a project is the present value of its estimated future (7) _____ discounted at the firm's (8) _____. This calculation uses cash flows rather than (9) _____ because it is a better measure of the (10) _____ and minimizes (11) _____. The only relevant cash flows are the net change in cash flows due to the project and are called (12) _____ cash flows. Although (13) _____ are irrelevant to a capital budgeting decision, (14) _____ should be included in the analysis. Corporate income taxes are considered because they reduce the cash flows. The appropriate tax rate to use is the (15) _____ rate which will be applied to additional income to the firm.

An investment project has three types of cash flows associated with it: the (16) _____, (17) _____ cash flows, and (18) _____ cash flows. The initial investment has three major components: the (19) _____, any change in (20) _____, and the (21) _____ when a currently owned asset is replaced.

The after-tax cash flows which result from using the new asset can be calculated as $(CFBT_t)(1 - T)$ plus $(Dep)(T)$. The latter term, $(Dep)(T)$, is called the (22) _____. The depreciation method relevant to cash flow determination is the one used for income tax purposes. The investor has a choice of the straight-line method or the (23) _____. An asset has one more year of tax depreciation than its class life suggests because of the (24) _____ convention, which limits the depreciation during the first and last years. At the end of the depreciation period, the asset's (25) _____ is reduced to zero.

When a capital project is ended, there may be cash flows in the last period called (26) _____ cash flows. These may arise from two sources: proceeds from the (27) _____ of the equipment or property and recovery of (28) _____. All of the cash flows directly attributable to a new asset should be considered in management's decision.

Acronyms You Should Know

ACRS	Accelerated Cost Recovery System
$CFAT_t$	Cash Flow After Tax during year t
$CFBT_t$	Cash Flow Before Tax during year t
MACRS	Modified Accelerated Cost Recovery System
T	Marginal Income Tax rate

Equations You Should Know

Cash flow$_t$	=	Cash receipts$_t$	-	Cash payments$_t$	(11-1)
$CFAT_t$	=	$CFBT_t$	-	Tax$_t$	(11-2)
$CFAT_t$	=	$(CFBT_t)(1 - T)$	+	$(Dep)(T)$	(11-3)
Incremental $CFAT_t$ =		$CFAT_t$ of new	-	$CFAT_t$ of old	(11-4)

Problems

11-1. *Depreciation.* A $5,000 computer for the office has a MACRS class life of three years.

A.   Calculate the straight-line depreciation schedule, assuming no salvage value and the half-year convention.

B.   Calculate the MACRS depreciation schedule, and determine the rounded annual percentage rates for later use.

11-2. *Sale of assets.* A machine with a depreciable basis of $45,000 has been depreciated four years under a MACRS class life of five years with half-year convention. The firm's marginal ordinary income tax rate is 34 percent. The capital gains tax rate is the same as the ordinary tax rate. Determine the loss, recapture of depreciation, and/or capital gain for each of the three sales prices given below. Calculate the taxes for each situation.

Sales Price
$5,000
$20,000
$50,000

11-3. *CFAT for expansion project.* Senoj Enterprises is considering the purchase of a new machine to expand its product line. Relevant information is given below. Calculate the after-tax cash flows expected from this project. Round answers to the nearest dollar.

Acquisition cost, including installation	$21,000
Depreciation	MACRS, 3-year class life
Useful life	5 years
Increase in NWC	$2,000
Salvage value at end of 5 years	3,000
Marginal income tax rate	34%
First-year revenues	$10,000
Annual increase in revenues	5%
First-year cash operating expenses	$4,000
Annual increase in cash operating expenses	6%

11-4. *CFAT for replacement problem.* Megabucks Manufacturing Company is analyzing the replacement of an old piece of equipment with a new, improved one. The equipment salesman says the new one will reduce operating expenses significantly. To verify the salesman's claims, a study to estimate future revenues and costs from this project was performed by an outside consulting firm. The study, which cost $1,500, was completed and paid for last month. The information from the study is given below for both the old and new equipment. Management has asked you to begin where the study left off and calculate the expected incremental cash flows from the proposed replacement.

Old equipment

Depreciation basis	$40,000
Depreciation method:	MACRS 5-year class life
Depreciation left:	2 years
Useful life left:	6 years
Current salvage value:	$7,000
Salvage value in 6 years:	$1,000
First-year revenues:	$48,000
Annual growth rate of revenues:	3%
Operating costs as a % of revenues:	60%

New equipment

Depreciation basis	$45,000
Depreciation method:	MACRS 5-year life
Project life:	6 years
Salvage value in 6 years:	$10,000
First-year revenues:	$50,000
Annual growth rate of revenues:	4%
Operating costs as a % of revenues:	40%
Increase in net working capital:	$2,500

General information

Marginal income tax rate:	34%
Marginal cost of capital:	12%
Round figures to nearest dollar.	

Determine initial cash flows, incremental operating cash flows, and terminal cash flows of the proposed replacement of old equipment with new equipment.

Answers to Chapter Summary

1.	classification		15.	marginal
2.	cash flows		16.	initial investment
3.	decision rules		17.	operating
4.	risk		18.	termination
5.	replacement		19.	acquisition price
6.	expansion		20.	net working capital
7.	cash flows		21.	salvage proceeds
8.	cost of capital		22.	tax shield
9.	accounting income		23.	MACRS
10.	net economic benefits		24.	half-year
11.	accounting ambiguities		25.	book value
12.	incremental		26.	termination
13.	sunk costs		27.	salvage
14.	opportunity costs		28.	net working capital

Problem Solutions

11-1. *Depreciation.*
A.   For straight-line depreciation for three years with zero salvage, the annual rate is $1/3 = 0.3333$ or 33.33%. The first year is only half this rate because of the half-year convention, which leaves the other half to be taken in the fourth year. We multiply the depreciation rate by the *initial depreciable value* of $5,000 (not the beginning balance) each year to get the annual expense.   The table below shows the results.

Year	Beginning Balance	Dep Rate	Dep Expense	Ending Balance
1	$5,000	16.67%	$833	$4,167
2	$4,167	33.33%	$1,667	$2,500
3	$2,500	33.33%	$1,667	$833
4	$833	16.67%	$833	-0-

B.   For MACRS three-year class life, we use 200% declining balance with the half-year convention. The rates are 200% of the straight-line rate, which is $(2)(33.33\%) = 66.67\%$. The first year is only half this rate because of the half-year convention. Multiply the depreciation rate times the *annual beginning balance* (not the initial depreciable value) each year. The final year is simply the amount that is left undepreciated at the end of the third year.

Year	Beginning Balance	Dep Rate	Dep Expense	Ending Balance	Rounded Percents
1	$5,000	33.33%	$1,667	$3,333	33%
2	$3,333	66.67%	$2,222	$1,111	45%
3	$1,111	66.67%	$741	$370	15%
4	$370	100%	$370	-0-	7%

In order to calculate the rounded percentage figures used by the IRS, we divide each year's depreciation expense by the *initial depreciable value* of $5,000 and round off the answer. As a practical matter these figures are available in IRS publications. The results are presented below.

A sample calculation for year 2 follows:

Dep expense   =   (Beginning balance)(Dep rate)
              =   ($3,333)(0.6667)
              = $2,222

Ending balance   =   Beginning balance -   Dep expense
                 = $3,333   - $2,222
                 = $1,111

Rounded %   =   Dep expense/Initial depreciable value
            = $2,222/$5,000
            =   0.45 or 45%

11-2. *Sale of assets.* The following relationships hold:

Sale price   <   Book value
results in a loss.

Sale price   =   Book value
results in neither a gain nor a loss.

Book value < Sale price < Depreciable basis
results in a recapture of depreciation.

Book value < Depreciable basis < Sale price
results in both a recapture of depreciation and a capital gain.

Historically, U. S. tax laws have distinguished between recaptured depreciation and capital gains when an asset is sold. Today the tax rate is the same for both types of gain. The distinction is still worth understanding, however, because the capital gains tax is a political issue of considerable importance. A capital gains rate below the ordinary tax rate is supposed to encourage long-term investment and accumulation of capital.

One school of thought, although there are others, behind the recapture of depreciation follows: The asset is supposedly losing value as it gets older. To reflect this loss of value to the firm, depreciation is deducted as an expense during the life of the asset, thereby reducing the income taxes paid by the company. If the asset is eventually sold for more than the book value, then the value actually lost apparently does not match the value assumed lost through the depreciation calculations. Then the IRS says that the firm took more expense that it really incurred, thereby reducing the taxes that it paid. Upon sale of the asset, the extra depreciation is "recaptured," and taxes are paid to make up for the earlier underpayment.

To solve the problem, we must first determine the book value of the asset. Use the rounded MACRS rates determined in Table 11-4 in the textbook. These are repeated here for convenience:

Year	%
1	20%
2	32%
3	19%
4	12%
5	12%
6	5%

The amount depreciated through four years is 20% + 32% + 19% + 12% = 83%.

Depreciable basis	$45,000
Accumulated depreciation (83% of $45,000)	37,350
Book value	$ 7,650

Scenario 1:	Sale price	$5,000
	Book value	7,650
	Loss	($2,650)
	Tax savings (34% times loss)	($901)

Scenario 2:	Sale price	$20,000
	Book value	7,650
	Recapture of depreciation	$12,350
	Taxes (34% times recapture)	$4,199

128

Scenario 3:

Sale price	$50,000	
Depreciable basis	45,000	
Capital gain		$5,000
Depreciable basis	$45,000	
Book value	7,650	
Recapture of depreciation		37,350
Total capital gain + recapture		$42,350
Tax on capital gain (34% times gain)	$1,700	
Tax on recapture (34% times recapture)	12,699	
Total tax		$14,399

As long as the ordinary tax rate and the capital gains tax rate are the same, the scenario 3 problem is a lot simpler, because we do not have to distinguish between recapture and capital gains.

Sale price	$50,000
Book value	7,650
Total capital gain + recapture	$42,350
Total tax (34% times gain + recapture)	$14,399

11-3. *CFAT for expansion project.*

There are three types of cash flows associated with a capital budgeting project: initial investment, operating cash flows, and terminal cash flows. We shall calculate each.

Initial Investment

The initial investment will be cash outflows to purchase the machine and to fund more working capital assets (accounts receivable and inventory).

Year 0:	Cost	($21,000)
	Increase in NWC	(2,000)
	Initial investment	($23,000)

Operating Cash Flows

Let's set up a table like the one in Table 11-5 in the textbook. We shall look at years 1 and 2 of each column separately; the subsequent years are calculated similarly. Following the sample calculations is a summary of the results.

Year 1:   Cash revenues, given $10,000

Revenues are given to grow at 5 percent per year, so multiplying by the factor (1 + growth rate) gives the next year's projected revenue.

Year 2:   Cash revenues   ($10,000)(1.05)   = $10,500

Data for cash expenses are given in a similar fashion. The calculations follow:

Year 1:   Cash expenses, given $4,000
Year 2:   Cash expenses   ($4,000)(1.06)   = $4,240

Year 1: $CFBT_1$ =   ($10,000 - $4,000)   = $6,000
Year 2: $CFBT_2$ =   ($10,500 - $4,240)   = $6,260

We need to calculate each year's depreciation expense using the rounded percentages we calculated in problem 1 above.

Depreciable basis $21,000

Year	Rate	Expense	
1	33%	$6,930	($21,000)(0.33) = $6,930
2	45%	9,450	($21,000)(0.45) = $9,450
3	15%	3,150	
4	7%	1,470	

Year 1:   Taxable income = ($6,000 - $6,930)   =   ($930) or -$930

Year 1:   Tax   =   ($930)(0.34)   =   ($316)

Year 1: $CFAT_1$ = $6,000 - ($316)   = $6,316

In the above calculation of $CFAT_1$ we subtract a negative tax, which has the effect of adding the two figures.

The results for five years follow:

Year	Cash Revenues	Cash Expenses	$CFBT_t$	Dep	Taxable Income
1	$10,000	$4,000	$6,000	6,930	(930)
2	10,500	4,240	6,260	9,450	(3,190)
3	11,025	4,494	6,531	3,150	3,381
4	11,576	4,764	6,812	1,470	5,342
5	12,155	5,050	7,105	0	7,105

Year	Tax	$CFAT_t$
1	($316)	$6,316
2	(1,085)	7,345
3	1,149	5,381
4	1,186	4,996
5	2,416	4,689

Terminal Cash Flow

Terminal cash flow in this problem consists of selling the machine at the end of the project and recovering any net working capital committed to the project. Recovering NWC means selling off all the inventory, collecting all the receivables, and paying all the bills brought on by using this equipment.

		$CFBT_t$	Tax	$CFAT_t$
Year 5:	Salvage	$3,000	$1,020	$1,980
	Recovery of NWC	$2,000		2,000
	Total			$3,980

Tax calculation:	Sale price	$3,000
	Book value	-0-
	Recapture	$3,000
	Tax (34% times $3,000)	$1,020

Now let's pull all of these three types of cash flows together into one schedule, as follows:

Year	Initial Investment	Operating $CFAT_t$	Terminal $CFAT_t$	Total $CFAT_t$
0	($23,000)			($23,000)
1		6,316		6,316
2		7,345		7,345
3		5,381		5,381
4		4,996		4,996
5		4,689	$3,980	8,669

11-4. *CFAT for replacement project.*

In this type problem we must determine the difference between the cash flows projected from the new equipment, if we purchase it, and the cash flows from the old equipment if we keep it. For starters we need depreciation schedules for both machines.

Depreciation schedule - old equipment

We need to prepare a depreciation schedule of the old machine for two reasons. First, we need the book value of the old to determine the tax liability as required in the initial investment section. And second, we need the annual depreciation expense for the operating cash flow calculations. We can begin using the rounded percentages for the five-year class life given previously. The table follows.

Year	Beginning Balance	Dep Rate	Dep Expense	Ending Balance
1	$40,000	20%	$8,000	$32,000
2	32,000	32%	12,800	19,200
3	19,200	19%	7,600	11,600
4	11,600	12%	4,800	6,800
5	6,800	12%	4,800	2,000
6	2,000	5%	2,000	0

Now we have the $6,800 book value at the end of year four for the initial investment calculation. We also have the fifth and sixth years' depreciation expense needed for calculating operating cash flows.

Depreciation schedule - new equipment

We need a depreciation schedule for the annual depreciation expense from the new machine.

Year	Beginning Balance	Dep Rate	Dep Expense	Ending Balance
1	$45,000	20%	$9,000	$36,000
2	36,000	32%	14,400	21,600
3	21,600	19%	8,550	13,050
4	13,050	12%	5,400	7,650
5	7,650	12%	5,400	2,250
6	2,250	5%	2,250	0

Initial investment

The initial investment consists of cash flows from purchasing the new equipment, selling the old, and any change in net working capital (NWC).

Cost of new equipment		($45,000)
Sale of old equipment		
Price	$7,000	
Book value	6,800 (See depreciation	
Gain	$200 schedule above.)	
Tax (34%)	$68	
Proceeds from sale of old (7,000 - 68)		6,932
Increase in NWC		(2,500)
Initial investment		($40,568)

The $1,500 spent for a study relating to this project is a sunk cost. The decision to spend it was made in the past. Those funds are long gone, cannot be recovered, and are not to be considered in the current decision.

Incremental operating cash flows

The operating cash flows are the heart of any industrial enterprise. For it to increase the value of the firm by replacing one machine with another that performs the same function, there must be some prospect of increased cash flows. These may arise from increased sales due to increased production capacity and from cost savings from more efficient equipment.

Here is a table summarizing the operating cash flows. An item-by-item explanation of the first line follows the table.

Year	New Revenue	Old Revenue	New-old Revenue	New Expense	Old Expense	New-old Expense	CFBT$_t$
1	$50,000	$48,000	$2,000	$20,000	$28,800	($8,800)	$10,800
2	52,000	49,440	2,560	20,800	29,664	(8,864)	11,424
3	54,080	50,923	3,157	21,632	30,554	(8,922)	12,079
4	56,243	52,451	3,792	22,497	31,471	(8,973)	12,766
5	58,493	54,024	4,469	23,397	32,415	(9,017)	13,486
6	60,833	55,645	5,187	24,333	33,387	(9,054)	14,242

Year	New Dep exp	Old Dep exp	New-old Dep exp	Taxable Income	Tax	CFAT$_t$
1	$9,000	$4,800	$4,200	$6,600	$2,244	$8,556
2	14,400	2,000	12,400	(976)	(332)	11,756
3	8,550	0	8,550	3,529	1,200	10,879
4	5,400	0	5,400	7,366	2,504	10,261
5	5,400	0	5,400	8,086	2,749	10,737
6	2,250	0	2,250	11,992	4,077	10,164

Now let's take this column-by-column for year 1.

New revenue for year 1 is given as $50,000. Year 2 will be 4% more or ($50,000)(1.04) = $52,000.

Old revenue for year 1 is given as $48,000. Year 2 will be 3% more or ($48,000)(1.03) = $49,440.

New - old revenue for year one is $50,000 - $48,000 = $2,000. This is the incremental revenue.

New expense is 40% of new revenue each year. For year 1 this is (0.40)($50,000) = $20,000.

Old expense is 60% of old revenue each year. For year 1 this is (0.60)($48,000) = $28,800.

Chapter 11: Capital Budgeting and Cash Flow Principles

New - old expense is for year 1 is $20,000 - $28,800 = ($8,800). This is the incremental expense. The negative sign means that the new expense is less than the old. That is, we are experiencing a cost savings. When we subtract a negative change in cost from a positive change in revenue, the result is to add the expense savings to the revenue.

Incremental CFBT$_t$ is the incremental revenue minus the incremental expense. For year 1 this is $2,000 - ($8,800) = $10,800. If the double negative bothers you, another way to look at this is to add the increase in revenues to the cost savings.

New depreciation expense is from the depreciation schedule developed above for the new equipment. For year 1 it is $9,000.

Old depreciation expense is from the depreciation schedule developed above for the old equipment. But remember, four years of the old machine's depreciable life is gone, so its year 5 five is the first year in our projection. The figure is $4,800. The old equipment is completely depreciated at the end of the sixth year of the old machine's life. Beginning in year 7 of the old machine's life (year 3 of the new machine's life), consequently, the old depreciation expense is $0.

New - old depreciation for year 1 is $9,000 - $4,800 = $4,200. This is the incremental depreciation expense.

Incremental taxable income is incremental CFBT$_t$ minus incremental depreciation expense. For year 1 this is $10,800 - $4,200 = $6,600.

Incremental tax is 34% of incremental taxable income. For year 1 this is (0.34)(6,600) = $2,244.

Incremental CFAT$_t$ is incremental CFBT$_t$ minus incremental tax. For year 1 this is $10,800 - $2,244 = $8,556.

Repeat these calculations for all six years of the planning horizon for the table above. This problem is "a natural" for an electronic spreadsheet.

Terminal cash flow

At the end of a project's life, there may be one-time cash flows specifically related to the end of the project. In a manufacturing firm environment, this usually means any salvage value of the new equipment (which will no longer be new), the opportunity cost of any forgone sale of the old equipment (which was sold at the beginning of the project), and recovery of net working capital committed to the project.

The problem states that both the old and the new equipment would have some market value at the end of the sixth year. Both would be depreciated to a zero book value. Any sale of either, therefore, would be fully taxable. Recovery of net working capital is not taxable because there is no profit involved. A table using figures given in the problem follows.

	Sale price	Book value	$CFBT_6$	Tax	$CFAT_6$
Sale of new equipment	$10,000	-0-	$10,000	$3,400	$6,600
Forgone sale of old	(1,000)	-0-	(1,000)	(340)	(660)
Recovery of NWC			2,500	-0-	2,500
Total					$8,440

Combined cash flows: Initial, operating, and terminal

As a matter of convenience, let's summarize all three types of cash flows in one table. This is easy with an electronic spread sheet and important for the arrangement of data for use in subsequent calculations, which will be addressed in the next chapter. All of these cash flows are incremental cash flows or changes from what would have been without the replacement.

Year	Initial Investment	Operating $CFAT_t$	Terminal $CFAT_6$	Total
0	($40,568)			($40,568)
1		$8,556		8,556
2		11,756		11,756
3		10,879		10,879
4		10,261		10,261
5		10,737		10,737
6		10,164	$8,440	18,604

Now we have a complete summary of the after-tax cash flows for the proposed replacement of old equipment with new equipment. In order to make a decision as to how this proposed replacement would affect the value of the firm, we shall turn to the next chapter to study decision techniques.

137

CHAPTER 12
CAPITAL-BUDGETING TECHNIQUES

Concepts to Understand

*   New fixed assets provide the company with cash flows after tax ($CFAT_t$), which are marginal revenues.

*   Investors, both stockholders and creditors, require a certain return to continue supplying capital to the firm. This required return is the marginal cost of capital, which is sometimes, but not always, used as the discount rate in capital budgeting problems.

*   Economic theory tells us that a company should invest in additional projects as long as the marginal revenue exceeds the marginal cost.

*   The present value of the expected future cash flows from a project is the value of that asset to the firm.

*   The initial investment or cash outlay is the cost of an asset to the firm.

*   The value of the firm is increased by the net present value of a project. The firm should not accept a project with a negative net present value because the value of the firm would decrease.

A Second Look

Capital budgeting is the framework for making decisions whether to or not to invest in long-term projects. An asset is valuable to the firm because it has the ability to produce cash flows. Estimation of future cash flows was the subject of the prior chapter. In this chapter we study analytical techniques to help us determine whether or not the projected cash flows of an asset will fulfill the rate-of-return requirements of the stockholders and creditors of the firm.

Three discounted cash flow (DCF) methods are presented: net present value (NPV), internal rate of return (IRR), and profitability index (PI). Any of these will help us maximize the owners' wealth. All three result in the same accept-reject decision for an individual project. They may, however, result in different rankings of several projects. They all use the same basic formula but solve for different variables.

Chapter 12: Capital-Budgeting Techniques

The NPV of a project is the amount by which the firm's value will increase or decrease if the project is accepted. In words, the equation is:

NPV = present value of expected future CFAT - initial investment.

Stated another way, the NPV is the dollar difference between what a project is worth and what it costs. If it is worth more than it costs, invest; otherwise, don't.

The IRR is the percentage discount rate that equates the present value of the cash flows with the initial investment. Another way to say the same thing is that the IRR is the discount rate that forces the NPV to equal zero. We use the same mathematical formula as with NPV but solve for the discount rate, instead of taking it as given:

Present value of expected future $CFAT_t$ = initial investment

The firm can raise money at the cost of capital, k, which is a rate sufficient to keep the stockholders and creditors supplying capital to the company. Management's question, then, is, "Are we willing to raise money at the rate k, and invest it at the IRR?" If the IRR is higher than k, the answer is "Yes."

The third criteria, the PI, is basically a benefit-cost ratio, utilizing the same calculations, rearranged for a third time:

PI = present value of expected future $CFAT_t$/initial investment

Here we have the value of a project divided by its cost or initial investment. It shows us the dollar amount of present value (benefit) a project provides per dollar of investment (cost). If a project provides more than one dollar of benefit per dollar of investment, we accept the project.

The payback period is a non-DCF method that is simple to calculate and easy to understand. It is, unfortunately, theoretically inferior to the DCF methods and does not provide a clue about the value of the firm.

The table below summarizes the methods. To save space, we'll abbreviate present value of the expected future $CFAT_t$ as PV and initial investment at period 0 as $CFAT_0$.

Method	Type	Formula	Disc rate	Units	Criteria	Decision
NPV	DCF	PV - $CFAT_0$	k	$	NPV>0	Accept
IRR	DCF	PV = $CFAT_0$	IRR	%	IRR>k	Accept
PI	DCF	PV/$CFAT_0$	k	$/$	PI>1	Accept
Payback	Non-DCF	Add $CFAT_t$	none	Yrs	Payback< standard	Accept

Taking the marginal revenue-marginal cost approach to investment decisions, an economist would contend that the firm should raise funds at the cost of capital to invest in all the acceptable projects available. This approach would maximize the value of the firm and the stockholders' wealth. This cannot always be done, however, because funding constraints, called capital rationing, often exist. They may be caused by management philosophy or institutional realities. In this case the IRR and/or PI may rank investment decisions better than NPV. Nonetheless, the total NPV of all projects accepted should be maximized and is still the ultimate criterion for investment decisions.

The NPV of a project is the value added to the firm if the project is accepted. Of the three criteria (NPV, IRR, and PI), NPV is the most clearly related to the financial objective of maximizing owners' wealth.

Chapter Summary

Capital budgeting decisions fall into three categories: the accept-reject decision, the (1) _____ choice decision, and the (2) _____ decision. Once cash flows have been projected for a proposed investment, the cash flows must be evaluated by some criterion to determine whether the firm should accept or reject the project. If choosing one project causes the rejection of another project on a functional basis, they are said to be (3) _____. If a firm cannot invest in all economically acceptable projects because funds are not available, the firm faces (4) _____.

Decision criteria which utilize the present value of expected future cash flows after tax are called (5) _____ methods. The *payback period* is the (6) _____ it takes to get back the initial investment in $CFAT_t$ on a non-DCF basis. If the payback period is less than the required payback period, the project is (7) _____. The required payback period is a (8) _____ figure that does not have a clear theoretical relationship to the value of the firm. Two other deficiencies of the payback criterion are that it does not take into account the (9) _____ of cash flows that occur within the payback period and it ignores any cash flows that occur (10) _____.

Net present value is the theoretically superior decision criterion. It is the present value of the (11) _____ from a project minus the (12) _____. A project is acceptable if the NPV is (13) _____. The discount used to calculate the NPV is usually the (14) _____ of the firm. The relationship showing the NPVs of a project at various discount rates is called a (15) _____. Acceptance of a project with a NPV of zero will earn the required return on the invested capital, but will not increase the (16) _____.

The *internal rate of return* is defined as the discount rate that equates the (17) _____ of expected future cash flows with the (18) _____.

A project is acceptable if the IRR is (19) _____. IRR is widely used in industry and often preferred over NPV. Sometimes nonconventional cash flow patterns will result in mathematical solutions of more than one IRR for a project, in which case interpretation of the multiple IRRs is difficult.

The *profitability index* is the ratio of the present value of the expected future cash flows to the initial investment. It is also known as the (20) _____. The PI tells us how many dollars of value we are getting for each dollar invested.

NPV, IRR, and PI always give the (21) _____ accept-reject decision on an individual project, but may sometimes give different (22) _____ of multiple projects. Conflicts may be caused by differences in (23) _____ or (24) _____. Since NPV is the amount by which the value of the firm should be increased by accepting a project, the NPV should be used to resolve any conflicts.

Mutually exclusive projects with unequal lives can be evaluated using a (25) _____. This method provides that the projects will be repeated until the lives are equal. Another method for dealing with the unequal life problem is the (26) _____.

Surveys of businesses indicate that a vast majority (86 percent) of large American corporations use DCF methods and many of them also use non-DCF techniques. Small firms are much less likely to use DCF methods because the expertise of owners often lies elsewhere, and the energy of owners is typically directed toward cash management which favors the payback method.

Acronyms and Notation You Should Know

$CFAT_0$	Initial Investment or Cash Flow After Tax at period 0
$CFAT_n$	Cash Flow After Tax during the last period, period n
$CFAT_t$	Cash Flow After Tax at period t
EAA	Equivalent Annual Annuity
IRR	Internal Rate of Return
k	Cost of Capital
NPV	Net Present Value
PI	Profitability Index

Equations You Should Know

Payback = Number of years to recover initial investment (12-1)

$$NPV = \sum_{t=1}^{n} CFAT_t/(1 + k)^t - CFAT_0 \qquad (12\text{-}2)$$

$$CFAT_0 = \sum_{t=1}^{n} CFAT_t/(1 + IRR)^t \qquad (12\text{-}3)$$

$$PI = \sum_{t=1}^{n} [CFAT_t/(1 + k)^t]/CFAT_0 \qquad (12\text{-}4)$$

Lotus Notes

Lotus 1-2-3[1] has a number of financial functions, which are useful for various types of analyses, as discussed in Chapter 4 of this *Study Guide*. For the present chapter, two functions are particularly helpful.

The first is @NPV(k,range). In this function "NPV" is a misnomer, because it takes the first cell in the range as period 1, not period 0. It discounts every cell in the range, including the first cell, back to period 0. What we should include in the range is $CFAT_t$ for t = 1 ... n. Then we can add $CFAT_0$ (a negative number) as usual to get the NPV. A cell entry for NPV as we define it would be:

$$@NPV(k, range \text{ containing } CFAT_1 \text{ to } CFAT_n) + CFAT_0$$

This is one reason we went to the trouble in the last chapter's problems to combine the cash flows into one column, with the initial cash outlay as a negative figure. This function will find the present value of any type cash flow pattern.

---

[1]Lotus 1-2-3 is a registered trademark of the Lotus Development Corporation.

The IRR is easy to calculate using present value interest factor tables if the $CFAT_t$ is an annuity, but can be really sticky if the $CFAT_t$ is uneven. The @IRR(guess, range) function calculates the IRR regardless of the type of cash flows. A cell entry to calculate the IRR might be:

@IRR(guess,range containing $CFAT_0$ to $CFAT_n$)

The term "guess" is a discount rate from which the program begins an iterative process to calculate the IRR. A modest rate, such as 0.1, will usually work. If you are searching for multiple IRRs, you may need to try additional "guesses" to see if you can change the answer. We could use k for a guess, but that is not necessary.

Note that the range contains the initial investment, $CFAT_0$, in the first cell as a negative number.

Problems

12-1. *Payback period with uneven cash flows.* $CFAT_t$ are given below for three projects.
A. Calculate the payback period for each.
B. Which are acceptable projects? What else do you need to know?
C. Rank the three projects in order of best to worst using the payback period criterion.
D. Explain how this problem demonstrates the two weaknesses of the payback period criterion.

Year	A	B	C
0	($10,000)	($10,000)	($10,000)
1	2,500	4,000	4,000
2	2,500	3,000	3,000
3	2,500	2,000	2,000
4	2,500	1,000	1,000
5	1,450	1,450	4,315

12-2. *NPV, IRR, and PI with uneven cash flows.* Use the $CFAT_t$ data from problem 1. The cost of capital for the firm is 12 percent.
A. Calculate NPV for each project.
B. Calculate the IRR for each project.
C. Calculate the PI for each project.
D. Which projects are acceptable with these criteria?

12-3. *Payback, NPV, IRR, and PI with annuity.* New Wave Seafood, Inc., is considering an expansion of their canning line. A new machine costing $190,000 is expected to produce $CFAT_t$ of $37,855 each year for 10 years. New Wave's cost of capital is 10 percent.
A.   Calculate the payback period.
B.   Calculate the NPV.
C.   Calculate the IRR.
D.   Calculate the PI.
E.   Is the project acceptable?

12-4. *Payback, NPV, IRR, and PI with uneven cash flows.* Use the data in problem 3 in Chapter 11 of this *Study Guide*. The cost of capital of the firm is 10 percent.
A.   Calculate the payback period.
B.   Calculate the NPV.
C.   Calculate the IRR.
D.   Calculate the PI.
E.   Is the project acceptable?

12-5. *Payback, NPV, IRR, and PI with uneven cash flows.* Use the data in problem 4 in Chapter 11 of this *Study Guide*. The cost of capital of the firm is 18%.
A.   Calculate the payback period.
B.   Calculate the NPV.
C.   Calculate the IRR.
D.   Calculate the PI.
E.   Should management accept or reject the project?

12-6. *Replacement chain and EAA.* Modgling Manufacturing Company is comparing two mutually exclusive conveyor systems, A and B, for the new assembly plant. Data for the two systems are given below. If system B is chosen, assume no increase in costs when it has to be replaced. The cost of capital is 15 percent.
A.   Calculate the NPV of each project for its given life. Which would you choose on the basis of these calculations alone.
B.   Calculate the NPV of B using the replacement chain technique. Which system would you choose on this basis?
C.   Calculate the EAA for each project. Which would you choose on this basis?

	System A	System B
Initial investment	($1,450,000)	($875,000)
Annual CFAT	$300,000	$275,000
Useful life - years	10	5

144

12-7. *NPV profile.* Angelo Drilling is considering two mutually exclusive projects, A and B. Both require large investments, but they have different lives. (This is not a situation for a replacement chain.) The data are given below:

	Project A	Project B
Initial investment	($25,000)	($30,000)
Annual $CFAT_t$	$8,110	$5,978
Useful life-years	6	10

A. Prepare a NPV profile for each project. Use discount rates of 0%, 5%, 10%, 15%, 20%, and 25%.
B. Sketch a graph of each NPV profile.
C. Identify the IRR of each project on your graph.
D. Which project would you chose in each of these ranges of discount rate: 0% - 5%, 5% - 15%, 15% - 24%, and above 24%? In which range is there a conflict between NPV and IRR?
E. If the firm's cost of capital is 10 percent, which project will increase the value of the firm more?

12-8. *Ranking conflicts with capital rationing.* Data for several projects are given below. Each project has a 10-year life. The $CFAT_t$ is an annuity. The cost of capital is 10 percent. All figures are in thousands of dollars.

Project	A	B	C	D	E	F
$CFAT_0$	$42	$45	$13	$100	$101	$39
$CFAT_t$	$10	$10	$2.7	$20	$15	$5

A. Calculate the NPV for each project. Round answers to the nearest thousand dollars, no decimals.
B. Calculate the IRR of each project. Round to the nearest whole percent.
C. If the firm has unlimited funds, which projects should it accept?
D. Suppose the firm has capital rationing such that it can invest only $100,000. Which projects would it accept if it ranked them by NPV and took the top projects? What total NPV would be added to the value of the firm?
E. Suppose the firm has capital rationing such that it can invest only $100,000. Which projects would it accept it ranked them by IRR and took the top projects? What total NPV would be added to the value of the firm?
F. Sketch a graph of the marginal revenue-marginal cost of capital schedules. Identify the acceptable projects.

Answers to Chapter Summary

1.	mutually exclusive	14.	cost of capital
2.	capital rationing	15.	NPV profile
3.	mutually exclusive	16.	value of the firm
4.	capital rationing	17.	present value
5.	DCF	18.	initial investment
6.	number of years	19.	greater than k
7.	acceptable	20.	benefit-cost ratio
8.	subjective	21.	same
9.	timing	22.	ranking
10.	after the payback period	23.	scale
11.	expected future CFAT	24.	timing
12.	initial investment	25.	replacement chain
13.	greater than 0	26.	EAA

Problem Solutions

12-1. *Payback period with uneven cash flows.*
A.   The initial investment is given as the negative figure in time period 0. We have to add up the annual $CFAT_t$ until we get an amount equal to the initial investment, which in this case is $10,000.

Payback = Number of years to recover initial investment   (12-1)

Project A: $2,500 + 2,500 + 2,500 + 2,500 = $10,000
The payback period is four years for A.

Project B: $4,000 + 3,000 + 2,000 + 1,000 = $10,000
The payback period is four years for B.

Project C: The payback period is also four years.

B.   We should either accept or reject all of these projects since they all have the same payback. We need a subjective accept-reject rule from management, however, because there is no theoretical tie-in to the value of the firm.

C.   There is no ranking these projects by payback. They all are equal if we go only by the four-year payback.

D.   The two weaknesses of the payback period are (1) timing of cash flows within the payback period and (2) cash flows beyond the payback period. Project A has even cash flows during the first four years, whereas, B and C have higher cash flows in the early years that decrease. Projects B and C are better if you consider the time value of money.

As for the second point, would you prefer $1,450 with B or $4,315 with C in the last year? Payback doesn't look beyond year four. With all of that in mind, project C appears to be the best of the lot. But we still do not know whether it will add to the value of the firm.

12-2.   *NPV, IRR, and PI with uneven cash flows.*
A.   To find the NPV we must find the PV of the $CFAT_t$ and subtract the initial investment. These present value calculations could be done any one of several ways: (1) formula, (2) tables, (3) financial calculator, or (4) electronic spreadsheet. We'll use the tables here.

We'll work through project A. B and C are similar. Since these $CFAT_t$ are not annuities, we must treat each year as a single payment to find the present value. We'll use equation 12-2, but set it up in tabular form for convenience.

$$\text{NPV} = \text{CFAT}_t \text{ discounted at cost of capital} - \text{CFAT}_0 \quad (12\text{-}2)$$

Year	A $CFAT_t$	12% PVIF	PV
1	$2,500	0.8929	$2,232
2	2,500	0.7972	1,993
3	2,500	0.7118	1,779
4	2,500	0.6355	1,589
5	1,450	0.5674	823
		Total PV =	$8,416
		$CFAT_0$ =	($10,000)
		NPV =	($1,584)

B.   The IRR for uneven cash flows can be done by the same four methods mentioned in part A for NPV. We'll use the trial-and-error method with the tables. The IRR is the discount rate that makes the PV of the expected future $CFAT_t$ equal to the initial investment. In the case of A, we need the PV to equal $10,000. We have already calculated the NPV, so let's use that information for a starting point, our first trial.

Trial #1:   12%   PV = $8,416   The PV is too low.

Now let's remember some of the present value relationships from Chapter 4. The present value decreases as the discount rate increases, and vice versa. We need $10,000 and got only $8,416. To raise the $8,416 we must lower the 12 percent. We are using equation 12-3.

$$\text{CFAT}_t \text{ discounted at IRR} \quad = \quad \text{CFAT}_0 \quad \quad (12\text{-}3)$$

Trial #2:   10%   PV = $8,825   The PV is still too low.

The calculations for this follow:

Year	A CFAT$_t$	10% PVIF	PV
1	$2,500	0.9091	$2,273
2	2,500	0.8264	2,066
3	2,500	0.7513	1,878
4	2,500	0.6830	1,708
5	1,450	0.6209	900
		Total PV =	$8,825
		CFAT$_0$ =	($10,000)
		NPV =	($1,175)

Because the PV is only $8,825, and we need $10,000, let's try a drastically lower discount rate.

Trial #3:   5%   PV = $10,001   Close enough! The IRR is 5 percent.

Year	A CFAT$_t$	5% PVIF	PV
1	$2,500	0.9524	$2,381
2	2,500	0.9070	2,268
3	2,500	0.8638	2,160
4	2,500	0.8227	2,057
5	1,450	0.7835	1,136
		Total PV =	$10,001 Close enough.
		CFAT$_0$ =	($10,000)
		NPV =	1

What does that mean? That means that if we invest $10,000 in this project and receive the CFAT$_t$ that are projected, we'll earn five percent. Doesn't sound like a great way to get rich quick.

C.   The PI is easy because we did most of the calculations when we calculated the NPV in part A. For project A the PV using 12 percent cost of capital is $8,416, and the initial investment is $10,000. Do not use the negative sign on the investment when calculating PI.

$$PI = \text{PV/Initial investment} \qquad (12\text{-}4)$$
$$= \$8,416/\$10,000$$
$$= 0.84 \quad \text{for project A.}$$

D.   Here are the answers for all three projects:

	A	B	C
NPV	($1,584)	($1,155)	$471
IRR	5%	6%	14%
PI	0.84	0.88	1.05
Payback	4	4	4

Now we can see that C is the only acceptable project, because the NPV = $471, which is greater than zero; IRR = 14 percent, which is greater than 12 percent, the cost of capital; and PI = 1.05, which is greater than 1.00. Notice that payback did not discriminate among the projects.

To interpret each of these criteria for the only acceptable project, C, the NPV means that the value of the firm will increase by $471 if we accept this project. The IRR means that we can earn 14 percent on this project. Since we can raise funds at 12 percent, we are happy to invest it at 14 percent. The PI means that we are getting $1.05 benefit for each $1.00 invested.

12-3.   *Payback, NPV, IRR, and PI with annuity.*
Problems with annuities are the easiest of all capital budgeting problems with the tables.

A.   To calculate the payback period with an annuity, all we have to do is divide the initial investment by the annual CFAT to see how long it takes to get our money back.

$$\text{Payback} = \$190,000/\$37,855$$
$$= 5 \text{ years (rounded off)}$$

B.   The NPV can be calculated using the present value interest factor tables to solve equation 12-2.

$$\begin{aligned}
\text{NPV} &= (\text{CFAT}_t)(\text{PVIFA}_{10\%, 10}) &-& \text{CFAT}_0 \\
&= (\$37,855)(6.1446) &-& \$190,000 \\
&= \$42,603
\end{aligned}$$

Note: Don't be alarmed if the your answers differ a little from these. Answers worked with the tables are less exact than those worked with a financial calculator or an electronic spreadsheet, primarily due to the number of decimal places carried in the tables.

C.   With an annuity, the trial-and-error method is not necessary. Equation 12-3 becomes:

$$\begin{aligned}
(\text{CFAT}_t)(\text{PVIFA}_{10\%, 10}) &= \text{CFAT}_0 \\
(\$37,855)(\text{PVIFA}_{10\%, 10}) &= \$190,000 \\
(\text{PVIFA}_{10\%, 10}) &= \$190,000/\$37,855 \\
&= 5.0192
\end{aligned}$$

This is the interest *factor*, not the interest rate. We must look in the table under 10 years for a figure close to 5.0192. Then look at the top of the column to find 15 percent. Thus,

$$\text{IRR} = 15\%.$$

D.   We have already done most of the calculations for the PI because it uses the same CFAT_t and present value interest factors as the NPV. Equation 12-4 with the tables becomes:

$$\begin{aligned}
\text{PI} &= (\text{CFAT}_t)(\text{PVIFA}_{10\%, 10})/\text{CFAT}_0 \\
&= (\$37,855)(5.0192)/\$190,000 \\
&= \$232,603/\$190,000 \\
&= 1.22
\end{aligned}$$

E.   The project is acceptable because the NPV > 0, the IRR > k, and PI > 1.00. The value of the firm will be increased by $42,603. Our investment will return 15 percent. We are buying $1.22 worth of future cash flows for each $1.00 invested. Note that these three criteria must necessarily give the same accept-reject decision. The payback period of 5 years doesn't really tell us much.

12-4. *Payback, NPV, IRR, and PI with uneven cash flows.*
If you worked problem 3 in the previous chapter, you have some idea of how much work it takes to get to the point of having projected cash flows to discount. We'll take them as given in this problem. The cost of capital is given as 10 percent.

Chapter 12: Capital-Budgeting Techniques

A.   Payback. We have to add each year's $CFAT_t$ until we get to the $CFAT_0$, which is $23,000. To do this let's make a column for cumulative $CFAT_t$.

Year	$CFAT_t$	Cumulative $CFAT_{t-}$
1	$6,316	$6,316
2	7,345	13,661
3	5,381	19,042
4	4,996	24,038 <-----
5	8,669	32,707

Since we're trying to get $23,000 out of this, the answer is between three and four years and much closer to four. If we want to be more precise, we shall have to assume that the cash flows are received evenly throughout the year. Then, we need $23,000 - $19,042 = $3,958 during the fourth year. As a percentage of the $4,996 to be received during the year, this would be $3,958/$4,996 = 0.79 of the year or about nine and one-half months. Thus the payback period is 3 years and 9 1/2 months.

B.   NPV. The easiest format for calculating the NPV using the present value interest factors is in table form. Multiply each annual cash flow by the interest factor and add the sums.

Year	$CFAT_{t-}$	10% PVIF	$(CFAT_t)(PVIFA)$
1	$6,316	.9091	$5,742
2	7,345	.8264	6,070
3	5,381	.7513	4,043
4	4,996	.6830	3,412
5	8,669	.6209	5,383
		Total PV =	$24,650
		$CFAT_0$ =	(23,000)
		NPV =	$1,650

C.   IRR. The IRR will have to be by trial-and-error unless we use a financial calculator or an electronic spreadsheet.

Trial #1: Let's take what we already know as the first trial. Ten percent is too low, because the PV discounted at that rate is $24,650, when we need only $23,000. To lower the $24,650 to $23,000 we must try a higher percentage rate.

Trial #2: Let's try 15 percent. Repeating the table just above, except with PVIFs for 15 percent gives us a PV of $21,751. We overdid it and went past $23,000. Try again.

Trial #3: Let's try 12 percent. This gives us $23,419. We're getting close.

Trial #4: Let's try 13 percent, since we need to use just a slightly higher rate. This gives us $22,840. Now we can see that the IRR is between 12 and 13 percent.

D.   PI. The PI is the ratio of the PV to the initial investment. Using the PV calculated in part B, we have:

$$
\begin{aligned}
PI &= \quad PV \text{ of } CFAT_t/CFAT_0 \\
&= \quad \$24,650/\$23,000 \\
&= \quad 1.07
\end{aligned}
$$

E.   Do we accept or reject? Accept, because NPV > 0, IRR > k, and PI > 1.00.

12-5.   *Payback, NPV, IRR, and PI.*
We'll take the $CFAT_t$ calculated in problem 4 in the prior chapter of this *Study Guide* and make an accept-reject decision.

A.   Payback. We'll set up a table and add the $CFAT_t$ until we reach $40,568, the amount of the initial investment.

Year	$CFAT_t$	Cumulative $CFAT_{t-}$
1	$8,556	$8,556
2	11,756	20,312
3	10,879	31,191
4	10,261	41,452

That's far enough. We can see that the payback period is between three and four years, and closer to four years when the cash flow reaches $40,568. Use the method in problem 4 above to get a more exact answer if you really want it.

B.   NPV. Let's set up a table with the $CFAT_t$ and the PVIFs for years 1 - 6. The cost of capital is 18 percent.

Year	$CFAT_t$	18% PVIF	$(CFAT_t)(PVIF)$
1	$8,556	.8475	$7,251
2	11,756	.7182	8,443
3	10,879	.6086	6,621
4	10,261	.5158	5,293
5	10,737	.4371	4,693
6	18,604	.3704	6,892

PV	$39,192
$CFAT_0$	(40,568)
NPV	($1,376)

C.   IRR. Because the $CFAT_t$ is not an annuity, we'll solve equation 12-3 for the IRR by trial-and-error with the PVIF tables. Using k = 18% above, we found that the PV was too low ($39,192 *vs.* $40,568). That means we have to use a lower discount rate to raise the $39,192 up to $40,568.

Trial #1:   17%. This results in a PV of $40,319, which is close. Maybe we can do better.

Trial #2:   16%. This rate gives us a PV of $41,497. Too high. The IRR is between 16 and 17%. Interpolation or a financial calculator or an electronic spreadsheet will give us 16.79 percent.

D.   PI. We can use the present value calculated in part B.

$$PI = \text{PV of } CFAT_t / CFAT_0 \qquad (12\text{-}4)$$
$$= \$39,192/\$40,568$$
$$= 0.97$$

E.   This project is unacceptable because NPV < 0, IRR < k, and PI < 1.00.

12-6. *Replacement chain and EAA.*
A.   The initial calculation of NPV for each project follows. The cash flows are both annuities, so the PVIFA tables can be used.

Project A: NPV   = $(CFAT_t)(PVIFA_{15\%, 10})$ - $CFAT_0$ (12-2)
                        = ($300,000)(4.8333)   - $1,450,000
                        = $1,505,631   - $1,450,000
                        = $55,631

Project B: NPV $=$ $(CFAT_t)(PVIFA_{15\%,5})$ - $CFAT_0$
         $=$ ($275,000)(3.1818) - $875,000
         $=$ $921,843 - $875,000
         $=$ $46,843

If we stopped here, we would opt for project A, since its NPV is larger. We cannot choose both because they are mutually exclusive.

B.   The life of project A is twice as long as that of project B, which invalidates the NPV comparison above. If project B were chosen, what would be done to fill the void at the end of its five-year life? It would be replaced by another identical project. So let's calculate the NPV for two consecutive projects B. Then we can compare ten years of service for A to ten years for B. This is called a replacement chain.

There are at least two ways to do this calculation. A time line will help us understand either method.

Year	$CFAT_t$ 1st B	$CFAT_t$ 2nd B	$CFAT_t$ Total
0	($875,000)		($875,000)
1	275,000		275,000
2	275,000		275,000
3	275,000		275,000
4	275,000		275,000
5	275,000	($875,000)	(600,000)
6		275,000	275,000
7		275,000	275,000
8		275,000	275,000
9		275,000	275,000
10		275,000	275,000

Let's repeat the total column below and treat it as one 10-year uneven cash flow. PVIFs for 15% are given. The third column is the product.

Year	$CFAT_t$ Total	15% PVIF	$(CFAT_t)(PVIF)$
0	($875,000)	1.0000	($875,000)
1	275,000	0.8696	239,130
2	275,000	0.7561	207,940
3	275,000	0.6575	180,817
4	275,000	0.5718	157,232
5	(600,000)	0.4972	(298,306)
6	275,000	0.4323	118,890
7	275,000	0.3759	103,383
8	275,000	0.3269	89,898
9	275,000	0.2843	78,172
10	275,000	0.2472	67,976
		NPV =	$70,132

Summing the last column gives us the NPV because time period zero outflows are included. When project B is used twice, consecutively, the replacement chain has a bigger total NPV than project A. This changed the preliminary decision we made in part A.

Now we shall calculate the replacement chain NPV by another method.
We already know that the first five-year project has a NPV of $46,843. Let's think about the problem as two projects with NPVs of $46,843 and make a time line to show them.

Year	NPV
0	$46,843
1	
2	
3	
4	
5	46,843
6	
7	
8	
9	
10	

The cash flows from the first five years give a NPV in period 0, and the second project B in years 6 - 10 result in a NPV of the same amount at the end of period 5. But the NPV in period 5 must be discounted back to period 0, as follows:

$$(NPV)(PVIF_{15\%,5})$$
$$(\$46,843)(0.4972) = \$23,290$$

The total NPV of both projects B is:

$$\$46,843 \quad + \quad \$23,290 \quad = \quad \$70,133$$

This is the same total NPV as we got with the first method. (The $1 difference is in rounding.)

C.　To find EAA for a project, we first have to calculate the NPV, which we have already done for both projects. Then we treat the NPV as if it were a PV; use k as given; and calculate the annuity. This is just like calculating the annual payment for a loan of the amount of the NPV. Go all the way back to equation 4-15, and substitute the new terminology.

$$PVA_n \quad = \quad (C)(PVIFA_{k,n}) \tag{4-15}$$
$$NPV \quad = \quad (EAA)(PVIFA_{k,n})$$

Project A:　
$$\begin{aligned} NPV &= (EAA)(PVIFA_{15\%,10}) \\ \$55,631 &= (EAA)(5.0192) \\ EAA &= \$55,631/5.0192 \\ &= \$11,084 \end{aligned}$$

Project B:　
$$\begin{aligned} NPV &= (EAA)(PVIFA_{15\%,5}) \\ \$46,843 &= (EAA)(3.352) \\ EAA &= \$46,843/3.352 \\ &= \$13,975 \end{aligned}$$

Notice that we used the original five-year life for project B.

Our choice on this basis would be project B because it has the larger EAA. This corresponds to the decision reached by the replacement chain.

12-7. *NPV profile.*
A.　A NPV profile is simply a table or graph of the project's NPV calculated with several different discount rates. In the previous problems, we calculated only one NPV with only one cost of capital. Now we are going to calculate NPVs at rates ranging from zero to 25 percent. We'll do sample calculations for project A. The rest are repetitious.

An electronic spreadsheet is convenient for this problem, because the calculations can be done rapidly and the data can be graphed within the spreadsheet. But we'll use the PVIFA tables here.

Project A

For 0%	NPV	=	$(CFAT_t)(PVIFA_{0\%,6})$	-	$CFAT_0$
		=	($8,110)(6.0000)	-	$25,000
		=	$23,440		

For 5%	NPV	=	$(CFAT_t)(PVIFA_{5\%,6})$	-	$CFAT_0$
		=	($8,110)(5.0757)	-	$25,000
		=	$41,162	-	$25,000
		=	$16,162		

For 10%	NPV	=	$(CFAT_t)(PVIFA_{10\%,6})$	-	$CFAT_0$
		=	($8,110)(4.3552)	-	$25,000
		=	$35,321	-	$25,000
		=	$10,321		

Continue this for 15, 20, and 25 percent. Do the same calculations for project B. The results follow:

Discount rate	NPV project A	NPV project B
0%	$23,660	$29,780
5%	16,164	16,161
10%	10,321	6,732
15%	5,692	2
20%	1,970	(4,937)
25%	(1,064)	(8,656)

These NPVs were calculated with an electronic spreadsheet, so the answers may differ slightly.

B.   A NPV profile graph of the two projects follows:

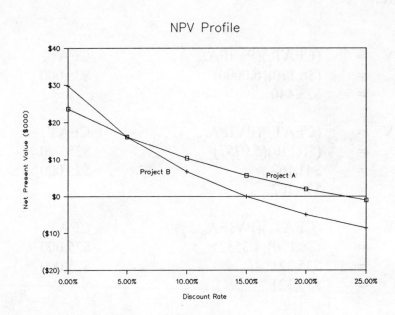

C.   The NPV of a project is zero when the IRR is used as the discount rate. The intersection of a project's NPV line on the x-axis shows the IRR, since that is where NPV equals zero. Project A's NPV is about 24 percent on the graph (23.66 percent to be exact), and B's IRR is 15 percent. You can scan the data above and come to the same conclusion.

D.   Both projects are acceptable at discount rates below 15 percent, but both cannot be accepted because they are mutually exclusive. If we chose on the basis of IRR alone, we would invest in A because its IRR of 24 percent is higher that B's 15 percent.

But our ultimate criterion must be to pick the project that will add the most to the value of the firm, and that depends on the cost of capital.

0% - 5%.   If the cost of capital is less than five percent, project B wins out on the NPV basis. There is, thus, a conflict below five percent because NPV dictates project B, and IRR recommends project A.

5% - 15%.   Above five percent there is no conflict as A has both the higher NPV and the higher IRR. In this range we would chose A, even though B would be acceptable if these projects were not mutually exclusive.

15% -24%.   In this range A is acceptable, but B in not acceptable because it has a negative NPV above 15 percent.

Above 24%.   At discount rates above A's IRR (23.66 percent rounded to 24

158

percent), neither project is acceptable.

E.   It the firm's cost of capital is 10 percent, management will chose project A and increase the value of the firm by $10,321,000.

12-8.   *Ranking conflicts with capital rationing.*
A.   Let's calculate the NPV for project A.

$$
\begin{aligned}
\text{NPV} &= (\text{CFAT}_t)(\text{PVIFA}_{10\%,10}) &-& \quad \text{CFAT}_0 \\
&= (\$10)(6.145) &-& \quad \$42 \\
&= \$61 &-& \quad \$42 \\
&= \$19
\end{aligned}
$$

The data were given as being in thousands, so we have rounded off to the nearest thousand dollars. The calculation is the same for the other projects. The data are presented along with other data in part C.

B.   To calculate the IRR for project A, where the cash flows are an annuity, we use the equation:

$$
\begin{aligned}
(\text{CFAT}_t)(\text{PVIFA}_{IRR,10}) &= \text{CFAT}_0 \\
(\$10)(\text{PVIFA}_{IRR,10}) &= \$42 \\
\text{PVIFA}_{IRR,10} &= \$42/\$10 \\
&= 4.2
\end{aligned}
$$

Looking in the table of present value interest factors for annuities, we find the IRR approximately equal to 20 percent.
        The process is similar for the remaining projects. The data from the problem is repeated, and the NPVs and IRRs are presented in part C below.

C.   To make a decision we need the data brought together so we can contemplate it. Here it is:

Project	A	B	C	D	E	F
CFAT$_t$	$10	$10	$2.7	$ 20	$15	$ 5
PV	$61	$61	$17	$123	$92	$31
CFAT$_0$	$42	$45	$13	$100	$101	$39
NPV	$19	$16	$ 4	$ 23	($9)	($8)
IRR	20%	18%	16%	15%	8%	5%

If the firm has unlimited access to funds, it should invest in all projects with a positive NPV. The same projects will have IRRs greater than the cost of capital, 10 percent. They should invest in projects A, B, C, and D. The value of the firm would be increased by the sum of the NPVs: $19 + $16 + $4 + $23 = $62 thousand. This is the value maximizing solution. An economist would argue that management should raise funds at 10 percent and invest in these four projects.

D.   But suppose the chief financial officer (CFO) is not an economist, and the firm has only $100 thousand to invest. This situation is called capital rationing. We are going to rank the projects by NPV in descending order along with their required investments. Then we shall add a row, titled "CFAT$_0$ Sum" to show the total investment at each step. Under project the A, the cumulative investment is the amount needed to take both D and A ($100 + $42 = $142).

Project	D	A	B	C	E	F
NPV	$ 23	$ 19	$16	$ 4	($8)	($9)
CFAT$_0$	$100	$ 42	$45	$ 13	$39	$101
CFAT$_0$ Sum	$100	$142	$187	$200	$239	$340

If we had only $100 thousand to spend and relied solely on this ranking by NPV, we would invest only in project D, the project with the highest NPV. The value of the firm would be increased by $23 thousand, the NPV of project D.

E.   Now rank them by IRR. They were ranked by IRR initially, but we did not know it then. Here is the IRR ranking with the CFAT$_0$ Sum row added.

Project	A	B	C	D	E	F
IRR	20%	18%	16%	15%	8%	5%
CFAT$_0$	$42	$45	$ 13	$100	$101	$ 39
CFAT$_0$ Sum	$42	$87	$100	$200	$301	$340

To use up our $100 thousand we can invest in projects A, B, and C. The total NPV of these three projects is $19 + $16 + $4 = $39 thousand. The value of the firm would be increased by this amount.

The firm value would be increased more by taking the three projects for $100 thousand rather than project D for the same investment. The ultimate criteria for is that the greatest total NPV should be obtained for the available funds.

F.   A graph to assist in the capital budgeting decision includes two schedules or curves: the investment opportunity schedule (IOS) and the marginal cost of capital schedule. The IOS shows the IRR and initial investment for each available project. The IOS is basically a marginal revenue curve. The marginal cost of capital curve is a horizontal line in this case, as the WACC does not change within the bounds of the problem. The capital budget graph follows:

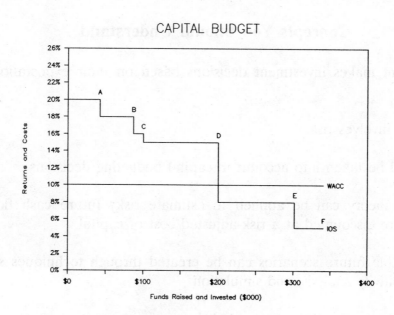

161

CHAPTER 13
CAPITAL BUDGETING AND RISK

Concepts You Should Understand

*   Management makes investment decisions based on their expectations about the future.

*   The future involves risk.

*   Risk should be taken into account in capital budgeting decisions.

*   Probability theory can be applied to estimate risky future cash flows after tax ($CFAT_t$), which are discounted at a risk-adjusted cost of capital.

*   Many possible future scenarios can be created through techniques such as worst case analysis, sensitivity analysis, and simulation.

*   An alternative approach to risk analysis is to remove risk from the expected $\overline{CFAT_t}$ by calculating certainty equivalents, which are discounted at a risk-free rate.

*   Multinational firms face international risks in addition to those facing domestic businesses.

A Second Look

Management should specifically recognize risk in its investment decisions. Risk measurement techniques are not perfect. We often use subjective input for quantitative models. We have two basic approaches for incorporating risk into NPV calculations. One is to allow for the risk, and the other is to remove it.

To allow for risk the $CFAT_t$ can be forecast with probability distributions and is called the *expected* $CFAT_t$. The appropriate discount rate for a risky stream of funds is a risky discount rate. A firm's average cost of capital is the appropriate discount rate for a capital budgeting project of average risk. This average rate can be adjusted up for more risky projects and down for less risky projects. The notation for the risk-adjusted discount rate is k*.

To remove risk from the calculated NPV, the risky cash flows are converted to risk-free cash flows called certainty equivalents. The conversion is accomplished by multiplying the risky cash flow by a certainty equivalent adjustment factor. The certainty equivalents are then discounted at a risk-free rate to give a risk-free NPV. On a practical basis, estimating the adjustment factor is sufficiently difficult that this method is little used.

The following table classifies the inputs and outputs to the NPV model:

NPV	Cash flows	Discount rate
Risky NPV	Risky $CFAT_t$	Risky k*
Certain NPV	Certainty Equivalent	Risk-free rate

Risk is specifically considered in capital budgeting by most major U. S. corporations.

Chapter Summary

Risk is the chance that the (1) _____ may not equal the expected outcome of an investment. The criteria used for evaluating potential investment projects should address the risk involved. The discounted cash flow methods require two major inputs: cash flows after tax ($CFAT_t$) and the cost of capital (k). Risk can be taken into account in either or both of these variables.

Two other names for the cost of capital are the (2) _____ and the (3) _____. Adjusting the discount rate for risk means using a (4) _____ than average rate for riskier projects and a (5) _____ lower rate for less risky projects. The notation for the risk-adjusted cost of capital is (6) _____. The amount of the adjustment is largely subjective.

The capital asset pricing model (CAPM) is theoretically appealing as a way to determine a risk-adjusted discount rate. The parameters required by this model are the (7) _____, the (8) _____, and the project's (9) _____. These three items are not easy to estimate. Estimating a project's beta by using the beta of the common stock of another company whose business is similar to the project is called the (10) _____. Because the CAPM measures market risk, it provides good results for a firm with a (11) _____ portfolio of assets. If a firm is not well diversified, total risk should be considered.

In addition to adjusting the discount rate, we need to calculate cash flows to take risk into account. Probability concepts developed in Chapter 5 can be applied to forecast future $CFAT_t$, which are referred to as (12) _____. Remember that the term "expected" means that the figure is backed up by a probability distribution. The

NPV becomes the *expected* NPV when it is calculated with (13) _____ and (14) _____.

Once the base case expected NPV has been established, management should consider some variations of the original scenario. One extreme is the (15) _____ analysis, wherein a combination of bad results in every realm is considered. This type analysis tends to temper optimism and to prompt management to ask if the firm could survive if the worst came to pass.

A systematic study of the effects of changes in forecasting variables is called (16) _____. Typically only one variable is changed at a time in order to see how sensitive the answer is to a change in that one variable. Electronic spreadsheets enable the analyst to answer "what-if" questions and to consider a broad range of possible economic scenarios.

A method of analysis that specifically incorporates probability distributions into a sensitivity analysis framework is called (17) _____. This differs from sensitivity analysis in that when the computer model is "run," it creates an economic environment from its probability distributions and gives an end result for that combination of variables. Many variables change at once giving the analyst a probable outcome.

Another approach to assessing the impact of risk on a project's acceptability is to calculate a certain (risk-free) NPV. The cash flows are adjusted to risk-free amounts, called (18) _____, which are discounted at a risk-free rate. This method is theoretically sound, but difficult in practice.

Capital budgeting in the international arena has additional risks beyond those faced in a domestic setting. These are primarily in the (19) _____ of funds, (20) _____ risk, and (21) _____ risk.

Many large U. S. corporations are concerned about project risk and use both quantitative and qualitative methods to assess its impact on the value of the company.

Acronyms and Notation You Should Know

a	Alpha (certainty equivalent adjustment factor)
CE_t	Certainty equivalent at time t
$\overline{CFAT_t}$	Expected cash flow after tax during period t
$CFAT_{tj}$	Cash flow after tax during period t for probability class j
k	Cost of capital
k*	Risk-adjusted cost of capital
k_{RF}	Risk-free rate of return
N	Number of outcomes, j, in $CFAT_{tj}$ probability distribution
$\overline{NPV}$	Expected after-tax net present value

Equations You Should Know

$$k_X = k \pm \text{Risk adjustment for project X} \tag{13-2}$$

$$k_X = k_{RF} + (k_M - k_{RF})\text{Beta}_X \tag{13-3}$$

$$\text{Total project risk} = \text{Market risk} + \text{Nonmarket risk} \tag{13-4}$$

$$\overline{NPV} = \sum_{t=0}^{n} \overline{CFAT_t}/(1 + k^*)^t \tag{13-5}$$

$$\overline{CFAT_t} = \sum_{j=1}^{N} (\text{Prob}_{tj})(CFAT_{tj}) \tag{13-6}$$

$$NPV = \sum_{t=0}^{n} CE_t/(1 + k_{RF})t \tag{13-A1}$$

Problems

13-1. *NPV.* Heather's Hatatorium is considering an expansion of retail space to accommodate a new product line. The addition of floor space would require an investment of $170,000. Heather has conducted a survey of Metroplex stores to determine the following probability distribution of cash flows for the first year of the new project.

Condition	Probability	CFAT$_t$
Real winner	0.10	$100,000
Pretty good	0.40	50,000
Not so hot	0.30	30,000
Terrible	0.20	20,000
Totals	1.00	

Subsequent years are expected to be the same as the first with the incremental cash flows being realized for six years.

For investments of average risk, Heather uses a discount rate of 12 percent. This project, however, is more risky than average, and she insists on expectations of a three percent risk premium or she will not commit funds to the expansion.

A. Calculate the expected CFAT$_t$.

Chapter 13: Capital Budgeting and Risk

B.	Calculate the risk-adjusted discount rate.
C.	Calculated the expected NPV.
D.	Should Heather accept or reject the expansion?
E.	As a matter of comparison, calculate the expected NPV using the average cost of capital without the risk adjustment. Did the adjustment alter the decision?

13-2. *Certainty equivalents.* Use the risky cash flows calculated for Heather's Hatatorium expansion in part A of problem 1 above. The rate of return on government bonds is eight percent. The following certainty equivalent adjustment factors have been determined.

Year	Alpha
0	1.00
1	.90
2	.85
3	.80
4	.75
5	.70
6	.65

A.	Calculate the certainty equivalent cash flows for each year.
B.	Calculate the NPV with the certainty equivalent method.
C.	Does the decision indicated agree with the one found by the risk-adjusted discount method used in problem 1?

Answers to Chapter Summary

1. actual outcome
2. discount rate
3. required rate of return
4. higher
5. lower
6. k*
7. risk-free rate of return
8. market rate
9. beta
10. pure-play technique
11. simulation
12. expected $CFAT_t$
13. $CFAT_t$
14. k*
15. worst case
16. sensitivity analysis
17. simulation
18. certainty equivalents
19. repatriation
20. political
21. exchange rate

Problem Solutions

13-1. *NPV.*

A.   The first step is to calculate the expected annual cash flow from the probability distribution. This uses methodology from Chapter 5 and equation 5-1. We multiply each probability by the associated return and add the products.

Condition	Probability	$CFAT_t$	$(Prob)(CFAT_t)$
Real winner	0.10	$100,000	$10,000
Pretty good	0.40	50,000	20,000
Not so hot	0.30	30,000	9,000
Terrible	0.20	20,000	4,000
Totals	1.00	$CFAT_t = $	$43,000

The expected $CFAT_t$ is $43,000 per year for six years.

B.   The risk adjusted discount can be found with equation 13-2. In this case the risk is greater than, not less than, average risk, so the adjustment increases the risk. You must choose the + from the ±.

$$k^* = k \pm \text{Risk adjustment} \qquad (13-2)$$
$$= 12\% + 3\%$$
$$= 15\%$$

Heather requires a return of 15% for investments of this risk level.

C.   The NPV is calculated as in Chapter 12, except the expected cash flows and the risk-adjusted discount rate are used. We are dealing with an annuity of $43,000 per year for six years. The risk-adjusted discount rate is 15 percent.

$$\overline{NPV} = \sum_{t=0}^{n} \overline{CFAT_t}/(1 + k^*)^t \qquad (13-5)$$

$$= (\overline{CFAT_t})(PVIFA_{15\%,6}) - CFAT_0$$
$$= (\$43,000)(3.7845) - \$170,000$$
$$= \$162,733 - \$170,000$$
$$= (\$7,267)$$

D.   Heather should reject the investment because the $\overline{NPV}$ is negative.

E.   What would the decision have been if we had neglected to recognize the added risk by adjusting the discount to 15 percent? Let's recalculate the $\overline{NPV}$ using 12 percent.

$$
\begin{aligned}
\overline{NPV} &= (\overline{CFAT_t})(PVIFA_{12\%,6}) &-& \quad CFAT_0 \\
&= (\$43,000)(4.111) &-& \quad \$170,000 \\
&= \$176,773 &-& \quad \$170,000 \\
&= \$6,773
\end{aligned}
$$

The decision at the average-risk cost of capital would have be to go ahead with the expansion. The risk adjustment changed the decision.

13-2. *Certainty equivalents.*
A.   Certainty equivalent adjustment factors (alpha) reduce a future, risky amount to an amount that the investor would accept without risk. Since the adjusted amount is a risk-free or certain amount, it is called a certainty equivalent (CE). Offered the opportunity to take either the risky cash flow or the CE, the investor would be indifferent between them.

For the financial manager to determine CE adjustment factors for the firm is a sizeable problem and not very widely attempted. CE alphas for a stream of cash flows may decrease into the future, because the farther in the future a cash flow is, the least sure one can be of its value. An investor, therefore, is willing to settle for a smaller certain amount in the far future than in the near future. This phenomenon is reflected in the alphas given in this problem.

The computations are easy enough. The first step is to multiply the risky cash flows by the alphas to reduce them to certainty equivalents. Then we discount them at the fisk-free rate. All of this can be accomplished in a table.

Year	Risky CFAT$_t$	Alpha	Certainty Equivalent	PVIF	8% PV
1	$43,000	.90	$38,700	.9259	$35,833
2	43,000	.85	36,550	.8573	31,336
3	43,000	.80	34,400	.7938	27,308
4	43,000	.75	32,250	.7350	23,705
5	43,000	.70	30,100	.6806	20,486
6	43,000	.65	27,950	.6302	17,613
				PV	$156,280
				CFAT$_0$	(170,000)
				NPV	($13,720)

C.   The negative $\overline{NPV}$ would cause the project to be rejected. This is consistent with the decision made in problem 1 with a risk-adjusted discount rate.

CHAPTER 14
COST OF CAPITAL

Concepts You Should Understand

*   People invest in a company because they expect a return on their investment.

*   The return they require is the same rate they could make on an alternative investment of the same risk. The rate they could have had on the alternative investment is an opportunity cost.

*   Management is responsible for using the funds in a manner which will earn the return that the investors require.

*   The cost of capital to the firm is the investors' required rate of return adjusted for taxes and flotation costs.

*   Each type of capital has its own cost.

*   The weighted average cost of capital (WACC) averages the costs of the individual components according to the proportions of those types in the capital structure.

*   The marginal cost of new funds, not historical cost, is important in investment decisions.

A Second Look

Stockholders and bondholders supply funds to a firm by buying stocks and bonds. These stockholders and bondholders expect management to purchase assets with the funds and earn enough to be able to pay interest on bonds and dividends on stock.   The investors have a world full of other investment opportunities available to them besides one particular company. There is an opportunity cost, consequently, when they invest in one company instead of another. The return they require on their investment in stocks or bonds is the opportunity cost that they could have received elsewhere for similar risk.

From management's viewpoint, the returns required by stockholders and bondholders are costs of capital to the firm. Management is interested in minimizing the weighted average capital cost to maximize the value of the firm. Management uses the weighted average cost of capital in determining its optimal capital structure and in making investment decisions. The weighted average cost of capital is often used as the discount rate in net present value (NPV) calculations and the hurdle rate for internal rate of return (IRR) comparisons, as seen in Chapter 12. It is the marginal cost in our marginal revenue-marginal cost analysis of investment projects.

The concepts deal with costs of new funds, not historical costs. Management must have new funds to invest in new projects. They concentrate on opportunity costs determined from the capital markets as the costs of capital. Costs should be on an after-tax basis.

The calculation of the weighted average cost of capital requires several steps:

(1) Calculate the cost of each type of capital (new debt, new preferred stock, new retained earnings, and new common stock).

(2) Calculate the weights of each type of capital.

(3) Use these costs and weights to calculate the weighted average cost of capital.

The following rules will help you with the calculations:

(1) Hold the weights of each type of capital constant. That is, all funds are raised in these proportions.

(2) If there is more than one source for a type of capital, use up the cheaper source before starting to raise funds from the more expensive source.

The Board of Directors, for example, has declared dividends which left $10 million for an addition to retained earnings. The firm's target capital structure is 40 percent debt and 60 percent equity. When management calculates the company's cost of capital, they should assume that they will use debt and new retained earnings until the earnings available for retention is used up. At that point management will begin using debt and new common stock for further financing. At all times they maintain the proportions of 40 percent debt and 60 percent equity. The problems presented will reiterate this concept.

Chapter Summary

When investors buy stocks or bonds from a company they require a return on their investment. Because they have the option of investing in other securities, their required rate is determined as an (1) _____. A firm's assets are financed by all sources of capital, which causes management to be interested in the overall cost or (2) _____. The proportions of the financing for the entire liability-capital side of the balance sheet is referred to as the (3) _____, while the weights of the long-term section is the (4) _____.

The cost of capital plays a critical role in maximizing the firm's value. One use is to determine the capital structure that results in the (5) _____ weighted average cost. The second role is in capital budgeting, where the cost of capital is used for the (6) _____ with NPV and the (7) _____ with IRR.

The cost of each type of long-term capital must be calculated individually, then averaged. The cost concepts are based on (8) _____ costs, not historical costs. An investor's required rate of return must be determined, then adjusted for the firm's specific (9) _____ and (10) _____. The cost to the company is the investors' required return after these adjustments.

The least costly source of capital is (11) _____; from the investors' viewpoint it is less risky than owing stock, and the (12) _____ is a tax-deductible expense. The required rate of return for common equity can be estimated by the (13) _____ model or the (14) _____. Ranked in terms of percentage cost from lowest to highest, the sources of capital are: debt, (15) _____, (16) _____, and new common stock.

The capital structure is the proportion or weight of each type of capital. Theoretically, the use of (17) _____ is preferable to book values for calculating the weights. These weights are used to calculate the weighted average cost of capital for the firm. This cost of capital is useful for capital budgeting decisions if we assume that both the (18) _____ and the (19) _____ of the investments stay at the current level.

The WACC of the last dollar raised is the (20) _____. As more and more funds are needed by the firm, the cost of individual components of capital may increase. When any individual cost increases, the WACC necessarily increases as well. This causes the marginal cost of capital (MCC) to (21) _____ as the quantity of funds raised increases. The point (amount of total financing) where the MCC increases is called a (22) _____ in the MCC schedule.

The MCC schedule and the (23) _____ are combined in the capital budgeting process. A graph containing both schedules give a clear picture of which projects should be accepted and which should be rejected. This is an application of marginal revenue-marginal cost theory.

Determining the WACC for small, privately owned, firms is generally considered (24) _____ difficult and subjective than for large corporations. Opportunity cost theory is basically sound for small firms, but data are not available to fit the models presented in this chapter.

Acronyms and Notation You Should Know

k	weighted average cost of capital (also k_{WACC} and WACC)
k_d	investors' required rate of return on debt
k_p	investors' required rate of return on preferred stock
k_e	investors' required rate of return on common equity
k_D	after-tax cost of debt
k_P	cost of preferred stock

Chapter 14: Cost of Capital

k_E	cost of common equity (either RE or CS)
k_{RE}	cost of retained earnings
k_{CS}	cost of common stock
k_{RF}	risk-free rate of return
k_M	expected rate of return on the market index
k_{WACC}	weighted average cost of capital (also k)
b	beta
T	marginal corporate income tax rate
f	flotation costs
d	expected constant preferred stock dividend
D_1	next expected common stock dividend
P_0	current market price of the stock (preferred or common)
g	expected future growth rate of common stock dividends
w_D	weight of debt in the capital structure
w_P	weight of preferred stock in the capital structure
w_{CS}	weight of common stock in the capital structure
WACC	weighted average cost of capital (also k)
BP_j	break point in the marginal cost of capital schedule caused by a change in the cost of type j capital
FA_j	amount of funds available from type j capital
W_j	weight of type j capital in the capital structure
MCC	marginal cost of capital
IOS	investment opportunity schedule

Equations You Should Know

$$k_D = \frac{(1 - T)}{(1 - f)} k_d \qquad (14\text{-}3)$$

$$k_P = \frac{d}{(1 - f)P_0} = \frac{k_p}{(1 - f)} \qquad (14\text{-}5)$$

$$k_e = D_1/P_0 + g \qquad (14\text{-}6)$$

$$k_e = k_{RF} + (k_M - k_{RF})\text{Beta} \qquad (14\text{-}7)$$

172

Chapter 14: Cost of Capital

$$k_{cs} = \frac{D_1}{(1-f)P_0} + g \qquad (14\text{-}9)$$

$$k_{RE} = k_e = D_1/P_0 + g \qquad (14\text{-}10)$$

$$k_{WACC} = \sum_{j=1}^{N} w_j k_j \qquad (14\text{-}11)$$

$$k_{WACC} = w_D k_D + w_P k_P + w_E k_E$$

$$BP_j = FA_j/W_j \qquad (14\text{-}12)$$

Problems

14-1. *k and BP.* Amalgamated Iron Works (AIW) has a capital structure with market values of debt of $500,000 and common equity of $300,000. During the coming year AIW expects to have $50,000 of earnings available for retention. New common stock can be sold at $25 per share with flotation costs of 20 percent. Stockholders expect a dividend next year of $2.50 per share and a growth rate of 10 percent ad infinitum. AIW can sell new bonds with a rate of 11.4 percent and flotation costs of five percent. The firm's marginal income tax rate is 25 percent.

A. Calculate the after-tax cost of debt.
B. Calculate the cost of retained earnings.
C. Calculate the cost of new common stock.
D. Calculate the weights in the capital structure.
E. Calculate the break point in the marginal cost of capital schedule caused when the firm runs out of earnings to retain and starts selling new common stock.
F. Calculate the WACC before the break point.
G. Calculate the MCC after the break point.

14-2. *k and BP.* Midnite Supply's capital structure consists of $60 million debt and $30 million common equity (market weights). Midnite plans an expansion of $60 million next year to meet growing demands. Management projects that $10 million will be available from earnings retention. Midnite's common stock is selling for $50 per share on the regional stock exchange. If new stock is sold, flotation costs will amount to 10 percent of the price. Next year's expected dividend of $5 per share is expected to grow at eight

percent per year *ad infinitum*. New bonds can be sold to yield the investor 9.7 percent, but flotation costs are three percent. The firm's marginal tax rate is 34 percent.
A.   Calculate the after-tax cost of debt.
B.   Calculate the cost of retained earnings.
C.   Calculate the cost of new common stock.
D.   Calculate the weights in the capital structure.
E.   Calculate the break point in the marginal cost of capital schedule caused when the firm runs out of earnings to retain and starts selling new common stock.
F.   Calculate the WACC before the break point.
G.   Calculate the MCC after the break point.

Answers to the Chapter Summary

1.	opportunity cost	13.	dividend growth
2.	weighted average cost of capital	14.	CAPM
3.	financial structure	15.	preferred stock
4.	capital structure	16.	retained earnings
5.	minimum	17.	market values
6.	discount rate	18.	capital structure
7.	hurdle rate	19.	riskiness
8.	future	20.	MCC
9.	taxes	21.	rise
10.	flotation costs	22.	break point
11.	debt	23.	IOS
12.	interest	24.	more

Problem Solutions

14-1. *k and BP.*
A.   Use equation 14-3 for the after-tax cost of debt.

$$k_D = \frac{(1 - T)}{(1 - f)}k_d \qquad (14\text{-}3)$$

$$= \frac{(1 - .25)}{(1 - .05)}(.114)$$

$$= .09 \text{ or } 9.00\%$$

B.   Since the company can retain earnings without incurring flotation costs, the cost of retained earnings is the same as the return required by stockholders.

$$k_{RE} = k_e = D_1/P_0 + g \qquad (14\text{-}10)$$
$$= \$2.50/\$25 + .10$$
$$= .20 \text{ or } 20.00\%$$

C.   The cost of new common stock is higher than retained earnings because of flotation costs.

$$k_{cs} = \frac{D_1}{(1 - f)P_0} + g \qquad (14\text{-}9)$$

$$= \$2.50/(1 - .2)(\$25) + .10$$
$$= .125 + .10$$
$$= .225 \text{ or } 22.5\%$$

D.   The weight of any type of capital is the amount of that type divided by the total capital. The sum of the weights must equal 1.00 or 100 percent.

$$\text{Total capital} = \text{debt} + \text{equity}$$
$$= \$500,000 + \$300,000$$
$$= \$800,000$$

$$\text{Weight of debt} = \text{debt/total}$$
$$= \$500,000/\$800,000$$
$$= .625 \text{ or } 62.5\%$$

$$\text{Weight of equity} = \text{equity/total}$$
$$= \$300,000/\$800,000$$
$$= .375 \text{ or } 37.5\%$$

As a check, the weight of debt + the weight of equity must = 1.00.

$$.625 + .375 = 1.00$$

E.   The break point is the total financing (debt and equity) that can be raised in the proportions (weights) using all of the $50,000 of new earnings that is available for retention but without selling new common stock. We shall use equation 14-12 and substitute retained earnings (RE) for the general form (j).

$$BP_j = FA_j/W_j \qquad (14\text{-}12)$$
$$BP_{RE} = FA_{RE}/W_{RE}$$
$$= \$50,000/.375$$
$$= \$133,333$$

This relationship might be easier to see by using the following table:

	Old Amount	Weight	New Amount
Debt	$500,000	.625	$83,333
Equity	300,000	.375	50,000
Total	$800,000	1.000	$133,000

This means that with $50,000 of earnings available to invest, the company can borrow $83,333 and invest the whole amount of $133,333. If the management wants to invest more than $133,333, it will have to borrow more money and sell new common stock for the equity portion of its financing.

F.   Financing before the break point consists of debt and retained earnings, so the WACC will be an average of those costs.

$$WACC = k = w_D k_D + w_{RE} k_{RE}$$
$$= (.625)(9.00\%) + (.375)(20.00\%)$$
$$= 13.125\%$$

G.   Financing after the break point consists of debt and new common stock, so the MCC will be an average of those costs.

$$MCC = k = w_D k_D + w_{CS} k_{CS}$$
$$= (.625)(9.00\%) + (.375)(22.5\%)$$
$$= 14.06\%$$

If the firm raises funds in excess of $133,333, each dollar will consist of $0.625 debt and $0.375 new common stock at a MCC of 14.06 percent.

14-2. *k and BP.*

A.   Use equation 14-3 for the after-tax cost of debt.

$$k_D = \frac{(1 - T)}{(1 - f)} k_d \qquad (14\text{-}3)$$

$$= \frac{(1 - .34)}{(1 - .03)}(.097)$$

$$= 0.0660 \text{ or } 6.60\%$$

B.   Since the company can retain earnings without incurring flotation costs, the cost of retained earnings is the same as the return required by stockholders.

$$\begin{aligned} k_{RE} = k_e &= D_1/P_0 + g \qquad (14\text{-}10) \\ &= \$5/\$50 + .08 \\ &= .18 \text{ or } 18.00\% \end{aligned}$$

C.   The cost of new common stock is higher than retained earnings because of flotation costs.

$$k_{cs} = \frac{D_1}{(1 - f)P_0} + g \qquad (14\text{-}9)$$

$$= \frac{\$5}{(1 - .10)(\$50)} + .08$$

$$= .1911 \text{ or } 19.11\%$$

D.   The weight of any type of capital is the amount of that type divided by the total capital. The sum of the weights must equal 1.00 or 100 percent.

$$\begin{aligned} \text{Total capital} &= \text{debt} + \text{equity} \\ &= \$60 + \$30 \\ &= \$90 \end{aligned}$$

177

$$\text{Weight of debt} = \text{debt/total}$$
$$= \$60/\$90$$
$$= .6667 \text{ or } 66.67\%$$

$$\text{Weight of equity} = \text{equity/total}$$
$$= \$30/\$90$$
$$= .3333 \text{ or } 33.33\%$$

As a check, the weight of debt + the weight of equity must = 1.00.

$$.6667 + .3333 = 1.00$$

E.   The break point is the total financing (debt and equity) that can be raised in the proportions (weights) using all of the $10 million of new earnings that is available for retention but without selling new common stock.

$$BP_j = FA_j/W_j \qquad (14\text{-}12)$$
$$BP_{RE} = FA_{RE}/W_{RE}$$
$$= \$10/.3333$$
$$= \$30 \text{ million}$$

This relationship might be easier to see by using the following table:

	Old Amount	Weight	New Amount
Debt	$60	.6667	$20
Equity	30	.3333	10
Total	$90	1.000	$30

This means that with $10 million of earnings available to invest, the company can borrow $20 million and invest the whole amount of $30 million. If the management wants to invest more than $30 million it will have to borrow more money and sell new common stock for the equity portion of its financing.

F.   Financing before the break point consists of debt and retained earnings, so the WACC will be an average of those costs.

$$WACC = k = w_D k_D + w_{RE} k_{RE}$$
$$= (.6667)(6.600\%) + (.3333)(18.00\%)$$
$$= 10.40\%$$

Let's calculate this one again using a table. This might make it easier to see.

	Amount	Weights	Costs	Weighted Costs
Debt	$60 million	0.6667	6.60%	4.40%
Equity	30	0.3333	18.00%	6.00
Total	$90 million	1.0000		10.40%

G.   Financing after the break point consists of debt and new common stock, so the MCC will be an average of those costs.

$$
\begin{aligned}
\text{MCC} \quad = \quad k \quad &= \quad w_D k_D \quad + \quad w_{cs} k_{cs} \\
&= \quad (.6667)(6.600\%) \quad + \quad (.3333)(19.11\%) \\
&= \quad 10.77\%
\end{aligned}
$$

Let's set this one up as a table and compare to the preceding table. The change is that the cost of new common stock is used instead of the cost of retained earnings. This change and the resulting change in the answer are boldfaced.

	Amount	Weights	Costs	Weighted Costs
Debt	$60 million	0.6667	6.60%	4.40%
Equity	30	0.3333	**19.11%**	**6.37**
Total	$90 million	1.0000		**10.77%**

If the firm raises funds in excess of the $30 million break point (calculated in part E), each dollar will consist of $0.60 debt and $0.30 new common stock at a MCC of 10.77 percent. The graph below shows the WACC before the break point and the MCC after the break point. The break point is the step-up in the marginal cost of capital graph on the following page:

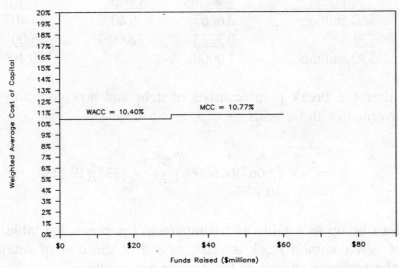

Marginal Cost of Capital

WACC = 10.40%

MCC = 10.77%

CHAPTER 15
LEVERAGE AND CAPITAL STRUCTURE

Concepts You Should Understand

*   Fixed operating costs cause a firm's earnings before interest and taxes (EBIT) to change by a greater proportion than sales change. This relationship is called operating leverage.

*   Business risk is the inherent uncertainty in EBIT and in the rate of return on total assets from operations (EBIT/TA).

*   Financial risk is the increased variability in earnings per share (EPS) and the increased probability of bankruptcy brought on by fixed financing costs.

*   When sales are climbing, leverage is good and increases stockholders' earnings more rapidly than sales increase. But when sales are declining, leverage is bad and decreases stockholders' earnings more rapidly than sales decrease.

*   The optimal capital structure is the combination of debt and equity that minimizes the weighted average cost of capital and maximizes the common stock price, according to traditional theory.

*   Fixed financial costs cause a firm's earnings per share to change by a greater proportion than EBIT change. This relationship is called financial leverage.

A Second Look

Fixed operating costs require the same payment each month (or year). The fixed costs do not increase or decrease when sales increase or decrease. Contrast that to raw materials cost; if sales increases, so does the raw materials cost. The presence of fixed costs causes EBIT (also called net operating income) to change more when sales change than it would if all costs were variable. This concept is called *operating leverage.*

Business risk is a combination of all the factors that cause the actual EBIT differ from the expected EBIT. Operating leverage contributes to business risk. Other variables held constant, the higher the operating leverage, the higher the business risk. A quantitative measure of operating leverage is the degree of operating leverage (DOL). Note that business risk and operating leverage depend on the firm's assets and are independent of the firm's capital structure.

Financial risk, however, is dependent on the capital structure. When debt or preferred stock is used as a source of funds, the interest or preferred dividends are fixed financial costs. When EBIT increases, these payments stay the same. The result is seen in increased variability of EPS. The more debt and preferred stock, the more *financial leverage,* and the more financial risk. The extreme effect of financial leverage is bankruptcy. A quantitative measure of financial leverage is the degree of financial leverage (DFL).

Financial leverage increases the risk caused by operating leverage. The combined leverage is measured by the degree of combined leverage (DCL).

How does financial leverage affect the value of the firm? This question has been the center of much debate over the past thirty-something years. The traditional theory holds that the value of the firm rises with the prudent use of debt, but that at some level of debt the probability of bankruptcy causes the value of the firm to stop rising and begin falling. The capital structure that results in the maximum value is the optimal capital structure.

Modigliani and Miller (M&M) proposed that there is no optimal capital structure in a hypothetical world of no taxes. The value of the firm is not affected by the mix of debt and equity financing.

If management believes the traditional theory, they should seek the optimal capital structure in their financing decisions. If they believe the ideal world of M&M, the financing mix is not important. A third theory is the pecking order hypothesis (POH). According to the POH, management does not set about achieving a particular capital structure, but uses retained earnings first, debt second, and new equity issues third. This order of preference for financing is the pecking order. Even so, the capital structure probably changes back-and-forth within some target range.

Chapter Summary

Changes in a company's sales cause greater percentage changes in the EBIT. The factor causing the increased variability is called (1) _____, which is the result of (2) _____ operating expenses. The degree of operating leverage (DOL) is the percentage change in (3) _____ caused by a change of one percentage point in (4) _____. The higher the firms' fixed costs relative to total costs, the higher the (5) _____ and the higher the break-even point, other things held constant.

Business risk is the (6) _____ in EBIT. A mathematical measure of business risk is the (7) _____ between the company's return on assets and the return on a market index. Return on assets for this purpose is called R and is calculated as (8) _____.

Financial leverage is the use of debt, preferred stock, or (9) _____ financing. Any of these result in a fixed cost: interest, preferred dividends, or a lease payment. The degree of financial leverage (DFL) is the percentage change in (10) _____ caused by a one percentage point change in (11) _____.
The (12) _____ is the percentage change in EPS caused by a change of one percentage point in sales.

Firms should consider the risk of combining high financial leverage with high operating leverage. Management of a company whose assets provide high operating leverage might consider using (13) _____ to offset it and reduce the (14) _____.

When a firm is considering two alternate financing plans, management may want to calculate the EPS at different levels of EBIT. At some level of EBIT, the EPS of the plans will be equal. This is called the EBIT-EPS (15) _____ or indifference point.

If financial leverage is used to increase EPS, the (16) _____ of the EPS may also increase. The risk of a stock is the (17) _____ between the rate of return on the stock and the rate of return on the (18) _____.
Finally, an increase in financial leverage leads to an increase in the riskiness of the stock. Too much leverage may ultimately result in bankruptcy.

An optimal capital structure is one which would (19) _____.
Traditional financial theory argues that the use of debt financing initially increases dividends proportionately more than it increases the (20) _____, up to some level of debt. Up to that point the stock price will increase. Beyond that point, however, investors perceive that the (21) _____ is increasing rapidly, causing the required return on equity to increase proportionately more rapidly the dividends. This relationship will cause the stock price to be (22) _____ at higher levels of debt. The amount of debt *does* affect stock price and an optimal capital structure *is* identifiable, according to the (23) _____.

In (24) _____ world of perfect capital markets and no taxes, the weighted average cost of capital is (25) _____ regardless of how much debt is used by the firm. The (26) _____, consequently, *is not* affected by the level of debt. There is *no* (27) _____, since any debt-equity combination is as good as any other.

When income taxes are introduced into the analysis, EBIT is distributed to three groups. The "I" in EBIT represents interest payments to (28) _____; the "T" is the tax payments to (29) _____; and whatever is left belongs to the (30) _____. As debt is introduced to the capital structure, the value of the firm increases by the amount of the present value of the (31) _____.
An offsetting factor, that reduces the value of the firm as the level of debt increases, is

the present value of expected (32) _____.

Additional considerations that are relevant to capital structure decisions include (33) _____ and (34) _____. The majority opinion appears to be that capital structure does matter, when all factors are considered.

One more hypothesis states that management prefers to finance assets using retained earnings first, then (35) _____, and, if necessary, new stock. The capital structure is determined passively as the sources of financing are depleted. This approach is called the (36) _____.

Acronyms and Notation You Should Know

$Corr_{RM}$	Correlation between return on assets and market return
$Corr_{rM}$	Correlation between return on stock and market return
Cov_{RM}	Covariance between return on assets and market return
Cov_{rM}	Covariance between return on stock and market return
d	Preferred dividend payments ($)
DCL	Degree of combined leverage (%)
DFL	Degree of financial leverage (%)
DOL	Degree of operating leverage (%)
EBIT	Earnings before interest and taxes ($)
EPS	Earnings per share ($ per share)
F	Fixed operating costs ($)
I	Interest payments ($)
L	Lease payments ($)
M&M	Modigliani and Miller
N	Number of shares of common stock
POH	Pecking order hypothesis
r	Rate of return on common stock (%)
R	Rate of before-interest-and-before-tax return on assets (%)
S	Sales ($)
T	Tax rate (%)
v	Ratio of variable cost to sales

Equations You Should Know

$$\text{DOL} = \frac{\% \text{ change in EBIT}}{\% \text{ change in sales}} = 1 + F/\text{EBIT} \qquad (15\text{-}1)$$

$$\text{Business risk} = \text{Cov}_{RM} = \text{Corr}_{RM}\sigma_R\sigma_M \qquad (15\text{-}2)$$

$$\text{DFL} = \frac{\% \text{ change in EPS}}{\% \text{ change in EBIT}} \qquad (15\text{-}3)$$

$$\text{DFL} = \frac{\text{EBIT}}{\text{EBIT} - I - L - d/(1 - T)} \qquad (15\text{-}4)$$

$$\text{DCL} = (\text{DOL})(\text{DFL}) \qquad (15\text{-}5)$$

$$\text{Cov}_{rM} = \text{Corr}_{rM}\sigma_r\sigma_M \qquad (15\text{-}6)$$

$$V = V_U + \text{Present value of interest tax shield} \qquad (15\text{-}9)$$

$$V = V_U + \begin{array}{c}\text{Present value of}\\ \text{interest tax shield}\end{array} + \begin{array}{c}\text{Present value of}\\ \text{expected}\\ \text{bankruptcy cost}\end{array} \qquad (15\text{-}10)$$

$$S^* = F/(1 - v) \qquad (15\text{-}B1)$$

Problems

The following annual data for Cee-Cee Enterprises apply to problems 1 - 6:

Cee-Cee Enterprises	
Sales	$300 million
Variable cost ratio	0.35
Fixed costs	$135 million
Interest payment	$ 20 million
Lease payment	$ 15 million
Preferred dividends	$ 5 million
Income tax rate	0.34
Number of shares	10 million

Chapter 15: Leverage and Capital Structure

15-1. *EPS.* Use the above data to calculate EBIT, net income, earnings available for common shareholders, and EPS.

15-2. *DOL, DFL, and DCL.* Use the above data and the EBIT from the previous problem to calculate the DOL, DFL, and DCL.

15-3. *EBIT.* Use the DOL to calculate the EBIT that would result from a sales increase of 10 percent. Repeat for a decrease of 10 percent.

15-4. *EPS.* Use the DFL to calculate the EPS that would result from an EBIT increase of 32.5 percent. Repeat for a decrease of 32.5 percent.

15-5. *EPS.* Use the DCL to calculate the EPS that would result from a sales increase of 10 percent. Repeat for a decrease of 10 percent. You should get the same answer as you did in the prior problem.

15-6. *Operating break-even sales.* Use the data above to calculate the operating break-even sales.

15-7. *Optimal capital structure.* Use the traditional approach to determine the optimal capital structure from the data below. Graph the relationships.

Debt to Total Capital	k_D	k_E
0.0	6.00%	12.00%
0.1	6.25%	12.25%
0.2	6.50%	12.50%
0.3	7.00%	13.00%
0.4	7.50%	14.00%
0.5	8.50%	16.00%
0.6	9.50%	19.00%

15-8. *EBIT-EPS.* Company X needs $240,000 in long-term financing for an expansion of its production facilities. It can borrow the money from the bank at nine percent or sell new stock at the market price of $32 per share. Flotation costs are 6.25 percent of the price of new stock, but there are no flotation costs on the bank loan. The price-earnings ratio after one year is expected to be nine times if they borrow the funds or 12 times if they sell new stock.

A.   Prepare an EBIT-EPS indifference point analysis with EBIT ranging from $0 to $150,000 in increments of $50,000.

B.   Calculate the EBIT-EPS indifference point.

Chapter 15: Leverage and Capital Structure

C.   Graph the relationship in part A.

D.   If EBIT is expected to be $100,000 after the expansion, should Company X use debt or equity financing if they are earnings maximizers? What if they are value maximizers?

Answers to Chapter Summary

1.	operating leverage	19.	maximize the stock price
2.	fixed	20.	required return on equity
3.	EBIT	21.	risk of bankruptcy
4.	sales	22.	lower
5.	DOL	23.	traditional theory
6.	inherent uncertainty	24.	Modigliani and Miller
7.	covariance	25.	constant
8.	EBIT/Total assets	26.	value of the firm
9.	lease	27.	optimal capital structure
10.	EPS	28.	creditors
11.	EBIT	29.	government
12.	DCL	30.	owners
13.	less financial leverage	31.	interest tax shield
14.	combined leverage	32.	bankruptcy costs
15.	break-even point	33.	agency theory
16.	standard deviation	34.	asymmetric information
17.	covariance	35.	debt
18.	market index	36.	POH

Problem Solutions

15-1.   *EPS*. To calculate EPS, let's work through an income statement. Figures are in millions, except for per share data.

Sales	$300
Variable costs (.35)($300)	105
Fixed costs	135
EBIT	$ 60
Interest expense	20
Lease payment	15
Earnings before taxes	$ 25
Taxes (.34)($25)	8.5
Net income	$ 16.5
Preferred stock dividends	5
Earnings available for common	$ 11.5
EPS ($11.5/10)	$1.15

15-2. *DOL, DFL, and DCL.* We can calculate these using the equations.

$$
\begin{aligned}
\text{DOL} &= 1 + \text{F/EBIT} \\
&= 1 + 135/60 \\
&= 1 + 2.25 \\
&= 3.25
\end{aligned}
$$

$$
\begin{aligned}
\text{DFL} &= \text{EBIT/[EBIT - I - L - d/(1 - T)]} \\
&= 60/[60 - 20 - 15 - 5/(1-.34)] \\
&= 60/[60 - 20 - 15 - 7.58] \\
&= 60/17.42 \\
&= 3.44
\end{aligned}
$$

$$
\begin{aligned}
\text{DCL} &= \text{(DOL)(DFL)} \\
&= (3.25)(3.44) \\
&= 11.18
\end{aligned}
$$

Now, just what do these mean? The DOL means that if there is a one percent change in sales, EBIT will change by 3.25 percent. The DFL means that if there is a one percent change in EBIT, there will be a 3.44 percent change in EPS. The DCL means that if there is a one percent change in sales, there will be a 11.18 percent change in EPS.

15-3. *EBIT.* For a sales change of 10 percent, EBIT will change by 32.5 percent [(10%)(DOL) = (10%)(3.25) = 32.5%]. The original sales and EBIT are shown with the increase and the decrease.

Original sales	$300.0 million
Original EBIT	$60.0 million
Sales + 10%	$330.0 million
EBIT + 32.5%	$79.5 million
Sales - 10%	$270.0 million
EBIT - 32.5%	$40.5 million

15-4. *EPS.* For a 32.5% change in EBIT, EPS will change by 111.8 percent [(32.5%)(DFL) = (32.5%)(3.44) = 111.8%].

Original EBIT	$60.0 million
Original EPS	$1.15 per share
EBIT + 32.5%	$79.5 million
EPS + 111.8%	$2.44 per share
EBIT - 32.5%	$40.5 million
EPS - 111.8%	($0.14) per share

15-5. *EPS.* We shall get the same results using DCL with the 10 percent sales change as we did using the DFL with the EBIT change. The DCL from question 2 above is 11.18.

Change in EPS	=	(Change in sales)(DCL)
	=	(10%)(11.18)
	=	111.8%

Original Sales	$300.0 million
Original EPS	$1.15 per share
Sales + 10%	$330.0 million
EPS + 111.8%	$2.44 per share
Sales - 10%	$270.0 million
EPS - 111.8%	($.14) per share

Chapter 15: Leverage and Capital Structure

15-6. *Operating break-even sales.* We can use equation 15-A1 from Appendix 15-A to calculate the dollar volume of sales necessary to break even or make an EBIT of $0. At this level of sales, the firm would be in big trouble because they cannot make their interest or lease payments.

$$
\begin{aligned}
S^* &= F/(1 - v) \qquad\qquad\qquad\qquad\qquad\qquad\qquad\qquad (15\text{-}A1)\\
&= \$135{,}000/(1 - .35)\\
&= \$207.692 \text{ million}
\end{aligned}
$$

15-7. *Optimal capital structure.*

Under the traditional approach we calculate the weighted average cost of capital, k, for each level of debt. The capital structure with the minimum k is optimal. We use equation 14-11 for each debt-to-total capital ratio.

A sample calculation for 10 percent debt-to-total capital ratio is given. The weight for equity is 1 minus the weight for debt. Calculations for the other levels are similar.

$$
\begin{aligned}
k &= w_D k_D \qquad + \qquad w_E k_{RE} \qquad\qquad\qquad\qquad\qquad (14\text{-}11)\\
&= (.1)(6.25\%) \ + \ (.9)(12.25\%)\\
&= 11.65\%
\end{aligned}
$$

The following table summarizes the results.

Debt to Total Capital	k_D	k_E	k	
.0	6.00%	12.00%	12.00%	
.1	6.25%	12.25%	11.65%	
.2	6.50%	12.50%	11.30%	
.3	7.00%	13.00%	**11.20%**	Optimal
.4	7.50%	14.00%	11.40%	
.5	8.50%	16.00%	12.25%	
.6	9.50%	19.00%	13.30%	

A graph of the data in the above table follows. The optimal capital structure is 30 percent debt-to-total capital.

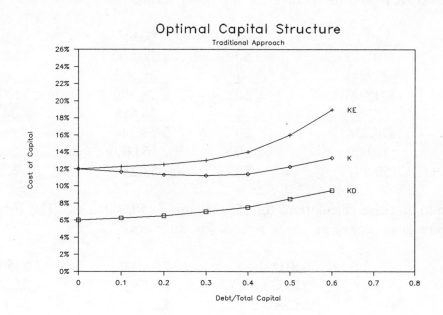

15-8. *EBIT-EPS*.

A.   The object is to prepare partial income statements to determine the EPS at different levels of EBIT for both possible forms of financing. We can then compare the results and determine which way to finance, considering our expectations for future EBIT.

Before starting the partial income statements, we need to calculate the interest payment if the funds are borrowed and the number of shares of stock to be sold if equity is used.

Annual interest payment   = (rate)(principal)
      = (0.09)($240,000)
      = $21,600

If stock is sold, the net to the company will be:

Net to company   =   (price)(1 - flotation)
      =   ($32)(1 - .0625)
      = $30

To raise $240,000 it will be necessary to sell 8,000 shares ($240,000/$30/share). The total old and new shares will be 24,000 (16,000 old + 8,000 new shares).

Now let's prepare partial income statements for $0 EBIT and for $100,000 EBIT as samples. Then we'll give the results for the other levels.

	Debt	Equity	Debt	Equity
EBIT	$0	$0	$100,000	$100,000
Interest	21,600	0	21,600	0
EBT	($21,600)	$0	$ 78,400	$100,000
Taxes	(7,344)	0	26,656	34,000
Net income	($14,256)	$0	$ 51,744	$ 66,000
# shares	16,000	24,000	16,000	24,000
EPS	($0.89)	$0	$3.23	$2.75

You should do these calculations for $50,000, and $150,000, also. The EPS for each level of EBIT are given below as check figures for your work.

EBIT	$0	$50,000	$100,000	$150,000
EPS-debt	($0.89)	$1.17	$3.23	$5.30
EPS-equity	$0	$1.38	$2.75	$4.13

B.   At some level of EBIT, EPS under the debt financing option will equal EPS under the stock financing option. Instead of using the income statement format, we set it up in equation form. We can omit lease payments and preferred dividends from the equation, since there are none in this problem. The unknown is EBIT.

$$\text{EPS with debt} \quad = \quad \text{EPS with stock}$$

$$\frac{(EBIT - I)(1 - T)}{N} = \frac{(EBIT - I)(1 - T)}{N}$$

$$\frac{(EBIT - 21{,}600)(1 - .34)}{16{,}000} = \frac{(EBIT - 0)(1 - .34)}{24{,}000}$$

Now we must solve this equation for EBIT. Simplifying, we see that:

$$(EBIT - 21,600)(.66)(24,000) = (EBIT)(.66)(16,000)$$
$$(15,840)EBIT - 342,144,000 = (10,560)EBIT$$
$$(5,280)EBIT = 342,144,000$$
$$EBIT = \$64,800$$

The EPS will be equal at $64,800 of EBIT, regardless of which type financing is used. Let's figure the EPS under each alternative to check our solution.

	Debt	Equity
EBIT	$64,800	$64,800
Interest	21,600	0
EBT	$43,200	$64,800
Taxes	14,688	22,032
Net income	$28,512	$42,768
# shares	16,000	24,000
EPS	$1.78	$1.78

It worked! EPS is $1.78 either way at an EBIT of $64,800.

C.   A graph of the EBIT-EPS relationship puts EBIT on the horizontal axis because it is the independent variable. That is, "EBIT happens," and EPS depends on EBIT. You may observe the indifference point where the two lines intersect at EBIT of $64,800 and EPS of $1.78 on the following EBIT-EPS indifference analysis graph.

EBIT—EPS Indifference Analysis

Chapter 15: Leverage and Capital Structure

D.   If Company X's chief financial officer's (CFO) best guess is that EBIT after the expansion will be $100,000, what should she recommend? If the goal is to maximize EPS, she would recommend debt financing because EPS is projected at $3.23 versus $2.75 for stock financing, based on the calculations in part A.

But what about stock price? One way to project stock price, if a company has a fairly stable price-earnings ratio (P/E), is to project EPS and multiply by the projected P/E. In this case the analyst thinks that the earnings will be valued more highly by the marketplace if the risk of debt is not present. That translates into a higher P/E for the stock financing alternative. We need to calculate price under each type of financing.

	Debt	Stock
EPS	$3.23	$2.75
P/E	9	12
Price	$29.11	$33.00

Thus, the CFO will recommend stock financing if she wants to maximize share price and believes the projections. This illustrates that earnings maximization and value maximization may not always coincide.

CHAPTER 16
DIVIDEND POLICY

Concepts You Should Understand

*   Dividends are the most important method of distributing cash to stockholders.

*   One of the major unresolved issues in financial management today is in regard to exactly how dividend policy affects stock price.

*   In Modigliani and Miller's perfect economic world, dividends do not affect the value of the firm.

*   Under real-world conditions there are conflicting views. Higher dividends may be favored because of reduced risk and significant transactions costs. Lower dividends, on the other hand, may be favored because of differential tax treatment for the stockholder and flotation costs for the firm.

*   Stock dividends and stock splits cut the stockholders' pie into more pieces, but do not alone make the pie larger.

A Second Look

A company's earnings belong to the stockholders. The board of directors decides whether these earnings will be paid out as dividends to the owners or used to purchase more assets for the business.   Dividend policy is inextricably combined with the capital structure problem, because earnings that are invested in additional assets also increase the equity portion of capital.

If less of the earnings is paid out and more is reinvested, then the company's assets and dividends should grow at a faster rate than if the payout ratio were higher. Investors would not care whether they get their cash now (through higher dividends) or later (through higher growth), if they could buy and sell stock without transactions costs and if effective income taxes were the same for dividends and capital gains.

Any stockbroker, however, will tell you that investors like stable per-share dividends with long, unbroken payment records.   Furthermore, the dividends should be increased periodically, when earnings justify it.   And never, never reduce or omit a quarterly payment. These are the rules of the game by which many directors try to play.

195

Several theories are worth reiterating. The dividend preference theory says that investors are willing to pay more for stock with high payout ratios (high current dividends and low reinvestment rate) than with low payout ratios. The high near-term dividends are viewed as less risky than future dividends and capital gains. Thus a higher discount rate, reflecting lower risk, is used and results in a higher stock price, other things the same.

The clientele theory suggests that companies have a clientele of stockholders who seek them out for their dividend policy. A firm should generally maintain its dividend policy rather than adjusting it radically from year to year.

The residual theory of dividends states that the firm invests in every acceptable project; then, if any earnings are left, it pays dividends.

Stock repurchases are another method to distribute dividends to stockholders. The resulting treasury stock reduces equity. Repurchases would not affect share price in perfect markets.

Stock dividends and splits affect price, *per se,* because the number of shares of stock is changed. Investors' wealth is not affected.

Chapter Summary

Three major ways for the board of directors to distribute cash to stockholders are (1) _____, (2) _____, and cash-financed (3) _____. Dividend policy concerns itself with the (4) _____ and (5) _____ of dividends. The dividend payout ratio is calculated by dividing the dividends per share (DPS) by the (6) _____.

Some theorists argue that dividends are irrelevant to the valuation of the firm. This stance depends on investors being able to (7) _____ if they want higher dividends (more cash), and to reinvest their (8) _____ if they prefer a lower payout. This argument requires perfect capital markets, which have no (9) _____, such as (10) _____ or (11) _____.
In the real world without perfect capital markets there are additional considerations.

The (12) _____ theory asserts that near-term dividends are (13) _____ than dividends expected far in the future. Investors prefer the certain, current dividends and capitalize them at a (14) _____, which causes a higher stock price, other things the same. For an investor to sell shares of stock to supplement dividend income is expensive because of (15) _____.
This theory supports a (16) _____ level of dividends.

One argument for a low level of dividends hinges on a higher marginal (17) _____ on cash dividends than on capital gains. The firm may also favor retaining more earnings and paying out less dividends if the firm has a substantial investment opportunity schedule. If the firm replaces earnings retention with the sales of new common stock, it incurs (18) _____ costs. The individual stockholders and the firm, itself, prefer lower dividends, according to this viewpoint.

One theory says that investors choose companies that pay the kind of dividends that they want. Investors requiring high current income buy stocks with high dividend yields, according to the (19) _____. Investors preferring capital gains will likewise purchase appropriate stocks.

Practical considerations affect dividend policy. One legal constraint is the (20) _____ rule, which allows dividends to be no larger than current net income plus cumulative (21) _____. Restrictive covenants in (22) _____ and income tax considerations may also mold dividend policy.

A firm with a large concentration of (23) _____ resting with one person or group, may refrain from paying dividends, preferring, instead to use available earnings for (24) _____. The company can thereby minimize its need for selling new stock, which would dilute the control of the current majority stockholders.

The (25) _____ theory of dividends states that companies use their earnings to invest in all acceptable investment opportunities, first. Then, if any earnings are left over, the residual is used to (26) _____. This is probably true in an aggregate economic sense, but would lead to fluctuating dividends if followed rigorously as an operating policy.

Boards of directors generally follow a policy of paying a per-share dividend that is (27) _____ and increases when justified by higher earnings and no (28) _____. This policy results in low variability (low risk) compared to a policy of a (29) _____, which would cause DPS to fluctuate in unison with EPS. In a very good year, an (30) _____ may be paid to distribute the exceptional earnings to shareholders.

Four dates are important in dividend payment procedures. In order of occurrence these are the (31) _____, the (32) _____, the (33) _____, and the (34) _____.

A stockholder who wants to purchase more shares with a dividend payment may enroll in a (35) _____ plan. This is particularly attractive to small investors who would have excessive transactions costs buying a few shares.

Stock may be repurchased by the issuing firm through (36) _____ or (37) _____. Repurchases may provide shares for executive (38) _____ and mergers and acquisitions. Repurchased stock is called (39) _____ and reduces (40) _____. Theoretically, a stock repurchase should have (41) _____ on the stock price, but may affect it in our imperfect world.

Stock dividends and stock splits create more or fewer pieces of paper, but do not affect the fundamental earnings power of the company. Many managers perceive that there is an (42) _____, and periodically use stock splits to adjust the price when it is outside the range. Neither stock dividends nor splits have any lasting effect on a shareholder's total wealth.

Acronyms and Notation You Should Know

DPS	Dividends per share
EPS	Earnings per share
NYSE	New York Stock Exchange

Equations You Should Know

Dividend payout ratio $=$ DPS/EPS $\qquad$ (16-1)

Problems

16-1. *Residual theory of dividends.* Big Country Food Processors has a capital structure with 20 percent debt, five percent preferred stock, and the rest common equity. It currently has identified three major investment opportunities with positive net present values. The three projects together require a $20 million investment. Big Country's management expects to have $9 million earnings available for dividends or retention. The firm's cost of capital is 13 percent over the relevant range of funds.
A. Determine exactly how the $20 million will be raised.
B. If the company follows the residual theory of dividends strictly, will it pay any dividends?

16-2. *Residual theory of dividends.* The Coast-to-Coast Truck Company has 65 percent debt and 35 percent common equity. The treasurer is planning on $105,000 to be available for dividends or retention. Acceptable projects requiring $200,000 total investment are available to the firm. If the board of directors adheres to the residual theory of dividends, will they declare dividends? If so how much?

16-3. *Stock split.* Manhattan, Inc., has the following common equity section on its balance sheet:

Common stock ($1.50 par, 300,000 shares)	$450,000
Additional paid-in capital	1,050,000
Retained earnings	$5,000,000
Total equity	$6,500,000

John owns 200 shares of stock. The market price of the stock is twice the book value.

198

The company is expected to pay a dividend of $1.80 per share during the coming year.

A.   What is the book value per share of common equity? What is the market price of a share of common stock?

B.   What is the total market value of John's stock? How much total dividends can he expect to receive?

C.   Prepare a common equity statement like the one above, assuming the company splits the stock three-to-one. What is the book value per share of common equity after the split? If the market-to-book ratio stays at two times after the split, what is the price per share?

D.   After the split, what is the total market value of John's stock? How much total dividends can he expect to receive?

16-4. *Stock dividend.*   The Red Arroyo Manufacturing Company has the following common equity section on its balance sheet:

Common stock ($1 par, 20,000,000 shares)	$5,000,000
Additional paid-in capital	225,000,000
Retained earnings	370,000,000
Total equity	$600,000,000

The stock is currently selling at a market-to-book ratio of 1.5. The expected annual dividend is $3 per share. Susie owns 500 shares of stock.

A.   What is the book value per share of common equity? What is the market price?

B.   What is the total value of Susie's stock? How much can she expect to receive in total dividends?

C.   Prepare a statement similar to the one above, assuming the board of directors declares a three percent stock dividend. What is the book value per share after the stock dividend? What is the market price, assuming the market-to-book ratio holds the same value? What will the new cash dividend per share be?

D.   What is the total market value of Susie's stock after the stock dividend? How much total cash dividends can she expect to receive?

Answers to Chapter Summary

1.	cash dividends	22.	bond indentures
2.	stock repurchases	23.	voting control
3.	mergers and acquisitions	24.	investment
4.	level	25.	residual
5.	stability	26.	pay dividends
6.	EPS	27.	stable
7.	sell some of their stock	28.	reductions or omissions
8.	dividends	29.	constant payout ratio
9.	friction costs	30.	extra dividend
10.	transactions costs	31.	declaration date
11.	flotation costs	32.	ex-dividend date
12.	dividend preference	33.	record date
13.	less risky	34.	payment date
14.	lower discount rate	35.	dividend reinvestment
15.	transactions costs	36.	tender offers
16.	high	37.	open-market purchases
17.	tax rate	38.	stock option program
18.	flotation	39.	treasury stock
19.	clientele effect	40.	common equity
20.	capital impairment	41.	no effect
21.	retained earnings	42.	optimal trading range

Problem Solutions

16-1. *Residual theory of dividends.*

A.   In this problem, we know how much total funds we need for the projects available to us. And from the way we learned to solve cost of capital problems in Chapter 14, we know to assume any new funds will be raised in the same proportions (weights) as the target or optimal structure given. All we have to do is to see how much equity we need and how much we have available from earnings.

The company's capital structure has 20 percent debt and 5 percent preferred stock. That leaves 75 percent common equity (1 - .20 - .05 = .75).

Equity needed	=	(.75)($20 million)	=	$15 million
Equity available from earnings retention				9
Additional equity needed				$ 6

The company needs $15 million in equity and has only $9 million available. It will have to sell new common stock to get the extra $6 million.

To maintain the present capital structure, it will also have to borrow money and sell new preferred stock in the following amounts:

New debt   =   (.20)($20 million)   = $4 million
New preferred   =   (.05)($20 million)   = $1 million

B.   The residual theory of dividends says that we'll use all the available earnings that we need, then pay dividends with the rest. There can be no dividends in this situation because we need all the earnings for investment. The following graph shows that only $12 million of investment can be undertaken using earnings retention as the only source of common equity. Financing of $20 million is required to accept all acceptable projects.

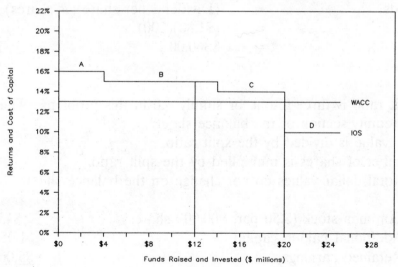

16-2. *Residual theory of dividends.* In order to maintain the given capital structure, 35 percent of the new funds must be equity.

Equity needed   =   (.35)($200,000)   = $70,000
Equity available from earnings retention   105,000
    Excess earnings available for dividends $35,000

201

The board of directors can declare dividends in the aggregate amount of $35,000.

16-3. *Stock split.*
A. Book value per share   =   Total equity/# shares
                           = $6,500,000/300,000
                           = $21.67

Market price   =   (Book value)(Market-to-book ratio)
               =   ($21.67)(2)
               = $43.33

B. John owns 200 shares of stock.

Market value of stock   =   (Market price per share)(# shares)
                        =   ($43.33)(200)
                        = $8,666.67

Dividends   =   (Dividend per share)(# shares)
            =   ($1.80)(200)
            = $360.00

C. The split ratio is three-to-one or simply 3.0 in this problem. There are only two changes in the equity section of the balance sheet:
(1) The par value is divided by the split ratio.
(2) The number of shares is multiplied by the split ratio.
Note that the total dollar values do not change on the balance sheet.

Common stock ($.50 par, 900,000 shares)	$450,000
Additional paid-in capital	1,050,000
Retained earnings	$5,000,000
Total equity	$6,500,000

The per share figures do change.

Book value per share   =   Total equity/# shares
                       = $6,500,000/900,000
                       = $7.22

Market price	=	(Book value)(Market-to-book ratio)
	=	($7.22)(2)
	=	$14.44

D.   After the split, John's total wealth should be the same as before the split. He now owns three times as many shares as before, 600 shares of stock (200 shares x 3), but the price is only 1/3 as much.

Market value of stock	=	(Market price per share)(# shares)
	=	($14.44)(600)
	=	$8,666.67

Likewise, his dividends per share will be 1/3 the pre-split amount or $0.60 (from $1.80/3). But his total payment will be the same because he has three times as many shares.

Dividends	=	(Dividend per share)(# shares)
	=	($.60)(600)
	=	$360

16-4. *Stock dividend.*

A.

Book value per share	=	Total equity/# shares
	=	$600,000,000/20,000,000
	=	$30.00

Market price	=	(Book value)(Market-to-book ratio)
	=	($30)(1.5)
	=	$45.00

B.   Susie owns 500 shares of stock.

Market value of stock	=	(Market price per share)(# shares)
	=	($45)(500)
	=	$22,500

Dividends	=	(Dividend per share)(# shares)
	=	($3)(500)
	=	$1,500

C.   When a stock dividend is declared, there are transfers on the balance sheet and per share market values are affected. Let's take this step-by-step.

$$
\begin{aligned}
\text{\# new shares} &= (\% \text{ of dividend})(\text{original \# shares}) \\
&= (.03)(20,000,000) \\
&= 600,000 \text{ shares}
\end{aligned}
$$

$$
\begin{aligned}
\text{Market value of} & \\
\text{stock dividend} &= (\text{\# new shares})(\text{market price}) \\
&= (600,000)(\$45) \\
&= \$27,000,000
\end{aligned}
$$

$$
\begin{aligned}
\text{Increase in} & \\
\text{common stock account} &= (\text{\# new shares})(\text{par value per share}) \\
&= (600,000)(\$1) \\
&= \$600,000
\end{aligned}
$$

$$
\begin{aligned}
\text{Increase in additional} & \\
\text{paid-in capital} &= \text{Market value of stock dividend - increase} \\
&\quad\quad \text{in common stock account} \\
&= \$27,000,000 - \$600,000 \\
&= \$26,400,000
\end{aligned}
$$

$$
\begin{aligned}
\text{Decrease in retained} & \\
\text{earnings} &= \text{Market value of stock dividend}
\end{aligned}
$$

With this information we can figure the new statement.

Common stock ($1 par, 20,600,000 shares)	$5,600,000
Additional paid-in capital	251,400,000
Retained earnings	343,000,000
Total equity	$600,000,000

The book value per share is now $600 million/20.6 million shares or $29.13. We could get the same result by dividing the old book value per share by (1 + the % dividend) or $30/(1.03) equals $29.13.

$$
\begin{aligned}
\text{Market price} &= (\text{Book value})(\text{Market-to-book ratio}) \\
&= (\$29.13)(1.5) \\
&= \$43.69
\end{aligned}
$$

The new cash dividend ought to be The old cash dividend divided by (1 + the % dividend) or $3/(1.03) equals $2.91.

D.   Susie owns the original 500 shares of stock plus three percent more shares or 515 shares (500 x 1.03).

Market value of stock	=	(Market price per share)(# shares)
	=	($43.69)(515)
	=	$22,500
Dividends	=	(Dividend per share)(# shares)
	=	($2.91)(515)
	=	$1,500

Thus, the stock dividend did not affect the stockholders total wealth.

CHAPTER 17
FINANCIAL PLANNING AND
CAPITAL MARKETS

Concepts You Should Understand

*   The business firm needs to project the amount of funds it will need in the future so that it can plan where to get them.

*   The general scheme to estimate future cash needs has three steps. The first is to project any change in sales. The funds required (uses of funds) to achieve the projected sales can then be estimated. And last, the sources of funds, including external financing needed, can be forecast.

*   A firm's three main uses of funds are investing in assets, repaying loans and other types of financing, and paying cash dividends.

*   A firm's three main sources of funds are cash flow from operations, the sale of assets, and new financing.

*   A company gets long-term funds from capital markets, either directly or through intermediaries.

*   Financial markets are quiet efficient, absorbing new information quickly and accurately. It is difficult, therefore, to add value to the firm by financing activities.

A Second Look

Financial planning is different from cash budgeting in that we are not looking for day-to-day inflows and outflows of cash. It is different from capital budgeting in that we are not trying to decide the merits of a particular investment project. We are planning the financial aspects of expansion and contraction of business.

Our time frame here is often a one-year planning period but can vary according the particular needs of a firm. We start out asking how much we expect to increase or decrease sales during the coming planning period. We are basically interested in the *change* in sales, because we already have sufficient assets to support our current sales level. If an increase in sales requires an increase in assets, then we must acquire the funds.

assets and pay for them. Shrinking sales can leave us with excess inventory, unused plant capacity, and more employees than we need. The main object of this exercise is to estimate future financing needs. Then we can arrange to meet the anticipated need for funds or to scale back operations.

The constant-percent-of-sales method of preparing a pro forma sources and uses of funds analysis is simple, straight forward, and produces good results in many instances. As with any financial model, you must *be careful that the model fits the application and that the underlying assumptions are appropriate.* Financing is accomplished through capital markets. The term capital markets covers a wide variety of institutional arrangements through which businesses and governments can get use of funds that savers and investors have to offer. Capital markets are thought to be quite efficient. That is, new information is reflected in securities prices rapidly and completely. This efficiency implies that it is difficult, if not impossible, to add value to the firm through special arrangements for funds.

Failure of management to provide external funds to support expanding sales can stifle a firm's growth and lead to stagnation and decline. The financial planning function is vital to the company's economic health.

Chapter Summary

Financial planning requires the projection of future financial statements, which are called (1) _____ statements. The (2) _____ method is a simple, yet useful, method to estimate future (3) _____ of funds.

Three major *uses* of funds are (4) _____, (5) _____, and (6) _____. The three most important *sources* of funds are (7) _____, (8) _____, and (9) _____. An estimate of new financing requirements in the future is the end product of the financial planning process.

The scenario for planning begins with estimating the future change in (10) _____. An increase in sales will almost surely require an increase in (11) _____ and may require an increase in (12) _____ as well. An increase in total assets will require new funds. Cash flow from operations is an (13) _____ source of funds because it does not involve outside investors. The sale of assets also produces funds, but management cannot sell assets required in the production process as a means to increase sales. Selling assets to provide funds is called (14) _____ financing. New financing from accounts payable and accruals is said to be (15) _____ because it increases automatically as sales increase. Arranged financing or (16) _____ financing needed is the balance figure and the sought-after answer in the planning problem. Once this figure is determined, management must sit back and decide where to get the money. If the figure is negative, they have to decide what to do with the surplus

To fulfill the requirement for external funds, the treasurer must raise long-term funds through the (17) _____. Some funds go directly from the investor to the firm through the sale of bonds and stock. Other funds are routed through (18) _____, which include (19) _____, (20) _____, and (21) _____. When treasurers negotiate directly with the friendly neighborhood banker, insurance company, or other supplier of funds, they are arranging (22) _____ in the (23) _____ market. Selling bonds or stock to the general public through an investment banker is a (24) _____, which is considered to be in an (25) _____ capital market.

When a new issue of securities (bonds or stock) is sold, either to the public or to an institution, the transaction is regarded as being part of the (26) _____ market. The distinguishing factor is that the firm receives new funds from the sale of new securities. In contrast, when one investor sells securities to another investor, funds are transferred between investors, but the company receives no new funds. This latter transaction is part of the (27) _____ market. The existence of secondary markets are helpful in pricing and selling new issues in the primary market.

Private placements have the advantages of (28) _____ and (29) _____. There is neither registration nor a (30) _____ for private placements, which reduces both costs and time. The waiting time has been reduced for public placements through the (31) _____ implemented in 1982. (32) _____ and (33) _____ are types of negotiated financing.

Efficient capital markets absorb new information (34) _____. This means that prices of securities are (35) _____ in light of all public information. Investors have many (36) _____ investments and sources of funds available to them. If new economic information occurs randomly and is quickly reflected in security prices, it is difficult for management to find one time that is better than another to issue new securities to raise funds. All in all, management is not likely to increase the value of the firm by its financing arrangements.

Another way to say that is that financing arrangements generally have NPVs of zero. (37) _____ markets are not so efficient as securities markets. The value of a tangible asset is derived from its use and the operating characteristics of the firm using it. Thus, positive NPVs are much more likely in investment activities than in financing activities.

International financing opportunities abound for larger firms. Multinational corporations may shop the world for lower interest rates, but will introduce the risk of fluctuations in (38) _____. Even if a firm does not seek financing abroad, it will face foreign competition for domestic funds.

Equations You Should Know

External financing needed =	Total uses of funds - (Cash flow from operations + sales of assets + spontaneous financing)	(17-4)
Fixed asset investment =	Expansion of fixed assets + replacement investments	(17-5)
Investment in assets =	Fixed asset investment + increase in current assets	(17-6)
Total uses of funds =	Investment in assets + repayment of financing + cash dividend payment	(17-8)
Cash flow from operations =	New income + depreciation	(17-9)

Problems

17-1. *External financing needed.* Beth owns a fast food chain named Beth's Burgers, Inc. With the introduction of a new menu item, Beth's Best Burger, she expects sales to soar, adding $4,000,000 to sales during the next fiscal year. Historically, current assets have averaged 15 percent of sales, while current liabilities have been 10 percent of sales. Fixed assets will increase by only five percent of sales. She expects to make a payment of $25,000 on a $200,000 long-term loan at the bank. She expects after-tax net income of $100,000 from the increase in sales. Depreciation expense is $28,000. She plans to pay herself a handsome dividend of $50,000 for her hard work. The rest of the CFAT will be reinvested in the burger chain. How much external financing will Beth need to achieve the projected increase in sales?

17-2. *External financing needed.* CLW Manufacturing monitors the various ratios shown below. The president thinks these relationships will hold in the future. She projects a sales increase of $500,000 for next year.

	% of Sales
Current assets	35%
Current liabilities	20%
Fixed assets	25%
Net profit margin	6%

In addition she expects the dividend payout ratio to be 30 percent and the increase in depreciation to be 20 percent of the increase in fixed assets. The company will make no payments on long-term debt principal and will not sell any assets. Use the constant-percent-of-sales method to project external financing needed.

Answers to Chapter Summary

1. pro forma
2. constant-percent-of-sales
3. sources and uses
4. investment in assets
5. repayment of financing
6. cash dividends
7. cash flow from operations
8. sale of assets
9. new financing
10. sales
11. current assets
12. fixed assets
13. internal
14. left-hand side
15. spontaneous
16. external
17. capital markets
18. financial institutions
19. deposit institutions
20. investment companies
21. contractual institutions
22. private placements
23. customer
24. public offering
25. impersonal
26. primary
27. secondary
28. speedier transactions
29. reduced flotation costs
30. waiting period
31. shelf rule
32. Term loans
33. leases
34. quickly and accurately
35. fair
36. alternative
37. real-asset
38. exchange rates

Problem Solutions

17-1. *External financing needed.*
The starting point to prepare a pro forma sources and uses of funds estimate is the sales projection. We need only deal with the changes, because the old level of sales is already funded. Beth expects fixed assets to increase by five percent of sales:

Expansion of fixed assets = (Fixed assets as % of sales)(Expected change in sales)
= (0.05)($4,000,000)
= $200,000

And as an approximation, we can say that:

Replacement of assets = depreciation expense
= $28,000

Now use equation 17-5 for the total expected investment in fixed assets.

Fixed asset investment = Expansion of fixed assets +
replacement investments   (17-5)
= $200,000 + $28,000
= $228,000

The expected increase in current assets is 15 percent of sales:

Increase in current assets = (Current assets as % of sales)(Expected change in sales)
= (.15)($4,000,000)
= $600,000

Now the total asset investment is:

Investment in assets = Fixed asset investment +
increase in current assets   (17-6)
= $228,000 + $600,000
= $828,000

Repayment of financing and dividends are given outright in the problem, so we can now find the total uses of funds using equation 17-8.

Total uses of funds $=$ Investment in assets +
repayment of financing +
cash dividend payment (17-8)
$=$ \$828,000 + \$25,000 + \$50,000
$=$ \$903,000

The added cash flow from the new operation is:

Cash flow from operations = New income + depreciation (17-9)
$=$ \$100,000 + \$28,000
$=$ \$128,000

 The problem does not mention the sale of any assets, so we have no choice but to assume there are no funds from that source.
 There are funds from the spontaneous increase in current liabilities projected at 10 percent of the increase in sales:

Spontaneous financing $=$ (Current liabilities as a % of sales)(Change in sales)
$=$ (.10)(\$4,000,000)
$=$ \$400,000

Now we can estimate the external financing needed.

External financing needed $=$ Total uses of funds -
(Cash flow from operations +
sales of assets +
spontaneous financing) (17-4)
$=$ \$903,000 - (\$128,000 + \$0 + \$400,000)
$=$ \$375,000

This means Beth will be knocking at the banker's door trying to borrow \$375,000 before the year is out.

17-2. External financing needed.
We can estimate the fixed asset investment to support the increase in sales. The expansion in fixed assets will be 25 percent of the increase in sales and the replacement depreciation will be 20 percent of the increase in assets. Depreciation is (.25)(500,000)(.2) or \$25,000.

Fixed asset investment $=$ Expansion of fixed assets +
replacement investments   (17-5)

$=$ (.25)($500,000)   +   (.25)($500,000)(.20)

$=$ $125,000   + $25,000

$=$ $150,000

The increase in current assets will be (.35)($500,000) or $175,000. Now we have the components for the investment in assets.

Investment in assets $=$ Fixed asset investment +
increase in current assets   (17-6)

$=$ $150,000   + $175,000

$=$ $325,000

Next we need to calculate the net income, dividends, and cash flow after tax from operations.

Net income $=$ (net profit margin)(sales)

$=$ (.06)($500,000)

$=$ $30,000

Dividends $=$ (Payout ratio)(net income)

$=$ (.30)($30,000)

$=$ $9,000

CFAT $=$ net income   +   depreciation

$=$ $30,000   + $25,000

$=$ $55,000

The total uses of funds can now be calculated.

Total uses of funds $=$ Investment in assets +
repayment of financing +
cash dividend payment   (17-8)

$=$ $325,000   + $0   + $9,000

$=$ $334,000

Spontaneous financing will be 20 percent of sales or $100,000. Now we are ready to pull the parts together to find the external financing needed.

External financing needed =   Total uses of funds -
                               (Cash flow from operations +
                               sales of assets   +
                               spontaneous financing)   (17-4)
                          = $334,000 - ($55,000 + $0 + $100,000)
                          = $184,000

The firm will be needing $184,000 financing from external sources to achieve its sales increase of $500,000.

CHAPTER 18
COMMON STOCK, PREFERRED STOCK, AND THE ISSUANCE OF SECURITIES

Concepts You Should Understand

*   A company increases its common equity by retaining earnings or by selling new common stock through either a general cash offer or a rights offering.

*   Common stockholders have the last claim to earnings when the firm is prospering and to assets when the firm is bankrupt.

*   Common stockholders vote to elect the board of directors and to amend the corporate charter and often have the right to maintain their proportionate share of ownership, which is called a preemptive right.

*   A company increases its preferred equity by selling new preferred stock.

*   Preferred stock is preferred over common stock in its claim to income when the firm is prospering and to assets when the firm is bankrupt. That is, preferred stock-holders' claims are ahead of common stockholders' claims.

*   Preferred stockholders usually do not have the right to participate in the management of the company by voting, and their return is usually limited to the fixed amount of their dividends. Creative uses of preferred stock financing do sometimes include voting rights, participating dividends, and other non-traditional rights.

*   A firm's management sells new common and preferred stock with the help of an investment banker, who serves in the capacities of advising, underwriting, and marketing.

A Second Look

The owners of a company are the common stockholders. They do not have hands-on management responsibilities, but they are responsible for electing the board of directors, who hire and fire management. Stockholders thus share control over the company.

Chapter 18: Common Stock, Preferred Stock, and the Issuance of Securities

When a firm sells a product or service, cash is collected by the company. Management uses these revenues to pay its bills, to pay interest, to pay taxes, and then to pay preferred stock dividends. After all of those payments, the earnings that are left belong to the common stockholders. The board of directors decides what to do with the earnings: pay dividends or retain earnings or some of both.

If the firm is faced with bankruptcy, assets may be auctioned off. In case of this event, there is usually not enough money to go around to everyone with a claim. Funds will be split up among creditors first, then preferred stockholders. Any shreds that are left will belong to the common stockholders. Common stockholders are called residual owners because in the cases of income and of bankruptcy, stockholders have the last claim.

From management's viewpoint stock has several advantages when compared to debt financing. Dividends can be omitted when times get tough; interest payments cannot. Stock does not have to be paid off; debt does. On the negative side, new stockholders get to vote, which reduces the amount of control the old stockholders had and can impede management functions. Earnings and dividends will be diluted because of the increased number of shares. The preemptive right is designed to rectify these negative aspects.

Preferred stock appears to have two sides, and what you see depends on how you view it. If you are a common stockholder, preferred stock affects you as debt does, because there is a fixed dividend payment, which is analogous to an interest payment. Preferred stock provides financial leverage for common stockholders. On the other hand, a creditor looks at preferred as providing a larger equity base. From management's viewpoint, a preferred stock dividend is not a tax deductible expense as is an interest payment. This contributes to the cost of preferred being higher than the after-tax cost of debt. Not all companies have preferred stock outstanding.

Many companies do not have to sell bonds or stock very often; several years may pass between major financing activities. A firm normally hires an expert to help prepare, price, and sell a new issue of securities. The expert is an investment banker, who, like any professional, has a lot of insight into market conditions, prices, and security features to make an issue successful.

When an investment banker, or a syndicate of investment bankers, underwrites an issue, they buy the stocks or bonds from the issuing firm at an agreed upon price plus a commission and/or fee. Then they sell the securities to the public, hoping to sell them at a higher price than they paid for them. The investment banker bears the risk that the issue will sell a lower price, as well.

A different arrangement is for the investment banker to sell the securities on a best-efforts basis. The investment banker receives a commission and makes his best effort to sell the securities, but does not guarantee the price. The investment banker plays an important role in raising funds for a company.

Chapter 18: Common Stock, Preferred Stock, and the Issuance of Securities

The following table summarizes the characteristics of common stock, preferred stock, and debt financing.

Comparison of Types of Long-Term Financing

	Common Stock	Preferred Stock	Debt
Life of security	Perpetual	Perpetual	Finite
Owners' control	May dilute	No effect[1]	No effect
Div/Int required	No	No[2]	Yes
Div/Int amount	Variable	Fixed[3]	Fixed
Div/Int tax deduction	No	No	Yes
Cost of capital	High	Medium	Low
Financial risk to firm	Decreases	Depends on viewpoint	Increases

Chapter Summary

A business raises funds internally from (1) _____ and (2) _____. Selling new stock and borrowing money are (3) _____ sources of funds. Stock financing may come from the sale of either common or preferred stock.

The maximum number of shares of common stock that a firm can issue without amending its charter is the number of shares (4) _____. Stock that has been issued, but is no longer (5) _____, is called (6) _____.

Common stockholders have claims against both the (7) _____ and the (8) _____ of the firm. In both cases they have a (9) _____ claim, meaning that, being the owners, they are last in line and get whatever is left after all other parties get their share. The claim against (10) _____ is recognized through the retention of earnings and depreciation to purchase assets and the payment of (11) _____. The claim against (12) _____ is primarily important if the firm is bankrupt and faces (13) _____ or is

---

[1]Preferred stock may have voting rights that will affect common stockholders' control.

[2]Preferred stock dividends are sometimes cumulative or otherwise require payment.

[3]Preferred dividends are sometimes participating or otherwise variable.

otherwise going out of business.

Common stockholders exert control over corporate activities primarily through voting for the (14) _____. This vote may be by majority vote or by (15) _____ voting, depending on the corporate charter. Stockholders have three rights to help preserve their control: the (16) _____ to maintain their proportionate share of ownership, the right to examine the (17) _____, and the right to get the names and addresses of other (18) _____. The temporary transfer of a stockholder's right to vote to another party is a (19) _____.

When new common stock is issued, the stockholders typically have the preemptive right to buy enough of the new shares to keep their proportionate ownership. But the existing stockholders may not want to exercise their rights or may not have the money to buy more shares. Instead they can (20) _____ the rights and receive some value for their loss of voting power. Or they can let their rights expire and lose wealth that could have been theirs.

From the viewpoint of management there are advantages and disadvantages to each type of financing. Failure to pay common or preferred (21) _____ cannot force a company into bankruptcy court as missing an interest payment can. Common stock does not have a (22) _____, so there is nothing to be repaid as there is with debt. Preferred stock may or may not have a maturity date or a conversion date specified in the indenture. The sale of new common stock presents the potential for (23) _____ of the old stockholders' control.

Preferred stock is preferred over common stock in its claims to both income and assets. In reference to income, preferred dividends are paid (24) _____ earnings can be retained or common dividends paid. Preferred dividends are always the same dollar amount, which is why preferred stock is classified as a (25) _____ security. Some preferred stock issues have a provision stipulating that anytime preferred dividends are omitted, common dividends cannot be paid until the preferred dividends are paid in arrears. These are called (26) _____. Although preferred stock does not have a maturity date, there may be ways to retire an issue. These include (27) _____ into common shares, a (28) _____ feature, and a (29) _____.

From the common shareholders' viewpoint, preferred financing provides (30) _____ without the stringent requirements associated with debt. Additional preferred does not dilute the voting rights of common shareholders. Preferred stock has (31) _____ in mergers and acquisitions. Preferred dividends are not a tax deductible expense, and the cost of preferred is between that of debt and common equity.

Securities are sold to the public through two methods: (32) _____ and (33) _____. A financial intermediary who works with a company to sell a new issue is an (34) _____. These intermediaries provide three major functions: (35) _____, (36) _____, and

Chapter 18: Common Stock, Preferred Stock, and the Issuance of Securities

(37)_____. In the underwriting phase, the investment banker bears the risk of price declines while selling the issue. Underwriters often spread the risk by forming a (38) _____ with each member taking part of the risk and part of the reward. If the investment banker is working on a commission without bearing any risk, it is a (39) _____ offering.

Other investment bankers and securities brokers may be enlisted to sell the issue on a commission basis, without risk bearing. These brokers constitute the (40) _____. The prospectus tells the details of the securities offering; preliminary prospectus is called a (41) _____. Flotation costs consist of the (42) _____ and the (43) _____.

The Securities and Exchange Commission (SEC) Rule 415 is known as the (44) _____. This rule allows an issue to be sold a little at a time during a (45) _____ period.

(46) _____ are stock sales to existing shareholders with preemptive rights rather than to the general public. Existing stockholders can purchase new shares below market price and protect their voting control. Flotation costs are lower for this type distribution than for a general cash offering.

Acronyms You Should Know

IPO	Initial public offering
SEC	Securities and Exchange Commission

Equations You Should Know

$$\text{Underwriter's spread} = \frac{\text{Gross sales proceeds - Net sales}}{\text{Gross sales proceeds}} \qquad (18\text{-}1)$$

Equations 18A-1, 18A-2, and 18A-3 refer to a rights offering of new common stock.

$$\text{\# new shares issued} = \text{New funds raised/Subscription price} \qquad (18\text{A-}1)$$

$$\text{\# rights per new share} = \text{\# rights issued/\# new shares} \qquad (18\text{A-}2)$$

$$\text{Cost of new share} = \text{Subscription price} + \text{\# rights per new share} \qquad (18\text{A-}3)$$

Problems

18-1. *Flotation costs.* Goforth, Inc., has decided to go for it and issue 3 million shares of common stock. The market price the day of issue was steady at $33 per share. Goldfinger Investment Banking Company paid Goforth $32.25 per share for the entire issue. Additional issue expenses for this common stock offering were $1.50 million.

A. Calculate the underwriter's spread as a percentage of Gross sales proceeds.

B. Calculate the total flotation costs as a percentage of gross sales.

18-2. *Rights offering.* An electric and gas utility company has 75 million shares of common stock authorized of which 25 million are outstanding. The company plans a rights offering of 5 million shares of common stock at a subscription price of $48 per share. The current market price is $50 per share.

A. How many rights will be issued? How many rights will it take to buy one new share of stock at $48?

B. What is the value of one right?

C. How much money would a stockholder with 100 shares of existing stock throw away if he received 100 rights and let them expire?

18-3. *Rights offering.* Blaze Industries, Inc., has 15 million shares of common stock outstanding with a current market price of $12 per share and par value of $0.50. The chief financial officer just released an announcement to the press that the company is planning a rights offering to increase their permanent equity base by $22.5 million. The new issue will have a subscription price of $11.25 per share. The company has 500,000 shares of $100-par preferred stock and 100,000 $1000-par bonds outstanding.

A. How many shares of new stock does Blaze need to issue to raise the required funds?

B. How many rights will be required to buy each new share?

C. What is the price of one new share?

D. What is the value of one right?

Answers to Chapter Summary

1.	retained earnings	24.	before
2.	depreciation	25.	fixed income
3.	external	26.	cumulative dividends
4.	authorized	27.	conversion
5.	outstanding	28.	call
6.	treasury stock	29.	sinking fund
7.	income	30.	leverage
8.	assets	31.	tax advantages
9.	residual	32.	general cash offer
10.	income	33.	privileged subscriptions
11.	dividends	34.	investment banker
12.	assets	35.	advising
13.	dissolution	36.	underwriting
14.	board of directors	37.	marketing
15.	cumulative	38.	syndicate
16.	preemptive right	39.	best-efforts
17.	firm's books	40.	selling group
18.	stockholders	41.	red herring
19.	proxy	42.	underwriting spread
20.	sell	43.	issue expenses
21.	dividends	44.	shelf rule
22.	maturity date	45.	two-year
23.	dilution	46.	Privileged subscriptions

Problem Solutions

18-1. *Flotation costs.*

A.   The gross proceeds is the market price times the number of shares sold.

Gross proceeds   =   ($33/share)(3 million shares)
                  = $99 million

The net sales is the price received by the issuing firm times the number of shares.

Net sales   =   ($32.25/share)(3 millions shares)
             = $96.75 million

Now use equation 18-1 to calculate the underwriter's spread.

$$\text{Underwriter's spread} = \frac{\text{Gross sales proceeds - Net sales}}{\text{Gross sales proceeds}} \qquad (18\text{-}1)$$

$$= (\$99 - \$96.75)/\$99$$
$$= 0.0227 \text{ or } 2.27\%$$

B.   Total flotation costs include the underwriter's spread and other issue costs.

Total flotation costs   =   ($99 - $96.75 + $1.50)/$99
                         =   0.0379 or 3.79%

18-2. *Rights offering.*
A.   One right will be issued for each share of outstanding stock, in this case 25 million rights. We can use equation 18A-2 to calculate the number of rights needed to purchase one new share of stock.

rights per new share   =   # rights issued/# new shares   (18A-2)
                          =   25/5
                          =   5 rights per new share

B.   Since it takes five rights and $48 to purchase one share of stock worth $50, each right ought to be worth:

Value of one right   =   ($50 - $48)/5 = $0.40

C.   A stockholder with 100 rights worth $0.40 apiece would throw away $40 by letting them expire.

18-3. *Rights offering.*
A.   The company needs to raise $22.5 million by selling stock at $11.25 per share. Use equation 18A-1.

new shares issued   =   New funds raised/Subscription price   (18A-1)
                       = $22.5 million/$11.25/share
                       =   2 million shares

B.   Since there are 15 million shares currently outstanding, they will have to issue 15 million rights, one for each outstanding share. Use equation 18A-2 for the number of rights per share of new stock.

# rights per new share	=	# rights issued/# new shares	(18A-2)
	=	15 million rights/2 million new shares	
	=	7.5 rights/new share	

C.   The price of one new share is given by equation 18A-3.

Cost of new share	= Subscription price	+	# rights per new share	(18A-3)
	= $11.25	+	7.5 rights	

D.   If the stock is selling for $12, 7.5 rights ought to be worth the $0.75 difference between the subscription price and the market price. This would be $0.10 apiece.

CHAPTER 19
BONDS AND CONVERTIBLE SECURITIES

Concepts You Should Understand

*   When a firm sells bonds, it is simply borrowing money through the mechanism of the capital markets.

*   Bondholders have claims that come before preferred and common stockholders on income for interest payments and on assets in case of bankruptcy. These claims are delineated in the bond indenture, and specific assets may be pledged as security.

*   At any time during the life of a bond, its value is the present value of the future cash flows expected by the bondholders, discounted at a rate reflecting the risk of the issue.

*   Junk bonds are risky bonds, rated BB (Ba) or lower, with correspondingly high interest rates.

*   Convertible bonds or convertible preferred stocks offer the owner the option to exchange the bond or preferred stock for common stock.

*   The market price of a convertible bond is its value as a bond if the stock price is below the conversion price. The convertible's price fluctuates with the stock price when the stock price is above the conversion price. The convertible bond thus offers the upside potential of the bond market and the downside protection of the bond market.

*   Convertible bonds have the advantages of being easier to sell to a broader range of the investing public and may eventually be converted into common stock, forgiving the debt and broadening the equity base of the firm.

A Second Look

The analysis of leverage on the variability of a firm's earnings per share and on its susceptibility to bankruptcy employs the same principles for both large and small companies. The institutional technicalities of how and from whom a company borrows money, however, often differ with its size. Bond financing is for large corporations and provides hugh amounts of capital worldwide for the promotion of business enterprise.

Bonds are long-term debt. Bondholders have a right to their interest payments before common stockholders have a right to any earnings to be retained or paid out as dividends. In case of bankruptcy, bondholders have a right repayment before the stockholders receive any funds. Bondholders are, thus, in a more secure position than stockholders, and expected bond yields will be lower than expected stock returns. This relationship is dictated by the ever-present risk-return tradeoff.

Several companies, including Standard and Poor's and Moody's, rate bonds as to their riskiness. The ratings range from AAA (the safest) to D (the riskiest). Numerous factors, both quantitative and qualitative, are taken into account in the ratings. Secured bonds have specific assets pledged to reduce their risk. The assets pledged are typically fixed assets. Unsecured bonds are called debentures.

The financial characteristics of a bond include the principal amount or face value of the bond, the coupon payment, which can be stated as the coupon rate, and the number of payments until maturity. The principal and the coupon do not change during the life of the bond. The market price does change, and it changes inversely to changes of the market rate of interest on bonds of similar risk.

Junk bonds have ratings of BB (Ba) or lower. The contrast is with investment grade bonds with AAA (Aaa) to BBB (Baa) ratings. Junk bonds may have been issued in the junk category or may have been issued as investment grade and subsequently deteriorated to junk status. These lower-quality bonds provide financing for many small, growing companies and for financial restructuring, such as leveraged buyouts.

Debt financing has gone international. Foreign bonds and Eurobonds abound and extend the reservoir of funds available for business. These also offer opportunities for portfolio managers who seek global diversification.

Convertible securities can be either bonds or preferred stocks. To an investor a convertible bond offers the best of two worlds: bonds and stocks. A preferred bond has limited downside risk, in that its price will not sink below its value as a bond as long as the company is solvent. On the other hand, it has unlimited upside potential, because its price will follow the price of the stock when the stock is above the conversion value. To a financial manager a convertible feature makes a bond issue a little easier to sell and holds out the hope that, if the company performs well, the debt will never have to be repaid. If the bonds are converted into common stock, the debt becomes equity. Of course, the bonds will have to be repaid if the stock does not increase in value enough to entice bondholders to convert.

Bond refunding means that a company sells new bonds and uses the funds to pay off old bonds. The main reason for doing this is that the interest rate on the new bonds is considerably lower than on the old bonds. In this case the firm has a sure-fire savings in reduced interest expense. A NPV analysis is used to determine when the interest-rate differential is sufficiently large to make a refunding advisable.

Warrants are added to bonds as something extra, in lieu of a higher interest rate.

The bondholder can sell the warrants and keep the bonds. A warrant is an option to buy a fixed number of shares of common stock at a given price until the warrant expires. If the warrants are exercised by the investors, the firm receives new funds and increases its common stock. To the investor a warrant offers the opportunity to make money if the price of the stock rises above the exercise price of the warrant. On the other hand, if the stock price stays below the exercise price until the expiration date, the warrants will expire worthless.

Chapter Summary

Bonds are long-term, fixed-income debt securities. The interest and principal must be paid when due or the bondholders may force the company into bankruptcy. The legal nature of bondholders' claims provide safety for the bondholders but represent risk to the management of the firm and the stockholders.

Bonds may be (1) _____, such as mortgage bonds, equipment (2) _____, and (3) _____ bonds. Unsecured bonds include (4) _____, subordinated debentures, and (5) _____ bonds. Debentures are backed by the good name of the company. In case of bankruptcy, a debenture that is subordinate to another will not be paid off until after the senior debenture has been paid. The firm must pay interest on income bonds only if the company has (6) _____ to pay it.

The contract that spells out all the details about a bond issue is called an (7) _____. A (8) _____ is appointed to look out for the interests of the bondholders, who may not keep up with activities of the firm on their own. The idea is that the company can take care of itself, but if the going gets rough the bondholders need someone to represent their interests. Portions of the indenture agreement, called (9) _____, restrict management from actions that would be detrimental to the bondholders.

The cash flows to a bondholder are fixed by contract with the bond issuer and consist of periodic interest or (10) _____ payments and a lump sum (11) _____ payment at maturity. The investor can reasonably expect to receive these payments unless the company encounters severe cash flow difficulties, in which case it may be a candidate for bankruptcy. The company often has ways available to retire a bond issue prior to maturity, including use of a (12) _____ and/or a (13) _____. The company may, at its option, pay off callable bonds early by paying the (14) _____, which is the face value plus a call premium. The company may retire bonds by buying them in the open market.

Ratings group bonds in risk classes for the convenience of investors. The two most widely known companies that rate bonds are (15) _____ and (16) _____. Investment grade bonds have ratings in the range of (17)

_____, whereas, junk bonds are rated (18) _____ and lower. Ratings go as low as (19) _____ for companies that are in default on payments to bondholders. The risk-return tradeoff applies to bonds as well as to other financial assets: the higher the rating, the safer the investment, and the lower the required return.

Junk bonds may be originally issued with speculative ratings, or they may be issued as investment grade and subsequently lose their quality rating when the company encounters financial difficulties. Issues that are downgraded from investment grade to junk status are known as (20) _____. Junk bonds are often used to finance (21) _____, wherein a group of investors buys the publicly held stock of a company, so that it becomes a closely held or private company. The junk bonds are sold to provide cash to buy the stock.

From the common stockholders' viewpoint financing with debt has the advantage that interest expense is a fixed payment that does not increase if profits increase. Any incremental earnings belong to the (22) _____. The flip side, of course, is that when earnings decline, interest must be paid, regardless. The after-tax cost of debt is lower than the cost of equity and lowers the weighted average cost of capital.

A bond issue of a U.S. company, underwritten and sold in France, and denominated in French francs, is an example of a (23) _____. A bond issue of a U.S. company, underwritten by an international syndicate, sold in various countries, and denominated in U.S. dollars, is an example of a (24) _____. The term Eurobond is a misnomer because the name actually applies to dollar-denominated bonds anywhere in the world.

Bonds and preferred stock may be convertible into (25) _____. The ratio of the number shares of common stock received for each bond (or each share of preferred stock) is the (26) _____. The effective price paid for each share of common is the (27) _____. Convertibles have limited (28) _____ and unlimited (29) _____. The price of the convertible security should not fall below the value of the (30) _____ if its convertible aspect were ignored. The price of the convertible will rise as the price of the common stock rises above the conversion price. The dollar value of converting one bond (or share of preferred stock) at the current market price of the common stock is the (31) _____. The price relationships are maintained by investors who engage in (32) _____, the simultaneous buying and selling of the same security to take advantage of price discrepancies between markets.

From management's viewpoint, an advantage of a convertible bond is that may be converted into common equity at some point in time. Thus, the equity base is broadened, interest payments cease, and the debt is forgiven. A convertible bond or preferred stock issue may appeal to a broader range of investors than a straight issue and increase its marketability. The conversion feature is referred to as an (33) _____ because it enhances the security offering. If the price of the common does not soon rise

enough to make conversion profitable, the issue is said to be (34) _____.
Conversions may be voluntary by the bondholder or forced by the company if the issue
has a (35) _____ or (36) _____. In either case
conversion will result in an economic advantage to the holder of the convertible security.

Warrants are another type of equity sweetener for bond issues. A warrant is an
option to buy a specified number of shares of common stock at a specified (37)
_____ during a specified (38) _____. Warrants are
detached from the bonds and traded separately in the securities markets. A warrant
should have some market value if the (39) _____ is greater than the
(40) _____. Investors should either exercise or sell their warrants and
options, since they eventually expire and are worthless thereafter.

Equations You Should Know

$$\text{Conversion ratio} = \frac{\text{Par value of conversion security}}{\text{Conversion price}} \qquad (19\text{-}1)$$

$$\text{Conversion value} = \text{Conversion ratio} \times \text{Common stock price} \qquad (19\text{-}2)$$

$$\%\ \text{conversion premium} = \frac{\text{Market value - conversion value}}{\text{Conversion value}} (100) \qquad (19\text{-}3)$$

The following equation applies to warrants if the stock price is greater than or
equal to the option price.

$$\text{Formula value} = (\text{Exercise ratio})(\text{Stock price - Option price}) \qquad (19\text{B-}1)$$

If the stock price is less than the option price, then

$$\text{Formula value} = 0$$

$$\%\ \text{premium} = \frac{\text{Market value - Formula value}}{\text{Formula value}} (100) \qquad (19\text{B-}2)$$

Acronyms You Should Know

LBO	Leverage Buyout
S&P	Standard & Poor's Corporation

Problems

19-1. *Bond refunding.* Five years ago the Jackrabbit Delivery Company sold $50 million of 15 percent, 30-year bonds. These bonds are callable after a five-year call protection period, which is now ended. The call premium is $150 per bond. The outstanding issue has $500,000 of unamortized flotation costs remaining. These costs will be amortized straight-line over the remaining 25 years of the old issue. Interest rates for bonds of the same risk are now 12 percent, and the outstanding bonds are selling for $1236.44.

Jack is considering refunding the old issue. New 25-year bonds could be sold at par with a 12 percent coupon rate. Flotation costs for the refunding would be $750,000 to be amortized over the 25-year life of the new issue. Jack's corporate tax rate is 34 percent. Should Jack refund?

19-2. *Warrants.* A warrant on AB Company gives the owner the option to purchase five shares of common stock at $25 per share. The warrant expires five years hence. The stock is currently selling for $17 per share and the warrant for $0.125 over the counter. What is the formula value of the warrant? Why is the market price greater than the formula value?

19-3. *Warrants.* A warrant on YZ Company gives the owner the option to purchase two shares of common stock at $25 per share. The warrant expires two years hence. The stock is currently selling for $29 per share and the warrant for $10.00 over the counter.
A. Calculate the formula value of the warrant.
B. Calculate the percentage premium for the warrant.
C. Why is this warrant selling at a premium?

Answers to Chapter Summary

1.	secured	21.	LBOs
2.	trust certificates	22.	stockholders
3.	collateral trust	23.	foreign bond
4.	debentures	24.	Eurobond
5.	income	25.	common stock
6.	enough earnings	26.	conversion ratio
7.	indenture	27.	conversion price
8.	trustee	28.	downside
9.	protective covenants	29.	upside
10.	interest	30.	bond or preferred stock
11.	principal	31.	conversion value
12.	call provision	32.	arbitrage
13.	sinking fund	33.	equity sweetener
14.	call price	34.	overhanging
15.	Moody's	35.	call provision
16.	Standard & Poor's	36.	acceleration clause
17.	AAA-BBB(Aaa-Baa)	37.	price
18.	BB(Ba)	38.	period
19.	D	39.	stock price
20.	fallen angel	40.	option price

Problem Solutions

19-1. *Bond refunding.* We'll approach this problem in three steps like any other capital budgeting problem. First, we'll determine our initial investment. Should we buy the bonds in the market or call them? The bonds are selling for $1236.44 and a bond with the call premium is $1150. So call them; it's cheaper. How many bonds are outstanding? $50,000,000/$1000 per bond = 50,000 bonds outstanding.

Initial investment		
Repayment of old bond principal		$50,000,000
Payment of call premium ($150 x 50,000 bonds)		7,500,000
Total payment to call old bonds		$57,500,000
Proceeds of new bond sale	$50,000,000	
Less flotation costs	750,000	
Net proceeds		49,250,000
Before-tax initial investment		$ 8,250,000

Now we need to determine how much tax savings are directly attributable to the decision to refund at the time of the refunding (time 0).

Tax deductible expenses
Call premium on old bonds $7,500,000
Unamortized flotation costs on old bonds   500,000
    Total tax-deductible expenses $8,000,000

Tax savings   =   (Tax rate)(Tax deductible expenses)
          =   (.34)($8,000,000)
          = $2,720,000

Now we are ready to put our before-tax initial investment on an after-tax basis.

Before-tax initial investment $8,250,000
Less tax savings   2,720,000
    After-tax initial investment $5,530,000

The next step is to calculate the annual cash flow from the proposed refunding. Our cash flow is in the form of **interest savings** each year. We shall look at the old bonds and the new bonds and take the difference.

Old bonds
Before-tax annual interest(.15)($50,000,000) $7,500,000

Annual tax deductible expenses:
    Interest expense $7,500,000
    Amortization of flotation costs
            ($500,000/25 years)   20,000
Total tax-deductible expenses $7,520,000

Annual tax savings (.34)($7,520,000)   2,556,800
    Annual after-tax interest payments $4,943,200

<u>New bonds</u>

Before-tax annual interest(.12)($50,000,000)	$6,000,000

Annual tax deductible expenses:

Interest expense	$6,000,000
Amortization of flotation costs	
($750,000/25 years)	30,000
Total tax-deductible expenses	$6,030,000

Annual tax savings (.34)($6,030,000)	2,050,200
Annual after-tax interest payments	$3,949,800

<u>Old bonds - new bonds</u>

After-tax interest payments on old bonds	$4,943,200
After-tax interest payments on new bonds	3,943,200
Annual after-tax interest savings	$1,000,000

The third step is to calculate the NPV of the savings. The only difference between this and any other capital budgeting project is that this cash flow is very low risk. The company, itself, makes the interest payments, so the savings are virtually assured. The initial expenses may not be exactly as projected, but they should be close. To adjust for the low risk we use the after-tax interest rate on the new bonds as the discount rate. The after-tax interest rate on the new debt is 12%(1 - .34) = 7.92%. Calling on Chapter 12, we use equation 12-2:

$$\text{NPV} = \sum_{t=1}^{n} \text{CFAT}_t/(1 + k)^t - \text{CFAT}_0 \qquad (12\text{-}2)$$

Since the cash flow is an annuity, we can use the PVIFA format. But we cannot use the tables because 7.92 percent is not in the tables. We can calculate the PVIFA as follows:

$$\text{PVIFA}_{k,n} = \frac{1 - \dfrac{1}{(1 + k)^n}}{k}$$

$$PVIFA_{7.92\%,25} = \cfrac{1 - \cfrac{1}{(1 + .0792)^{25}}}{.0792}$$

$$= \cfrac{1 - 1/6.722772}{.0792}$$

$$= \cfrac{1 - .148748}{.0792}$$

$$= .851251/0.792$$

$$= 10.7481$$

Now we can calculate the NPV using the PVIFA format.

$$NPV = CFAT(PVIFA_{7.92\%,25}) - CFAT_0$$

$$= \$1,000,000(10.7481) - \$5,530,000$$

$$= \$10,748,000 - \$5,530,000$$

$$= \underline{\$5,218,000}$$

Jackrabbit Delivery Company should refund because the NPV is positive and will increase the value of the firm.

19-2. *Warrants.* The warrant gives the investor the option to exchange the warrant and 5 shares x $25/share or $125 for five shares of stock with a market value of 5 shares x $17/share or $85. Not many folks will jump at a chance like that, so the formula value is zero. Yet, the warrant is selling for $0.125, which indicates that some people are speculating that the price of the stock will increase from its current $17 to above the exercise price of $25 during the five-years remaining in the life of the warrant.

Chapter 19: Bonds and Convertible Securities

19-3. *Warrants.*

A.   In this case the exercise price of $25 per share is below the market price of $29, so the formula value can be calculated with equation 19B-1.

Formula value   =   (Exercise ratio)(Stock price - Option price)   (19B-1)
                     =   (2)($29 - $25)
                     = $8

B.   Use equation 19B-2 to calculate the percentage premium.

$$\% \text{ premium} = \frac{\text{Market value - Formula value}}{\text{Formula value}}(100) \qquad (19B-2)$$

$$= \quad (\$10 - \$8)(100)/\$8$$
$$= \quad 25\%$$

Note: The 100 in the above equation is just to convert the decimal fraction (0.25) to a percentage.

C.   The warrant is selling at a premium because investors expect the stock price to increase from its current level.

CHAPTER 20
LEASE FINANCING
AND TERM LOANS

Concepts You Should Understand

*   Operating and financial leases are alternatives to financing assets with term loans, other long-term debt, or equity.

*   The present value of financial leases must be shown on both sides of a company's balance sheet because they represent long-term commitments similar to long-term debt.

*   The economic analysis of whether to buy or to lease an asset utilizes a net present value framework that compares the alternatives.

*   Term loans often have restrictive covenants designed to protect the lender from potential deterioration of the borrower's ability to pay.

*   The costs of term loans include interest, flotation costs, and possible loss of managerial discretion through restrictive covenants.

*   Term loans are more flexible than bond financing in terms of how quickly funds can be arranged, maturity, size, and renegotiation.

A Second Look

Businesses look for the most economical, most convenient ways to finance assets that creative management can think up. A straight-forward way to finance an asset is to borrow money from a financial institution in the form of a term loan. Another option that combines the acquisition of the asset and its financing is a lease.

An operating lease is a short-term, cancelable lease. More than one company will lease the asset during the asset's life. Items like automobiles and office copiers are often leased. This is a convenient method for a firm to gain use of a needed asset.

Sometimes a business needs a particular asset, such as a piece of manufacturing equipment, and also needs a source of funds for its purchase. The equipment manufacturer, at the same time, is looking for a way to make a sale. An alternative to the sale could be a financial lease. The firm leases the equipment from the equipment

235

manufacturer over long enough time period that the asset is paid for (fully amortized) by the end of the lease.

A financial lease is a long-term contractual liability to the lessee and must be included on the balance sheet. An equal amount is included as an asset. The amount to be entered on the balance sheet is the present value of the future lease payments. Finding the present value is called capitalizing the lease payments. The term capital lease is used as well as financial lease.

A financial lease is a form of financing and affects the firm's cash flows much like debt. Lease payments are tax-deductible expenses. The difference in the effect on a firm's income taxes is a critical result of the classification of a lease as operating or financial. A NPV framework can be used to analyze whether a firm should lease or buy a particular asset.

A brief and highly simplified comparison of operating and financial leases is in the following table:

	Operating	Financial
Term	Short-term	Life of asset
Cancelable	Yes	No
Service, maintenance, insurance	Lessor	Lessee
Capitalized	No	Yes
Amortized	No	Yes

Term loans are another type of long-term financing. These are simply loans with maturities ranging from one to 15 years. The lenders are typically commercial banks, insurance companies, pension funds, and finance companies. The lender may require collateral and insist upon restrictive covenants in the loan agreement to reduce the risk. Term loans are often fully amortized, which means that each payment consists of not only interest but also enough principal to pay off the loan over its life without a large payment at the end.

Term loans are readily available to most businesses, easy to negotiate, require minimal flotation costs, may be negotiated and renegotiated to fit the mutual needs of the borrower and lender, and may be the only source of debt financing available to small firms. Term loans add risk to the borrower and may restrict management's discretion in certain financial decisions.

Chapter Summary

Leases are financial arrangements that provide a firm with a specific asset and financing. In a lease agreement the owner of the asset is called the (1) _____, whereas, the (2) _____ uses the asset. A short-term, cancelable lease is an (3) _____ lease, and a long-term, noncancelable lease is a (4) _____ lease. Service, maintenance, and insurance for the leased asset are normally provided by the lessor for a(n) (5) _____ but not for a(n) (6) _____. In a financial lease the value of the asset is (7) _____ over the life of the lease. When a company A sells an asset to company B, then leases the asset from B, the transaction is called a (8) _____. Three main types of lessors are (9) _____, (10) _____, and (11) _____.

Financial leases are a form of (12) _____ and reduce the lessee's capacity to borrow from other sources. Lease payments are (13) _____ expenses for the lessee. The proper accounting treatment of lease financing is delineated in (14) _____.

There would be no economic reason for leases if firms could raise funds in (15) _____ capital markets. From the lessee's viewpoint there are several perceived reasons for leasing, including shifting the risk of (16) _____, conserving (17) _____, eliminating the problems of (18) _____, and preserving (19) _____. In reality all costs associated with these perceived reasons are passed along to the lessee. The main actual advantages of leasing to both the lessor and lessee derive from (20) _____ and from reduced (21) _____.

The economic analysis to decide whether to lease or buy is a three-step process. The first step is to calculate the net present value (NPV) of (22) _____ the asset outright. The second step is to calculate the (23) _____ NPV of leasing the asset. The third step is to choose the alternative with the higher positive NPV. In calculating the buy alternative NPV, the appropriate discount rate is the same as used by the firm for other projects of similar risk, often the weighted average (24) _____. The appropriate discount rate for the lease alternative, however, is the after-tax (25) _____. This analysis is the application of capital budgeting techniques to the specialized cash flows of leasing.

Leases are considered an alternative to financing with (26) _____. Firms usually obtain loans with maturities of three to five years from (27) _____, while (28) _____ and (29) _____ provide longer-term loans ranging up to 15 years. The borrowing company normally negotiates directly with the lender rather than employing an investment banker. If the lender perceives substantial risk involved in the loan, the lender may require (30) _____ to be pledged by the borrower. (31) _____ are often included in a loan agreement to enhance the safety of the loan by encouraging sound financial management on the part of the borrower. Restrictions often target both sides of the balance sheet, (32) _____, and management itself.

When calculating the cost of term loans, the nominal interest rate stated in the loan documents is not sufficient to give a true picture of the cost. The effective cost also needs to consider (33) _____ and (34) _____. Among the advantages of term loans over bonds are the speed at which loans can be negotiated, lower flotation costs,   and flexibility in negotiations with the lender.   The major disadvantage of term loans is the risk added to the firm by the commitment to fixed loan payments. Restrictive covenants are another disadvantage from management's viewpoint.

Small firms frequently have no choice between term loans and bonds because they are not large enough to raise funds through a bond issue. Small firms may, on the other hand, have access to lease financing.

Equations You Should Know

$$k = (1 - T) \times \text{Required rate of return on borrowing} \qquad (20\text{-}1)$$

$$C = V_0/\text{PVIFA}_{k,n} \qquad (20\text{-}2)$$

$$B_0(1 - f) = \sum_{t=1}^{n}[B_t + (1 - T)I_t]/(1 + k)^t \qquad (20\text{-}3)$$

$$k = (1 - T)(\text{Interest rate})/(1 - f) \qquad (20\text{-}4)$$

Problems

20-1. *Amortization schedule.* Prepare an amortization table for a $50,000 term loan to be repaid in three equal, annual installments. The interest rate is 15 percent.

20-2. *Effective cost of term loans.* Bubba's Bar-B-Que and Catering Service just signed a five-year note for $35,000 at 12 percent interest. Bubba's friendly neighborhood banker charged him loan initiation fees totaling $700. Bubba's booming business bumps him into a 25 percent marginal income tax bracket.

A.   Prepare a five-year amortization schedule.

B.   Determine the effective after-tax cost of the loan using equation 20-2.

C.   Determine the approximate effective cost of borrowing using equation

20-3.   *Lease vs. buy decision.*   Gator Photography is considering leasing processing equipment to open a new store in the mall.   They can lease the equipment from the manufacturer or buy it outright.

    If they purchase the equipment, the installed cost is $70,000.   MACRS depreciation with the half-year convention will be used with a five-year class life.   (Refer to Table 11-4 in the text for depreciation rates.)   A projections for cash flow before tax is given below. The firm is in the 34 percent marginal tax bracket and has a weighted average cost of capital of 14 percent.

    If they lease, the annual lease payment will be $15,000 for six years.   The payments are to be made at the beginning of each year.   Because of minor service calls by the manufacturer, Gator expects to save a small amount of operating expenses each year, given on an after-tax basis below.

Period	CFBT$_t$	Op cost savings
0	*	*
1	$20,000	$500
2	$20,800	$530
3	$21,600	$560
4	$22,500	$590
5	$23,400	$630
6	$24,300	$670

A.   Calculate the NPV to determine if the project is acceptable if the equipment is purchased.

B.   Calculate the NPV of the incremental cash flows if the equipment is leased.

C.   Should Gator Photography buy, lease, or neither?

Answers to Chapter Summary

1.	lessor	18.	equipment disposal
2.	lessee	19.	credit capacity
3.	operating lease	20.	tax advantage
4.	financial lease	21.	transactions costs
5.	operating lease	22.	buying
6.	financial lease	23.	incremental
7.	fully amortized	24.	cost of capital
8.	sale and leaseback	25.	cost of debt
9.	equipment manufacturer	26.	term loans
10.	financial institutions	27.	commercial banks
11.	leasing companies	28.	insurance companies
12.	debt	29.	pension funds
13.	tax-deductible	30.	collateral
14.	FASB #13	31.	restrictive covenants
15.	perfect	32.	cash flow
16.	obsolescence	33.	flotation costs
17.	working capital	34.	taxes

Problem Solutions

20-1. *Amortization schedule.*

The first step is to calculate the annual payment required to amortized the loan in three payments at 15 percent. Use equation 20-2 and the present value interest factor for annuities table. This is identical to finding payments as we did in Chapter 4.

$$C \quad = \quad V_0/\text{PVIFA}_{15\%,3} \qquad\qquad (20\text{-}2)$$
$$= \quad 50,000/2.2832$$
$$= \quad \$21,899.09$$

Using an electronic spreadsheet or a financial calculator will give a payment of $21,898.85, which is 24 cents lower than the one found with the tables. The difference is caused by rounding in the tables. The following schedule is based on the spreadsheet figure.

Chapter 20: Lease Financing and Term Loans

Period	Beginning Balance	Payment	Interest	Paid to Principal	Ending Balance
0	*	*	*	*	$50,000.00
1	$50,000.00	$21,898.85	$7,500.00	$14,398.85	$35,601.15
2	$35,601.15	$21,898.85	$5,340.17	$16,558.68	$19,042.48
3	$19,042.48	$21,898.85	$2,856.37	$19,042.48	$0

First-year calculations follow:

Interest   =   (interest rate)(beginning balance)
                  =   (.15)($50,000)
                  = $7,500

Paid to principal   =   Payment - interest
                  = $21,898.85 - $7,500
                  = $14,398.85

Ending balance   =   Beginning balance - Paid to principal
                  = $50,000 - $14,398.85
                  = $35,601.15

20-2. *Effective cost of term loans.*
A.   We need to find the annual payment at 12 percent for five years. Use equation 20-2 and the PVIFA table.

$$C = V_0/PVIFA_{12\%, 5} \tag{20-2}$$
$$= \$35,000/3.6048$$
$$= \$9,709.28$$

This answer is only six cents off of the spreadsheet answer of $9709.34. The calculations are identical to those in problem 20-1 above. The amortization schedule follows:

Period	Beginning Balance	Payment	I_t Interest	B_t Paid to Principal	Ending Balance
0	*	*	*	*	$35,000.00
1	$35,000.00	$9,709.34	$4,200.00	$5,509.34	$24,490.66
2	$24,490.66	$9,709.34	$3,538.88	$6,170.46	$23,320.20
3	$23,320.20	$9,709.34	$2,798.42	$6,910.92	$16,409.28
4	$16,409.28	$9,709.34	$1,969.11	$7,740.23	$8,669.05
5	$8,669.05	$9,709.34	$1,040.29	$8,669.05	$0

B.   Now to adjust for the flotation costs and the tax effect, we can use equation 20-3. The term $B_0(1 - f)$ is the amount of the loan minus the flotation costs. In this problem the flotation costs are given as $700, so there is no need to convert to a percentage, f, until we get to part C. Here we know that we got only $35,000 minus $700 or $34,300.

The term B_t corresponds to our column headed Paid to Principal. The term I_t corresponds to the column headed Interest. Since the tax rate is 25 percent, $(1 - T)$ is 0.75. Multiplying this by I_t we get the column below. Then add the Paid to Principal to the $(1 - T)I_t$ to get the numerator on the right side of equation 20-3.

Period	$(1-T)I_t$	$B_t + (1-T)I_t$	$CFAT_t$
0	*	*	($34,300.00)
1	$3,150.00	$8,659.34	$8,659.34
2	$2,654.16	$8,824.62	$8,824.62
3	$2,098.82	$9,009.73	$9,009.73
4	$1,476.84	$9,217.06	$9,217.06
5	$780.21	$9,449.27	$9,449.27

Combining the cash flows, we get the $CFAT_t$ column below. Then to find the effective rate, we must solve the problem for the internal rate of return. We can use the trial-and-error method with the table of present value interest factors for single payments. Remember, the object is to get the NPV to equal zero. Let's try 10 percent.

Period	$CFAT_t$	$PVIF_{10\%}$	PV
0	($34,300.00)	1.0000	($34,300.00)
1	$8,659.34	.9091	$7,872.21
2	$8,824.34	.8264	$7,292.67
3	$9,009.73	.7513	$6,769.01
4	$9,217.06	.6830	$6,295.25
5	$9,449.27	.6209	$5,867.05
		Total	($203.81)

Chapter 20: Lease Financing and Term Loans

We got a negative $203.81 when we wanted $0. That is as close as we are going to get with the tables. The actual IRR calculated with a spreadsheet is 9.77 percent, which is not in the table.

Now, what have we determined? The cost of borrowing to this company is only about 10 percent instead of the 12 percent rate stated in the loan. The factor that lowered it is putting the interest payment on an after-tax basis. The flotation costs raised the rate slightly, but not nearly so much as the tax deduction lowered it.

C.   Now let's try the quick-and-dirty method of equation 20-4. We need to put the flotation costs on a percentage basis: $700/$35,000 = 0.02 or 2 percent. Now we are ready to plug into the equation.

$$k \quad = \quad (1 - T)(\text{Interest rate})/(1 - f) \qquad\qquad (20\text{-}4)$$
$$= \quad (1 - .25)(.12)/(1 - .02)$$
$$= \quad 0.0918 \text{ or } 9.18\%$$

This result of 9.18 percent is not real close to the actual of 9.77 percent. The approximation of 10 percent using the tables without interpolating was somewhat better.

20-3. *Lease vs. buy decision.*
A.   Beginning with $CFBT_t$, we need to calculate $CFAT_t$. The MACRS depreciation rates from Table 11-4 in the textbook are 20, 32, 19, 12, 12, and five percent for years one through six. Each rate is multiplied by the cost of $70,000 to get that year's depreciation expense. For example, year one's depreciation expense is (.20) ($70,000) or $14,000.

Period	$CFBT_{t-}$	Dep Exp	Taxable Income	34% Tax	$CFAT_t$
0	*	*	*	*	($70,000)
1	$20,000	$14,000	$6,000	$2,040	$17,960
2	$20,800	$22,400	($1,600)	($544)	$21,344
3	$21,600	$13,300	$8,300	$2,822	$18,778
4	$22,500	$8,400	$14,100	$4,794	$17,706
5	$23,400	$8,400	$15,000	$5,100	$18,300
6	$24,300	$3,500	$20,800	$7,072	$17,228

Taxable income is $CFBT_t$ minus depreciation expense. Taxes are 34 percent times the taxable income. $CFAT_t$ is $CFBT_t$ minus taxes.

Now we must find the NPV of this stream of cash flows. The cost of capital is given as 14 percent and should be used as the discount rate on the project itself. Use the PVIF table for the factors below. Multiply each PVIF times each $CFAT_t$ to get the present value of the $CFAT_t$s. Sum the PVs, including the initial cash outlay in period 0 to get the NPV.

Period	$PVIF_{14\%}$	PV of $CFAT_t$
0	1.0000	($70,000)
1	0.8772	$15,755
2	0.7695	$16,424
3	0.6750	$12,675
4	0.5921	$10,484
5	0.5194	$9,505
6	0.4556	$7,849
	NPV	$2,692

The project, itself, without a lease acceptable because of its positive NPV.

B.   Now let's consider the leasing alternative. The benefits of leasing in this problem are twofold. First, Gator does not have to pay out the initial $70,000 to purchase the asset, so we can consider this an inflow in the lease analysis. The second benefit is a given annual operating cost savings. Because the operating savings increases taxable income, taxes take a bite out of the savings. We must, then put the cost savings on an after-tax basis by multiplying by (1 - T), which is (1 - .34).
These are in the table below.

What does Gator lose with the lease? He loses the tax shield of deducting depreciation expense, and he has to pay the $15,000 per year lease payment. The lease payment is tax deductible and must also be multiplied by (1 - T). A rather tricky point in this problem is that the lease payments are at the beginning of each year, rather than at the end. Thus the payments fall in periods 0 through 5 instead of 1 through 6. These various cash flows are shown below.

Period	Dep expense	Lost Dep tax shield	Op cost savings	A/tax Op cost savings	Investment not made
0	*	*	*	*	$70,000
1	$14,000	($4,760)	$500	$330	
2	$22,400	($7,616)	$530	$350	
3	$13,300	($4,522)	$560	$370	
4	$8,400	($2,856)	$590	$389	
5	$8,400	($2,856)	$630	$416	
6	$3,500	($1,190)	$670	$442	

Period	Lease payment	A/tax Lease payment	Incremental $CFAT_t$ with lease	$PVIF_{8\%}$	PV
0	*	*	$60,100	1.0000	$60,100
1	($15,000)	($9,900)	($14,330)	0.9259	($13,268)
2	($15,000)	($9,900)	($17,166)	0.8573	($14,717)
3	($15,000)	($9,900)	($14,052)	0.7938	($11,155)
4	($15,000)	($9,900)	($12,367)	0.7350	($9,089)
5	($15,000)	($9,900)	($12,340)	0.6806	($8,399)
6	$0	$0	($748)	0.6302	($471)
				NPV	$3001

The incremental $CFAT_t$ column is the sum of the investment not made, the lost depreciation tax shield, the after-tax cost savings, and the after-tax lease payment. The second year, for example is - $7,616 + $350 - $9,900 = - $17,166.

The cost of debt is given as 12.12 percent. The after-tax cost of debt is calculated as (12.12 percent)(1 - .34) equals 8.00 percent, which is to be used as the discount rate. This lease alternative is also acceptable, as it has a positive NPV.

C.   Gator should lease the equipment because that alternative has the greater NPV and will increase the value of the firm more than the buy alternative.

CHAPTER 21
MERGERS AND CORPORATE RESTRUCTURINGS

Concepts You Should Understand

*   Corporate restructuring is making major changes in the assets and liabilities in a short period of time, such as is accomplished through mergers, consolidations, and acquisitions.

*   Methods of payment may be cash, stock, debt securities or practically any combination that is agreeable to all parties. Taxation and voting control are important determinants of the financing arrangements.

*   Accounting practices affect the reported earnings and book values of merged firms. The ability of the market to evaluate the data and properly reflect it in the price supports the claims of market efficiency.

*   The advantages of mergers must be evaluated by both firms involved from the viewpoint of their own stockholders. The NPV framework is the best approach, which is supplemented by consideration of market value exchange ratios and price-earnings ratios.

*   Differences of opinion often lead to takeover fights between the companies, encouraging the development of numerous defensive strategies for companies that do not wish to be combined.

*   A leveraged buyout involves a group of investors, often a group of the firm's managers, borrowing funds to buyout the stock of the company, taking it private.

A Second Look

Firms sometimes venture away from the daily business routine to attempt major shifts in their assets or capital. Mergers and other types of corporate restructurings often make the headlines because of their magnitude and the flamboyant personalities involved. The decades of the 1960s and the 1980s were packed with mergers and acquisitions. Corporate raiders appear on TV expounding upon the benefits to stockholders of the companies they are trying to acquire. Management of the target companies often disagree and a takeover battle ensues.

Mergers may expand a company's existing business or provide a stake in an entirely unrelated enterprise. Mergers may be paid for with cash or securities. Stockholders of both firms are faced with decisions involving complex financing and looming uncertainty about the future prospects of the combined businesses.

Among the highly technical accounting problems faced by management are the tax consequences and the after-merger financial reporting. One nonfinancial problem is the merging of personnel in the companies. Upper management, in fact, often gives the impression that they are more worried about their own jobs than about the wealth of the stockholders.

Mergers must look good when they are proposed, or they would not be undertaken. But, after the fact, what are the long-term results? Empirical studies indicate that the stockholders of the firm which is purchased usually fair rather well. After all, the offer must be attractive enough to entice stockholders into giving up what they have and entering the new deal. The stockholders of the acquiring firm, however, do not always come out so well, because they apparently pay too much.

Leveraged buyouts (LBOs) are a special type of takeover in which a group of investors buys the stock of a company from its public owners, so that the company ends up privately owned by the group of investors. The group is often a team of the company's own managers who decide they would like to run the company to suit themselves and reap the profits. They raise the funds to buy the stock with some equity of their own and a lot of debt, frequently junk bonds and bank loans. Investment bankers are typically involved in mergers and LBOs for expert advise, financial arrangements, and salesmanship.

Chapter Summary

Corporate restructuring means huge and sudden changes in a company's assets and/or liabilities. Mammoth changes do not occur from normal business transactions; they are brought about by intentional actions, often by an outsider. Restructuring usually takes the form of a (1) _____, a (2) _____, or an acquisition. We shall refer to all business combinations as mergers, hereinafter, as a matter of not naming all three types each time they are referred to collectively. A merger that combine two companies in the same line of business is a (3) _____. When a firm combines with one of its suppliers or customers, a (4) _____ merger has taken place. When two companies in unrelated businesses join forces, the combination is a (5) _____ merger.

Two independent firms may formally pursue some objective together, without merging, in a (6) _____. A (7) _____ is a holding company that owns the stock of a (8) _____.

When a merger occurs, payment must be made by one firm to buy the common stock of another. Payment may take many forms, the most common being (9) _____, (10) _____, or (11) _____. For payment received by the stockholders of the acquired (selling) company to be tax-free in the year of the payment, the payment must be in (12) _____ securities. This latter term means common stock or preferred stock that has the right to vote like common stock.

When firms merge the accounting records of the two companies must be consolidated to provide an accurate picture of the resulting entity. Two accounting methods are used. The market value of the seller's assets and a goodwill account is established under the (13) _____ method. Only the book value of the acquired assets is recorded under the (14) _____ method. Because of higher depreciation expense under the (15) _____ method, cash flows are larger with this method. Accounting earnings, on the other hand, are bigger under (16) _____.

Management is presumably working to maximize the stockholders' wealth. Mergers may contribute to this goal if the new company experiences (17) _____, wherein the combined effort is more efficient than the previous individual efforts and not simply larger. Growth, itself, may be an adequate goal for some managements. And sometimes there may be a (18) _____ if one firm has been experiencing tax losses that could shield income of the other from income taxes.

Diversification of a firm's business endeavors is a questionable reason for mergers because the stockholders can diversify their individual portfolios by buying stock of other companies. Another questionable reason for mergers is (19) _____, which may be due more to accounting methods than to economic enhancement of earnings power.

Evaluation of mergers is apparently highly complex; otherwise, how could investment bankers command fees in the multimillions to arrange the big deals? A (20) _____ based on projected post-merger cash flows is the logical approach for management. The beleaguered stockholder, however, has little information to go on, and is likely to rely on two well-known ratios: (21) _____ and (22) _____. Evaluations by the buyer are sometimes too high, causing the firm winning the bid to pay too much for the acquired firm. This phenomenon is called the (23) _____.

The offer by one company to buy stock from the stockholders of another company is a (24) _____. For the offer to be successful, the offered price must be well above the (25) _____ of the target company's stock. Historically, takeover targets have included companies that are (26) _____; that have low (27) _____; and that have low (28) _____.

Various defensive tactics have been designed for managements that want to fight takeover bids of other companies. These tactics include (29) _____, (30)

_____, (31) _____, and (32) _____.
Leveraged buyouts result in a company's stock being bought from the general public so that ownership is concentrated in the hands of a few individuals.

Acronyms and Notation You Should Know

LBO	Leveraged Buyout
P/E	Price-earnings ratio

Equations You Should Know

$$\text{Market value exchange ratio} = \frac{\text{Market value of cash and securities offered to seller's stockholders}}{\text{Market value of seller's stock}} \qquad (21\text{-}1)$$

$$\text{P/E exchange ratio} = \text{(Buyer's P/E)/(Seller's P/E)} \qquad (21\text{-}2)$$

Problems

21-1. *P/E exchange ratios.* BB Manufacturing, Inc., is considering buying CC Tool and Die Company. BB's earnings per share (EPS) is $12, and its price is $180 per share. CC's EPS is $3, and its price is $30. Calculate the P/E of each company and the P/E exchange ratio.

21-2. *Market value exchange ratio.* The Martin-Glover Company (MGC) is trying to entice the stockholders of Big Country Wholesalers (BCW) to tender their stock for one of three offers. MGC's stock closed at $35 per share yesterday and BCW's at $45. The terms of each package are as follows:

Package 1:   5 shares MGC stock for 3 shares BCW stock
Package 2:   3 shares MGC stock plus $20 cash for 2 shares BCW stock
Package 3:   1 MGC bond with a market value of $1125 for 20 shares BCW stock

If you were a Big Country stockholder, which deal would you prefer?

Answers to Chapter Summary

1.	merger	17.	synergy
2.	consolidation	18.	tax advantage
3.	horizontal	19.	earnings growth
4.	vertical	20.	NPV analysis
5.	conglomerate	21.	market value exchange ratios
6.	joint venture	22.	P/E exchange ratios
7.	parent	23.	winner's curse
8.	subsidiary	24.	tender offer
9.	cash	25.	market price
10.	common stock	26.	cash rich
11.	convertible securities	27.	debt-to-equity ratios
12.	voting equity	28.	P/E ratios
13.	purchase	29.	publicity campaign
14.	pooling of interests	30.	stock purchases
15.	purchase	31.	legal tactics
16.	pooling of interests	32.	defensive mergers

Problem Solutions

21-1. *P/E exchange ratios.*
First we need to calculate the P/Es for each company.

P/E for BB = $180/$12 = 15

P/E for CC = $30/$3 = 10

Now we can use equation 21-2 to calculate the P/E exchange ratio.

P/E exchange ratio = (Buyer's P/E)/(Seller's P/E) (21-2)
  = 15/10
  = 1.5

Chapter 21: Mergers and Corporate Restructurings

21-2. *Market value exchange ratio.*

A good way to approach this problem is to use the market value exchange ratio, equation 21-1, and choose the highest ratio.

$$\text{Market value exchange ratio} = \frac{\text{Market value of cash and securities offered to seller's stockholders}}{\text{Market value of seller's stock}} \tag{21-1}$$

Package 1 ratio = (5 shares)($35)/(3 shares)($45)
                 = 1.30

Package 2 ratio = [(3 shares)($35) + $20]/(2 shares)($45)
                 = 1.39

Package 3 ratio = $1125/(20 shares)($45)
                 = 1.25

From the sellers' viewpoint, they are getting $1.39 worth of stock and cash per $1.00 of BCW stock tendered with package 2. Since that's the highest ratio, it's preferred.

CHAPTER 22
INTERNATIONAL FINANCIAL
MANAGEMENT

Concepts You Should Understand

*   International financial management is extremely important in terms of investments, financing, sales, and purchases for businesses in today's ever-shrinking world.

*   International finance for a multinational corporation has both additional risks and additional opportunities compared to a domestic company.

*   One major category of risk is foreign exchange risk, which is the fact that when funds are to be received or paid in the future in a foreign currency, the value relative to the domestic currency is not certain.

*   Political risk is another area of concern. This deals with problems such as cash flow restrictions imposed by other countries (meaning they won't let you bring your profits home), expropriation of assets by a foreign government (meaning they steal your factory), and innumerable lesser problems.

*   International currency markets offer means of reducing foreign exchange risk for the multinational corporation.

*   The opportunities for a company to invest in projects in countries around the world are much broader than for domestic firms and have different risk-return considerations.

*   International financial markets offer much broader opportunities for raising short-term and long-term funds than are available in any one country.

A Second Look

International finance is constantly growing in importance. Companies trade with each other around the world. Communications link businesspersons around the globe as if they were across town. The names of many multinational corporations (MNCs) are household words to most of us because of the products we use. The financial networks for implementing trade, transferring funds, investing, and raising capital are rising to meet the needs of an international clientele.

The MNC is faced with the risk that cash flows in another country in another currency will change in value relative to the home currency. Exchange rates change constantly under the system of floating exchange rates. This risk can be reduced by several risk management techniques, including forward or futures transactions in the foreign currency markets. Another aspect of exchange-rate risk is translations risk, which is the risk that balance sheet assets and liabilities change in value due to exchange rates.

The *interest rate parity theorem* (IRPT) says that a forward exchange rate takes into account the difference between interest rates in the two countries. If US$0.58 (0.58 U.S. dollars) will buy 1DM (one deutsche mark), for example, the spot exchange rate is US$0.5800/DM. Suppose we expect interest rates to be six percent per year (6.0/4 quarters per year = 1.5 percent for three months) in the U.S. and four percent per year (one percent per three months) in Germany. If we invested $.058 in the U. S. and 1DM in Germany for three months, we would have $0.5887 and 1.01DM at the end of three months. At the beginning of the three-month period when the spot rate is $0.58/DM, the forward rate should be $0.5887/1.01DM or $0.5829/DM.

The *purchasing power parity theorem* (PPPT) is similar to the IRPT, except that inflation rates are substituted for interest rates. Forward exchange rates are believed to include expectations about both inflation and interest rates.

International investment decisions utilize the same capital budgeting techniques as domestic projects, but projecting cash flows and assessing risk are considerably more complex. Future exchange rates, inflation rates, and numerous political considerations need to be addressed to reach a valid decision.

MNCs may find it advantageous to raise funds in foreign markets because of favorable interest rates, lack of certain domestic restrictions, and any number of reasons. International financing is facilitated through international banks, institutions like the World Bank, and institutions involved in money and capital markets.

Chapter Summary

International finance includes activities in currency markets, money markets, and capital markets. An MNC that starts or buys a business or a tangible asset in a foreign country is said to have made a (1) _____. Companies that conduct a large part of their business in foreign countries are known as (2) _____.

An exchange rate quoted in terms of the home currency per unit of the foreign currency (US$0.58/DM from the U.S. viewpoint, for example) is a (3) _____ quote, and the reciprocal (1.7241DM/US$) is an (4) _____ quote. Exchange rates for buying and selling today are (5) _____ rates, while rates contracted for delivery in the future are called (6) _____ rates.

Contracts, often between a international firm and a bank, for large, individualized amounts of currency for future delivery are (7) _____. Standardized currency contracts traded on organized exchanges, such as the International Monetary Market, are called (8) _____. Either type contract can be used to guarantee a price for currency needed at some point in the future.

Floating exchange rates change constantly. If the home currency appreciates against a foreign currency, the home currency will buy more of the foreign currency, making foreign goods cheaper in terms of the home currency. The possibility of an adverse effect of exchange rate changes on a firm's financial statements is (9) _____ risk. The Statement of Financial Accounting Standards (SFAS) No. 52 mandates that translation be done with (10) _____ exchange rates.

Six methods for managing transactions risk are to do nothing, to conduct all business transactions in the (11) _____, to (12) _____ in the foreign exchange markets, to engage in (13) _____, to balance the assets and liabilities invested in foreign currencies, and to move funds among countries to take advantage of changing exchange rates.

The decision to build a factory (or make any other investment) in a foreign country involves more considerations than to build one at home. The future direction of exchange rates is a major factor. Other factors include (14) _____ and interest rates in the foreign country. The available capital markets and political stability of the foreign country also complicate the decision. The tax structure of the foreign country often favors certain functional operations over others. Manufacturing firms, for example, may be taxed a lower rates than financial institutions. There are often restrictions on a parent company's taking funds out of a host country. There may also be tariffs, quotas, and possible takeover by the foreign government, which is called (15) _____.

International finance has much specialized terminology. Funds denominated in one currency and deposited in another country are called (16) _____. U.S. dollars on deposit in a Swiss bank, for example, are Eurodollars. The bench mark interest rate for Eurodollar loans is the (17) _____. If a U.S. firm issued bonds in Japan, denominated in Japanese yen, they would be (18) _____. If a U.S. company issued bonds denominated in U.S. dollars in Japan and several European countries, they would be (19) _____.

In order to facilitate trade among countries, several instruments are used to assure payment for goods shipped to foreign countries. These instruments are a letters of credit, drafts, and (20) _____. Without these, there would be intolerable risk involved in shipping merchandise to international markets.

Acronyms and Notation You Should Know

CD	Certificate of Deposit
FASB	Financial Accounting Standards Board
FDI	Foreign direct investment
i_F	Foreign interest rate
i_{US}	U.S. interest rate
I_F	Foreign inflation rate
I_{US}	U.S. inflation rate
IMM	International Monetary Market
IRPT	Interest rate parity theorem
LIBOR	London Interbank Offered Rate
MNC	Multinational corporation
N	Number of months in the forward contract
PPPT	Purchasing power parity theorem
SFAS	Statement of Financial Accounting Standards
X_0	Spot exchange rate (US$/foreign currency)
X_1	Forward exchange rate (US$/foreign currency)

Equations You Should Know

$$\text{Cost of cover} = \frac{X_1 - X_0}{X_0} \times \frac{12}{N} \qquad (22\text{-}1)$$

$$X_1/X_0 = (1 + i_{US})/(1 + i_F) \qquad (22\text{A-}1)$$

$$X_1/X_0 = (1 + I_{US})/(1 + I_F) \qquad (22\text{A-}2)$$

Problems

22-1. *Interest rate parity theorem.* The direct spot exchange rate between U.S. dollars and Japanese yen is US$0.007241/YN. Interest rates on 90-day instruments are six percent per annum in the U.S. and eight percent per annum in Japan. If IRPT holds, what is the 90-day forward exchange rate?

22-2. *Purchasing power parity theorem.* The indirect spot rate between Swiss francs and U.S. dollars is 1.4625SF/US$. Inflation is expected to be five percent per annum in the U.S. and 7.2 percent in Switzerland. If PPPT holds, what is the 180-day forward exchange rate?

22-3. *Investing.* You live in the U.S. and have $1 million which you are considering investing in German (deutsche) marks. The spot rate is $0.6865/DM and the one-year forward rate is $0.6660/DM. The one-year interest rate is 6.5 percent in the U.S. and 6.0 percent in Germany.
A. How many dollars will you have at the end of one year if you invest in the U.S.?
B. If you exchange your dollars for marks and invest in Germany, how many marks will you have at the end of one year?
C. You can guarantee yourself the forward exchange rate one year from now by selling marks forward. Suppose you did this as well as exchanging your marks and investing in Germany (as in part B). At the end of one year, how many dollars will you get when you exchange your investment in marks plus the interest in marks for dollars at the rate in your forward contract?
D. Which is the better deal, A or C?

Answers to Chapter Summary

1.	foreign direct investment	11.	home currency
2.	multinational corporations	12.	cover or hedge
3.	direct	13.	currency swaps
4.	indirect	14.	inflation rates
5.	spot	15.	expropriation
6.	forward	16.	Eurocurrencies
7.	forward contracts	17.	LIBOR
8.	currency futures	18.	foreign bonds
9.	translations	19.	Eurobonds
10.	current	20.	banker's acceptances

Chapter 22: International Financial Management

Problem Solutions

22-1. *Interest rate parity theorem.*

The 90-day interest rates are .06(90 days/360 days) = .015 in the U.S. and .08(90/360) = .02 in Japan. Use equation 22A-1.

$$X_1/X_0 \quad = \quad (1 + i_{US})/(1 + i_F) \qquad\qquad (22A\text{-}1)$$

$$X_1/.007241 \quad = \quad (1 + .015)/(1 + .02)$$

$$
\begin{aligned}
X_1 \quad &= \quad (.007241)(1.015)/(1.02) \\
&= \quad \$0.007206/YN
\end{aligned}
$$

22-2. *Purchasing power parity theorem.*

First, let's change this to a direct rate because equation 22A-2 was given for direct rates. The direct rate is just the reciprocal of the indirect rate.

$$1/1.4625SF/US\$ \quad = \quad US\$0.6838/SF$$

The inflation rate for 180 days ought to be half of the annual rate, so the U.S. 180-day rate is .025 and the Swiss rate is .036.

Now we can use equation 22A-2.

$$X_1/X_0 \quad = \quad (1 + I_{US})/(1 + I_F) \qquad\qquad (22A\text{-}2)$$

$$X_1/.6838 \quad = \quad (1 + .025)/(1 + .036)$$

$$
\begin{aligned}
X_1 \quad &= \quad (.6838)(1.025)/(1.036) \\
&= \quad US\$0.6765/SF
\end{aligned}
$$

22-3. *Investing.*

A.   The investment of $1 million in the U.S. would increase by 6.5 percent.

$$\$1,000,000(1.065) \quad = \quad \$1,065,000$$

Chapter 22: International Financial Management

B.   At the spot rate of $0.6865/DM, you could exchange your $1 million for:

$$\$1,000,000/\$0.6865/DM \quad = \quad 1,456,664.2DM$$

At 6 percent interest this would grow to 1,544,064DM by the end of one year.

$$1,456,664.2DM(1.06)= \quad 1,544,064DM$$

C.   This scenario has three steps. First, you convert your $1,000,000 at the spot rate of $0.6865/DM for 1,456,664DM (as in part B). At the same time you enter a forward contract to sell DM one year from now at $0.6660/DM. Second, you invest your 1,456,664DM in Germany at six percent, which gives you 1,544,064DM at the end of the year (as in part B). Third, at the end of the year you convert your 1,544,064DM back into $ at the $0.6660/DM rate specified in the contract you made a year ago. (The spot rate may now be higher or lower, but you have a contract rate of $0.6660/DM.) The calculation follows:

$$1,544,064DM(\$0.6660/DM) = \quad \$1,028,346.60$$

Through this three-step process you have ended up with $1,028,347 less any expenses incurred in the initial currency exchange and in the forward contract.

D.   You would be better off investing in the U.S. and getting $1,065,000 than exchanging, investing, and converting back into $1,028,346.60 in this case.